ZERO TRUST CNAPP

Cloud Native Application Protection Platform

Protect Code, Cloud, Clusters, Containers and LLMs

Definitive Guide

Atharva Shah
Gaurav Mishra
Rahul Jadhav

"Build to Runtime" Security
5 REASONS ACCUKNOX IS YOUR ZERO-TRUST CLOUD SECURITY TOOL

1 EFFORTLESS
Agentless: Onboard, Detect, and Protect in Minutes, AI-LLM Powered!

2 EXTENSIVE
Secures VMs, K8s, IaC Assets for Multi-cloud and On-premise

3 EFFECTIVE
Inline Remediation to Prevent "Zero Day" Attacks Instead of Post-attack Mitigations

4 OPEN SOURCE
Powered by KubeArmor, 750,000+ Downloads and Increasing

5 INNOVATIVE
10+ Patents, Secure IoT/Edge, 5G Workloads, LLMs

AccuKnox CNAPP Definitive Guide

Copyright © 2024 AccuKnox
All rights reserved.

ACKNOWLEDGEMENTS

A comprehensive book like this would not be possible without the support of a number of our colleagues.

Ms. Laura Niespolo for her amazing artistic talents that led to the book cover design
Ms. Debjani Roy and Ganaraj Sawant, for graphics and formatting.
Ms. Jen Wilson, for amazing wordsmithing and editorial support.
Syed Hadi for being a meticulous project manager and helping us stick to the aggressive schedule we set out for ourselves.

All of our colleagues whose knowledge, expertise, support and encouragement helped us immensely.

We sincerely hope this book makes a token contribution to your efforts to deliver highly efficient and secure Cloud Services to your stakeholders. I hope you enjoy reading this as much as we enjoyed writing this.

Atharva Shah, Gaurav Mishra, Rahul Jadhav

I have a lot to be thankful for. All my life I have received help, support, and motivation from known and unknown individuals. My wife, Priti, and my daughter, Gauri have stood steadfast with me, encouraging me to tread difficult paths. This book would not exist without the support and motivation from my peers and team at AccuKnox. Special thanks to Nat Natraj, my mentor and CEO of AccuKnox, for encouraging me to push the boundaries.

Rahul Jadhav | CTO & Co-Founder
AccuKnox

This extensive guide on AccuKnox's Enterprise CNAPP solutions was a labour of love, made possible by my cherished family and my distinguished colleagues' constant support and assistance. My path has been anchored by my parents' principles of diligence, fortitude, and intellectual curiosity, for which I will always be thankful. I owe a debt of appreciation to our visionary leaders, Nat, Rahul, and Gaurav, for giving me this chance, which has enabled me to achieve new heights as well as to our outstanding teammates, Laura, Debjani, Ganaraj, Syed, and Jen, whose knowledge and imagination brought this book to life. May it encourage businesses to accept the transformative potential of AccuKnox's solutions in their pursuit of cloud security excellence.

Atharva Shah | Technical Content Writer
AccuKnox

I would like to express my deepest gratitude to the following people for their unwavering support throughout this journey. To my parents, for their constant love and encouragement that fueled my passion for learning. To my spouse, for her understanding and patience during countless hours dedicated to this project. And to my incredible colleagues at AccuKnox, whose expertise, collaboration, and dedication were instrumental in bringing the AccuKnox Zero Trust book to fruition.

Gaurav Mishra | Product Manager
AccuKnox

FOREWORD

I am thrilled to write this preamble note.

In our discussions with hundreds of end-customers, and partners (resellers, distributors, MSSPs) it became very clear that they were looking for a reasonably comprehensive overview of key concepts and technical details of Zero Trust and in particular Zero Trust CNAPP (Cloud Native Application Protection Platform). While the analysts (Gartner, Forrester, IDC, TAG Cyber, Kuppinger Cole, GigaOM, etc.) have done a great job of addressing bits and pieces of the subject, a holistic coverage of Zero Trust CNAPP was lacking. Consequently, our Solution Engineers were expending time and effort on educating the target audience. We felt there had to be a more efficient and more scalable approach. I made a casual suggestion to a few of our team members, and before I knew it, Gaurav Kumar Mishra, with the support of Rahul Jadhav and Atharva Shah, shared a reasonably well-thought-out book outline. It became clear that we had the making of what I would consider a Definitive Guide to Zero Trust CNAPP.

This complements the excellent reports by the analysts. Since it is written by practitioners who spend a good part of their day in the design, architecture, engineering, development, and deployment of Cloud Security solutions, this comes from the "school of hard knocks" and will appeal to practitioners.

I believe you will find this to be a very informative guide in your journey to implement Zero Trust Cloud Security solutions.

I would like to thank my colleagues, Atharva, Gaurav, and Rahul for taking precious time away from their "day job" and personal commitment to devote to this book. We would like to thank you for your time.

Nat Natraj
CEO & Co-Founder
AccuKnox

AccuKnox CNAPP Definitive Guide

CONTENTS

Chapter 1. Introduction 1
Chapter 2. What is Zero Trust 2
Chapter 3. Why Zero Trust...Why Now 5
    Section 3.1. Kubernetes Security 6
Chapter 4. CNAPP 16
    Section 4.1. ASPM (Application Security Posture Management) 19
    Section 4.2. CSPM (Cloud Security Posture Management) 24
    Section 4.3. KSPM (Kubernetes Security Posture Management) 29
    Section 4.4. Alert Fatigue & Prioritizing Vulnerabilities with AccuKnox 33
    Section 4.5. KIEM (Kubernetes Identity and Entitlement Management) 35
    Section 4.6. CWPP (Cloud Workload Protection Platform) 38
    Section 4.7. Inline Mitigation vs. Post-Attack Remediation 43
    Section 4.8. GRC (Governance, Risk, and Compliance) 49
    Section 4.9. CDR (Cloud Detection & Response) 54
    Section 4.10. IaC (Infrastructure as Code) Security 58
    Section 4.11. Capturing Forensics 61
    Section 4.12. Enterprise Integration 66
    Section 4.13. EDR (Endpoint Detection and Response) Integration 72
    Section 4.14. SIEM (Security Information and Event Management) Integration 76
    Section 4.15. Ticketing Systems 79
Chapter 5. Zero Trust CNAPP Use Cases 86
    Section 5.1. Application Firewalling 86
    Section 5.2. Microsegmentation 89
    Section 5.3. Network Firewalling 90
    Section 5.4. Securing Secrets 93
    Section 5.5. Securing Data Science Access 98
    Section 5.6. Crypto Attacks 101
Chapter 6. Kubernetes Security Best Practices 106
Chapter 7. Admission Controllers - where do they fit in 110
Chapter 8. Layered Security 114

- Chapter 9. Deployment Workflow 118
  - Section 9.1. Deployment Models - Public Cloud 119
  - Section 9.2. Deployment Models - Private Cloud 139
- Chapter 10. Advanced Capabilities 146
  - Section 10.1. Securing Edge/IoT Assets 153
  - Section 10.2. Securing 5G Assets 157
  - Section 10.3. Securing LLMs (Large Language Models) 161
- Chapter 11. Customer Case Studies 166
- Chapter 12. Analyst Accolades 169
- Chapter 13. Partners 170
- Chapter 14. Differentiators 171
- Chapter 15. Appendix 173
- Chapter 16. About AccuKnox 177

Chapter 1   INTRODUCTION

The Cloud Security industry has evolved significantly over the past decade. The industry evolution can be segmented into the following phases:

Phase 1	Basic CSPM (Cloud Security Posture Management) solutions
Phase 2	Point products (CSPM), CWPP (Cloud Workload Protection Platform), GRC (Governance Risk and Compliance)
Phase 3	Advanced point products which addressed the unique security challenges associated with Kubernetes: KIEM (Kubernetes Identity and Entitlement Management) and KSPM (Kubernetes Security Posture Management)
Phase 4	Due to increased integration costs, and the industry trend towards "platformization," there has been an increased demand from customers towards an integrated stack resulting in CNAPP (Cloud Native Application Protection Platform)
Phase 5	In the post-SolarWinds, Log4J era, governments have been encouraging organizations (Public and Private) to adopt a Zero Trust posture, resulting in Zero Trust CNAPP

The following sections provide an overview of key architectural and functional concepts involved in Zero Trust CNAPP. Prior knowledge of the Cloud (Public Cloud, Private Cloud) and Kubernetes will help you to understand and utilize the information and guidelines provided in this book.

Chapter 2   What is Zero Trust

Zero Trust is a security model that assumes all users, devices, and resources are untrusted by default, regardless of their location or network. It advocates continuous verification of identities, devices, and activities before granting access to resources, enforcing the principle of least privilege, and implementing robust security controls across the entire digital estate.

Why is Zero Trust Important?

Traditional perimeter-based security models are no longer effective in today's interconnected and distributed computing environments. With the rise of cloud computing, remote work, and the increasing sophistication of cyber threats, the traditional "trust but verify" approach has become inadequate. Zero Trust addresses these challenges by eliminating the concept of a trusted network and adopting a "verify, then trust" mindset.

How is Zero Trust Accomplished?

Implementing Zero Trust involves several key components:

Identity and Access Management (IAM): Robust authentication and authorization mechanisms ensure that only legitimate users and devices can access resources based on their roles and privileges.

Micro-Segmentation: Networks are divided into smaller, secure zones, with access controlled at a granular level, reducing the attack surface and limiting lateral movement.

Encryption: Data is encrypted at rest, in transit, and use, protecting it from unauthorized access and ensuring confidentiality.

Continuous Monitoring: User, device, and network activities are continuously monitored, enabling prompt responses to anomalies detected.

Automation and Orchestration: Security policies and controls are consistently applied across the entire IT environment through automation and orchestration, reducing the risk of human error and increasing operational efficiency.

Zero Trust Architecture: A typical Zero Trust architecture includes the following components:

Identity Provider (IdP): Centralizes management of user identities and authentication.

Policy Engine: Defines and enforces access policies based on user, device, and resource attributes.

Policy Administrator: Manages and updates access policies based on changing business requirements and threat landscape.

Policy Enforcement Point (PEP): Enforces access policies at various points within the network and applications.

Monitoring and Analytics: Collects and analyzes security data from various sources to detect and respond to threats.

Zero Trust Adoption Timeline

Year	Event
1974	Saltzer and Schroeder introduced the "Least Privilege" principle at MIT.
1977	Ken Thompson delivers the "Trusting Trust" lecture, highlighting the challenges of secure computing.
1984	RSA and Diffie-Hellman algorithms introduce public-key infrastructure (PKI) for secure communications.
2003	The Jericho Forum introduces the concept of "de-parameterization" in security.
2010	John Kindervag of Forrester Research coins the term "Zero Trust."
2019	SolarWinds supply chain attack highlights the need for a Zero Trust approach.
2023	CISA issues Emergency Directive 21-01, urging federal agencies to adopt Zero Trust architectures.

Zero Trust Tenets

1. The network is always assumed to be hostile.
2. Assume threat actors are already inside your network.
3. Network locality (segmentation) is not sufficient for deciding trust in a network.
4. Every device, user and network flow is authenticated and authorized.
5. Policies must be dynamic and calculated from as many sources of data as possible.
6. The device is no longer the border. A service identity/user is the new border.

7. Containers, serverless and cloud are the new disruptors of traditional security architecture.

Key Differentiators

1. **Continuous Verification**: Unlike traditional security models, Zero Trust continuously verifies user identities, device posture, and activity patterns before granting access.
2. **Least Privilege Access**: Access is granted based on the principle of least privilege, ensuring users and devices have only the minimum necessary permissions.
3. **Micro-Segmentation**: Networks are segmented into secure zones, limiting the impact of a potential breach and reducing the attack surface.
4. **Comprehensive Visibility**: Zero Trust provides comprehensive visibility into user, device, and network activities, enabling effective threat detection and response.
5. **Context-Aware Policies**: Access policies are dynamic and based on contextual information, such as user roles, device posture, and risk profiles.

Zero Trust is a fundamental shift in cybersecurity thinking, recognizing that traditional perimeter-based security models are no longer sufficient in today's interconnected and distributed computing environments. By adopting a "never trust, always verify" approach, Zero Trust enhances an organization's security posture, reduces the risk of data breaches, and enables more secure and efficient operations.

Key takeaways

- Assume all users, devices, and resources are untrusted by default.
- Continuously verify identities, devices, and activities before granting access.
- Implement robust authentication, authorization, and encryption mechanisms.
- Segment networks and limit access based on the principle of least privilege.
- Monitor and analyze security data to detect and respond to threats promptly.
- Automate and orchestrate security policies and controls across the entire IT environment.

Embracing Zero Trust is not just a technology implementation but a cultural shift in how organizations approach security. It requires a holistic approach, involving people, processes, and technology, to effectively protect against evolving cyber threats and enable secure digital transformation.

Chapter 3   Why Zero Trust…Why Now

Cybersecurity threats have been on the rise ever since the birth of the PC. Threats were further exacerbated by the growth of networking and later the internet. While threats have been on the rise steadily since then, since COVID we have seen an alarming rise in cybersecurity threats. While the SolarWinds and Log4J attacks took the world by shock, these very recent public cases make it imperative that organizations invest in Zero Trust security.

BNN Bloomberg — TECHNOLOGY | Company News | News Wire — Jan 17, 2024

JPMorgan Sees Hacking Attempts on Systems Double to 45 Billion Per Day

"JPMorgan Chase, the largest US bank by assets, now invests $15 billion a year and employs 62,000 technologists to, in part, help fortify its defense against cyber crimes, said [Mary Callahan Erdoes](#), head of JPMorgan Chase's asset and wealth management division, at the World Economic Forum in Davos, Switzerland, on Wednesday.

JPMorgan now spends about $15 billion on technology every year as part of its attempts to bolster its cyber defenses, Erdoes said. That figure has been on the rise in recent years: JPMorgan previously said it spent about $14.3 billion on technology in 2022.

Erdoes also said the company has nearly 62,000 technologists who are also helping to secure its systems."

THE WALL STREET JOURNAL.

The Audacious MGM Hack That Brought Chaos to Las Vegas

A gang of young criminals. A more than $30 million ransom. Casinos in disarray. Six days inside the cyberattack that put corporate America on notice.

March 29, 2024

The gang behind the MGM hack call themselves Star Fraud, and investigators say they sprung out of a sprawling online community called the Com. Virtually unheard of five years ago, the Com has become one of the top cybersecurity problems facing the U.S.

Com hackers have stolen millions of dollars in cryptocurrency heists. They have driven teenagers to despair with sextortion schemes. They have successfully masqueraded as FBI agents to trick Apple and Meta into revealing the home addresses and phone numbers of their users. They have hired criminals to throw Molotov cocktails or even fire guns at the homes of rivals. They've hacked into Microsoft, Nvidia, Uber, and Samsung. They've stolen the source code to an unreleased version of the videogame "Grand Theft Auto," and tried to extort millions from dozens of companies around the world.

Change Healthcare's ransomware attack costs edge toward $1B so far

First glimpse at attack financials reveals huge pain

Connor Jones   Tue 16 Apr 2024   12:50 UTC

UnitedHealth, parent company of ransomware-besieged Change Healthcare, says the total costs of tending to the February cyberattack for the first calendar quarter of 2024 currently stands at $872 million. That's on top of the amount in advance funding and interest-free loans UnitedHealth provided to support care providers reeling from the disruption, a sum said to be north of $6 billion.

Section 3.1   Kubernetes Security

Kubernetes is the most widely used open-source platform for container orchestration. It automates a variety of container management-related operations. Deployment, scalability, testing, management, etc. all are simplified. Let us look at some typical Kubernetes blunders that most businesses make. The list includes all the major problems faced by several enterprises that have adopted Kubernetes. Testing in a Kubernetes environment demands a full understanding of the platform's architecture and components. Without thorough testing practices in place, organizations usually encounter unexpected bugs or failures in their applications. Effective management of Kubernetes clusters is also crucial for smooth operations. This chapter explores common Kubernetes security risks and provides mitigation strategies to fortify your Kubernetes deployments.

Top 10 Kubernetes Mistakes to Avoid

Kubernetes Mistake	Security	Availability	Scalability	Resource Efficiency	Maintainability	Compliance	Cost
Exposed Secrets	4	2	1	1	2	3	1
Inadequate RBAC	4	2	1	1	3	3	1
Unpatched Vulnerabilities	4	3	2	1	2	4	3
No Resource Limits	2	3	3	4	2	1	4
Unmonitored Resources	2	2	2	3	2	1	2
Using Host Path Volumes	3	1	2	1	2	2	1
Privileged Containers	4	2	3	3	3	3	2
Skipping Config Backups	3	2	1	1	2	2	2
Deprecated API Usage	3	2	1	1	2	2	1
Ignoring Network Policies	4	2	3	2	3	3	2
Manual Scaling	2	3	3	3	2	1	2
No Failover Planning	3	4	2	2	2	2	2
Unencrypted Data Transit	4	2	2	2	2	3	1
Pod Misconfigurations	3	2	2	2	2	2	2

Kubernetes Mistake	Security	Availability	Scalability	Resource Efficiency	Maintainability	Compliance	Cost
Using Default Credentials	4	2	1	1	1	4	1

Security Risks in Kubernetes

Exposed Secrets - Improperly managed secrets, such as passwords, API keys, and other sensitive data, can lead to unauthorized access and data breaches. High-profile incidents like the Tesla AWS breach have highlighted the severe consequences of exposed secrets in Kubernetes environments.

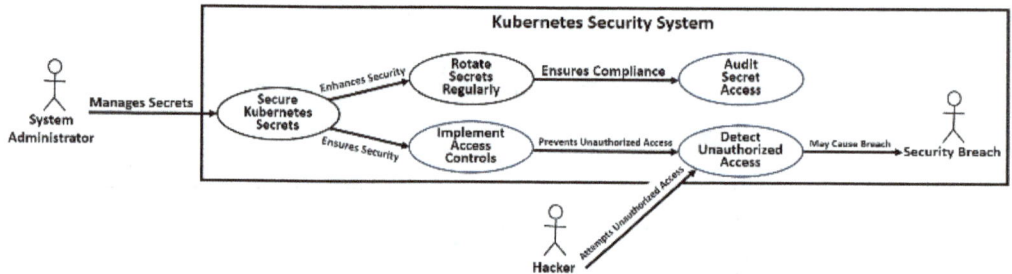

FIGURE 1.   KUBERNETES EXPLOIT SCENARIO

Inadequate Role-Based Access Control (RBAC) - Weak RBAC settings can grant excessive permissions to users, increasing the risk of accidental or malicious actions that disrupt services or expose sensitive data. Implementing and regularly reviewing RBAC policies is crucial for maintaining a secure Kubernetes environment.

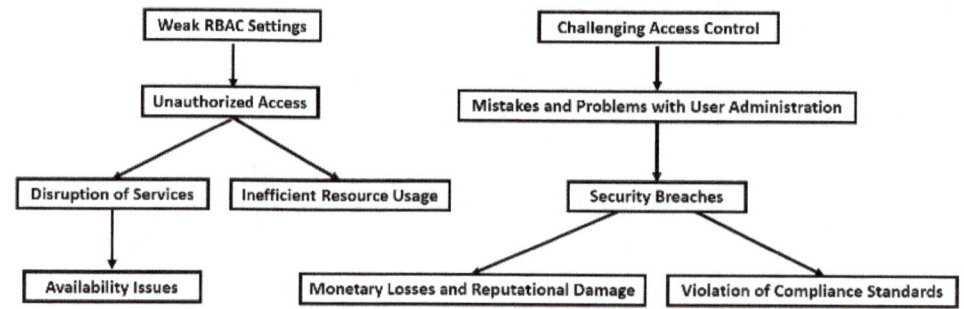

FIGURE 2.   ROLE BASED ACCESS CONTROL

Unpatched Vulnerabilities - Failing to promptly patch known vulnerabilities in Kubernetes components or applications can expose clusters to various attacks, compromising security, availability, and compliance.

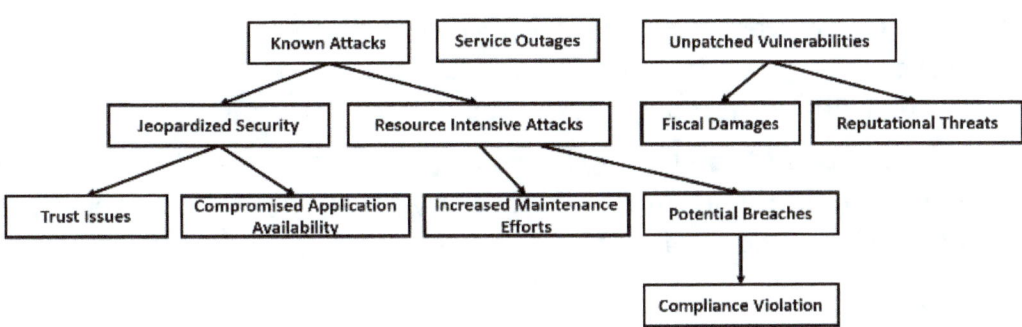

FIGURE 3. UNPATCHED VULNERABILITIES LEAVE SYSTEMS AT RISK

No Resource Limits - Without resource limits, Kubernetes pods can consume excessive system resources, leading to resource exhaustion attacks and degraded performance for other services.

Unmonitored Resources - Lack of monitoring can leave security breaches, performance issues, or scaling problems undetected, potentially leading to prolonged service disruptions and compliance violations.

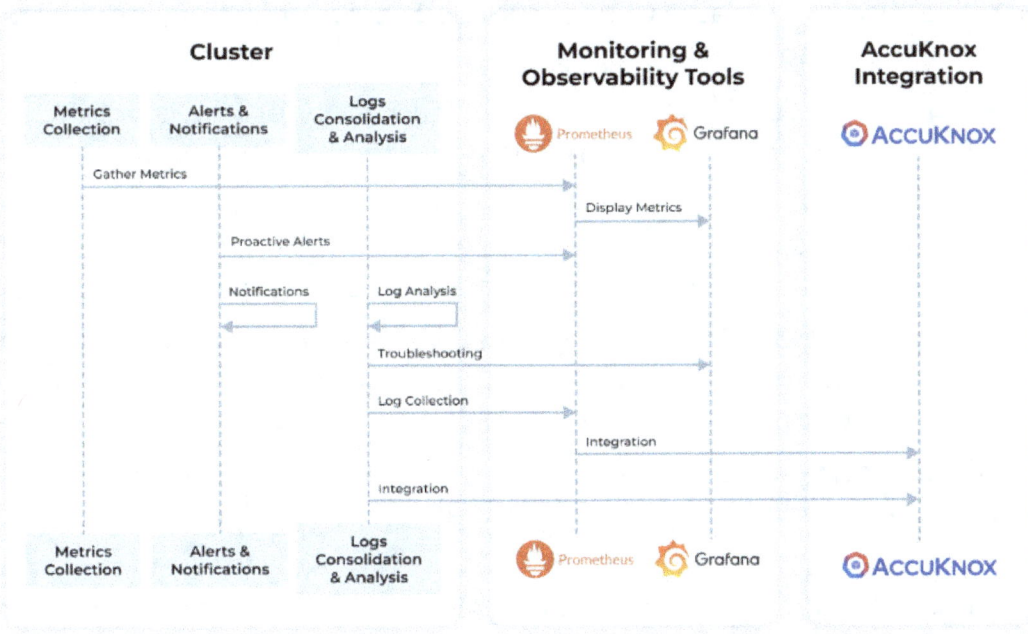

FIGURE 4. CLUSTER MONITORING ARCHITECTURE

Privileged Containers - Running containers with elevated privileges increases the attack surface and the risk of compromising the host system if the container is breached.

Skipping Configuration Backups - Neglecting to back up Kubernetes configurations can hinder recovery efforts in the event of misconfigurations, failures, or security incidents, potentially leading to data loss and prolonged downtime.

Reliance on Deprecated APIs - Using deprecated Kubernetes APIs can expose clusters to known vulnerabilities and compatibility issues, hindering security, scalability, and maintenance efforts.

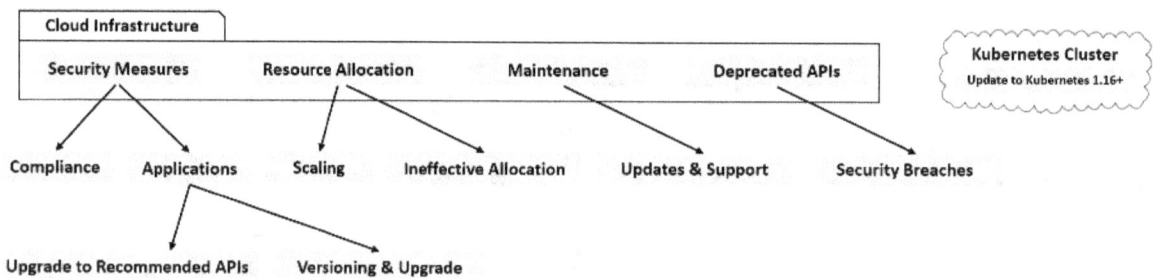

FIGURE 5.   KUBERNETES CLUSTER CLOUD INFRASTRUCTURE

Ignored Network Policies - Failing to implement and maintain network policies can leave Kubernetes pods vulnerable to unauthorized communication, increasing the risk of intrusion or data leakage.

Manual Scaling - Manual scaling processes can lead to under-provisioning or over-provisioning issues, affecting application performance, security, and resource efficiency.

No Failover Planning - Lack of failover planning can result in extended downtime and service disruptions in the event of component failures or unexpected traffic spikes.

Unencrypted Data Transit - Transmitting sensitive data without encryption can expose it to eavesdropping and interception, violating compliance regulations and increasing the risk of data breaches.

Pod Misconfigurations - Misconfigured Kubernetes pods can introduce vulnerabilities, expose services to unauthorized access, and cause performance issues or downtime.

Using Default Credentials - Failing to change default credentials in Kubernetes components or applications can provide an easy entry point for attackers, compromising the entire cluster.

Mitigation Strategies - To mitigate the security risks associated with Kubernetes deployments, organizations should implement the following strategies:

  a. **Secure Secret Management**
     Use Kubernetes Secrets or external secret management tools like HashiCorp

AccuKnox CNAPP Definitive Guide

Vault or CyberArk Conjur to securely store and manage sensitive data. Regularly rotate secrets and implement access controls and encryption to prevent unauthorized access.

b. **Implement Robust RBAC**
Enforce the principle of least privilege by implementing Role-Based Access Control (RBAC) in Kubernetes. Regularly review and update RBAC policies to ensure they align with evolving security requirements.
AccuKnox solutions offer RBAC with strict GRC rulesets.

```yaml
apiVersion: rbac.authorization.k8s.io/v1
kind: ClusterRole
metadata:
  name: cluster-iam-role
rules:
- apiGroups: [""]
  resources: ["pods"]
  verbs: ["get", "list"]
```

SSH keys, passwords, and other private information are kept in Kubernetes Secrets. They become git accessible when they are checked out of the IaC repository. Organizations are adopting DevSecOps more frequently as a result of its significance.

c. **Establish Patch Management**
Implement a regular patch management process to promptly address known vulnerabilities in Kubernetes components and applications. Automate patch deployment and leverage vulnerability management tools to prioritize and address vulnerabilities effectively.

d. **Set Resource Limits** Configure resource limits for CPU and memory in Kubernetes pods to prevent resource exhaustion attacks and ensure fair distribution of resources across applications. Configure resource requests and limits properly to maintain optimal [Kubernetes cluster operation](https://www.accuknox.com/blog/securing-your-kubernetes-cluster-defense-in-depth-kyverno-kubearmor) and application reliability. Take a look at this illustration of setting a limit to 1000 millicores CPU and 128 mebibytes, and setting a quota for requests to 400 millicores CPU and 128 mebibytes.

```yaml
containers:
- name: accuknox-test
   image: ubuntu
```

```
      resources:
        requests:
          memory: "128Mi"
          cpu: "400m"
        limits:
          memory: "256Mi"
          cpu: "100m"
```

e. **Monitor Kubernetes Resources**

Implement monitoring and observability tools like Prometheus and Grafana to collect and analyze Kubernetes metrics. Set up alerts and notifications to proactively identify and respond to performance issues, security breaches, or scaling problems. Let's imagine that, because of their complicated operations, your pods always take longer than 30 seconds to gracefully end. If you want extra time for cleanup in this situation, you may change the grace period to 45 or 60 seconds.

```
apiVersion: v1
kind: Pod
metadata:
  name: container10
spec:
  containers:
    - image: ubuntu
      name: container10
  terminationGracePeriodSeconds: 60
```

f. **Restrict Privileged Containers**

Avoid running containers with privileged access unless necessary. Implement Pod Security Policies (PSPs) to enforce least privilege principles and limit the permissions granted to containers.

Namespace Based Security

Namespaces offer logical division inside a cluster, enabling various projects or teams to work together without problems. The advantage is that it eliminates team interference and promotes parallel work in the same cluster. The default namespace could be adequate for small teams with a modest number of microservices (for example, 5–10). However, different namespaces are suited for better administration in larger companies or teams that scale quickly. A cluster's several namespaces enable communication while providing logical separation. Failure to utilize distinct namespaces may result in accidental interference with the work of other teams. To properly arrange services, it is advised to define and utilize various namespaces.

Confused regarding policy specifications? Refer to KubeArmor's pre-packaged policies and outlines here > https://docs.kubearmor.io/kubearmor/documentation/host_security_policy_specification

Here's how you can create resources inside the namespace:

```yaml
apiVersion: v2
kind: Pod
metadata:
  name: pod110
namespace: test-env
  labels:
     image: pod110
spec:
  containers:
- name: prod110
  Image: ubuntu
```

Track and Organize with Labels

Labels are key-value pairs that help manage and organize resources within your Kubernetes cluster. They improve control and visibility into how objects and services interact.

```yaml
apiVersion: v2
kind: Pod
metadata:
  name: my-pod
  labels:
       environment: dev-env
       team: test02
spec:
  containers:
  - name: test02
       image: "Ubuntu"
       resources:
       limits:
       cpu: 2
```

Audit Logs Save the Day!

Audit logs record API requests made to the kube-apiserver. They can help diagnose issues and identify suspicious activity. Here's how to enable audit logging with a sample audit.log policy:

Enable Audit Logging:

```
--audit-policy-file=/etc/kubernetes/audit-policy.yaml --audit-log-path=/var/log/audit.log
```

Sample Audit Log Policy (Pods)

```yaml
apiVersion: audit.k8s.io/v3
kind: Policy
omitStages:
  - "RequestReceived"
rules:
  - level: RequestResponse
    resources:
      - group: ""
        resources: ["pods"]
  - level: Metadata
    resources:
      - group: ""
        resources: ["pods/log", "pods/status"]
```

Use livenessProbe and readinessProbe

Liveness and readiness probes monitor application health within pods. They determine if a pod is functioning and ready to receive traffic. Here's an example of liveness probe using an HTTP path.

```yaml
apiVersion: v3
kind: Pod
metadata:
  name: container201
spec:
  containers:
```

AccuKnox CNAPP Definitive Guide

```yaml
- image: ubuntu
  name: container201
  livenessProbe:
    httpGet:
      path: /staginghealth
      port: 8081
```

Key Differentiators

AccuKnox Enterprise CNAPP (Cloud-Native Application Protection Platform) is an end-to-end solution designed to address the security challenges associated with Kubernetes deployments. It leverages a Zero Trust security approach to prevent unauthorized access, backdoor operations, network interface manipulation, file system modifications, process execution, and administrative function abuse.

1. **Enforcing Compliance:** Identifiying and fixing security misconfigurations, ensuring adherence to industry standards.

2. **Real-Time Threat Detection:** Whitelisting to prevent suspicious activity and offer comprehensive visibility into your applications.

3. **Ransomware Protection:** Dedicated safeguards for secret management solutions like HashiCorp Vault and CyberArk Conjur.

4. **Continuous Monitoring:** Continuous monitoring of workloads and integration with SIEM tools for centralized security analysis.

Key Takeaways

By preventing assaults on pods, containers, and virtual machines (VMs), AccuKnox fortifies containerized systems. It prevents harmful behavior before it starts by simplifying the enforcement of intricate Linux security procedures. For more predictability, AccuKnox unifies security by bridging the gap between Linux security modules and Kubernetes security. It guarantees security independent of the cloud, preserving interoperability with various cloud service providers. For improved security, AccuKnox implements granular workload control by limiting operations inside workloads. It makes the process of creating and managing security rules easier by enforcing them instantly upon definition. To strengthen network security, AccuKnox controls communication between containers, securing communication routes in the process. For native security enforcement, it works smoothly with Kubernetes. AccuKnox also works with others to provide 5G zero-trust security solutions that use future-proof security protocols.

Chapter 4   CNAPP

How does Gartner Define CNAPP?

Cloud-native application protection platforms (CNAPPs) are a unified and tightly integrated set of security and compliance capabilities designed to secure and protect cloud-native applications across development and production. CNAPPs consolidate a large number of previously siloed capabilities, including container scanning, cloud security posture management, infrastructure as code scanning, cloud infrastructure entitlement management, runtime cloud workload protection and runtime vulnerability/configuration scanning.

As per Gartner:

- Optimal security of cloud-native applications requires an integrated approach that starts in development and extends to runtime protection.

- Implement an integrated security approach that covers the entire life cycle of cloud-native applications, starting in development and extending into production.

- Integrate security into the developer's toolchain so that security testing is automated as code is created and moves through the development pipeline, reducing the friction of adoption.

- Acknowledge that perfect apps aren't possible and focus developers on the highest severity, highest confidence and highest risk vulnerabilities to avoid wasting developer's time.

- Scan development artifacts and cloud configuration comprehensively and combine this with runtime visibility and configuration awareness to prioritize risk remediation.

- Favor CNAPP vendors that provide a variety of runtime visibility techniques, including traditional agents, Extended Berkeley Packet Filter (eBPF) support, snapshotting, privileged containers and Kubernetes K8s integration to provide the most flexibility at deployment.

AccuKnox CNAPP Definitive Guide

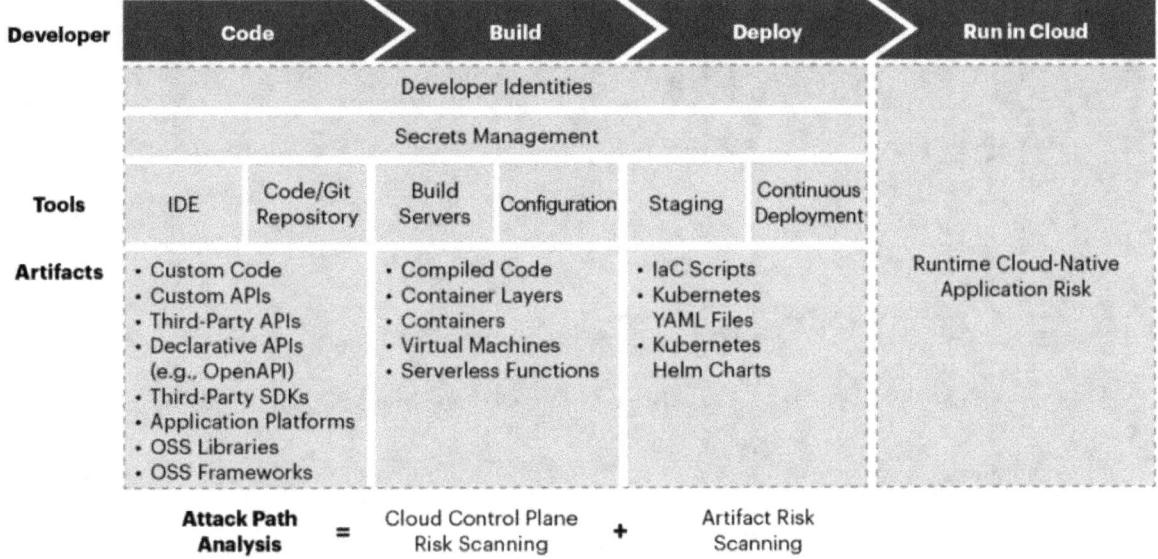

FIGURE 6. CODE-TO-CLOUD RISK VISIBILITY, PRIORITIZATION, AND REMEDIATION

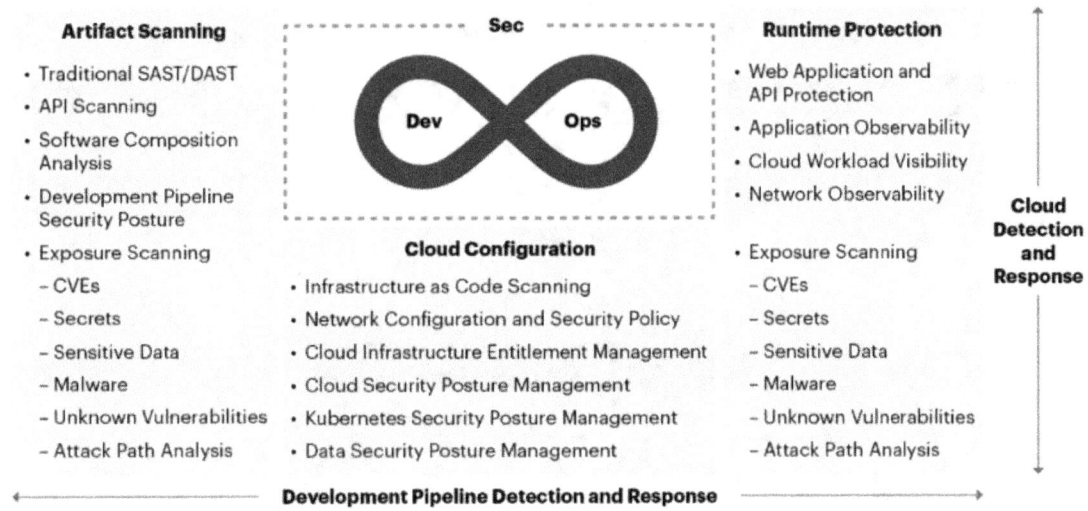

FIGURE 7. GARTNER'S DETAILED CNAPP VIEW

AccuKnox CNAPP Definitive Guide

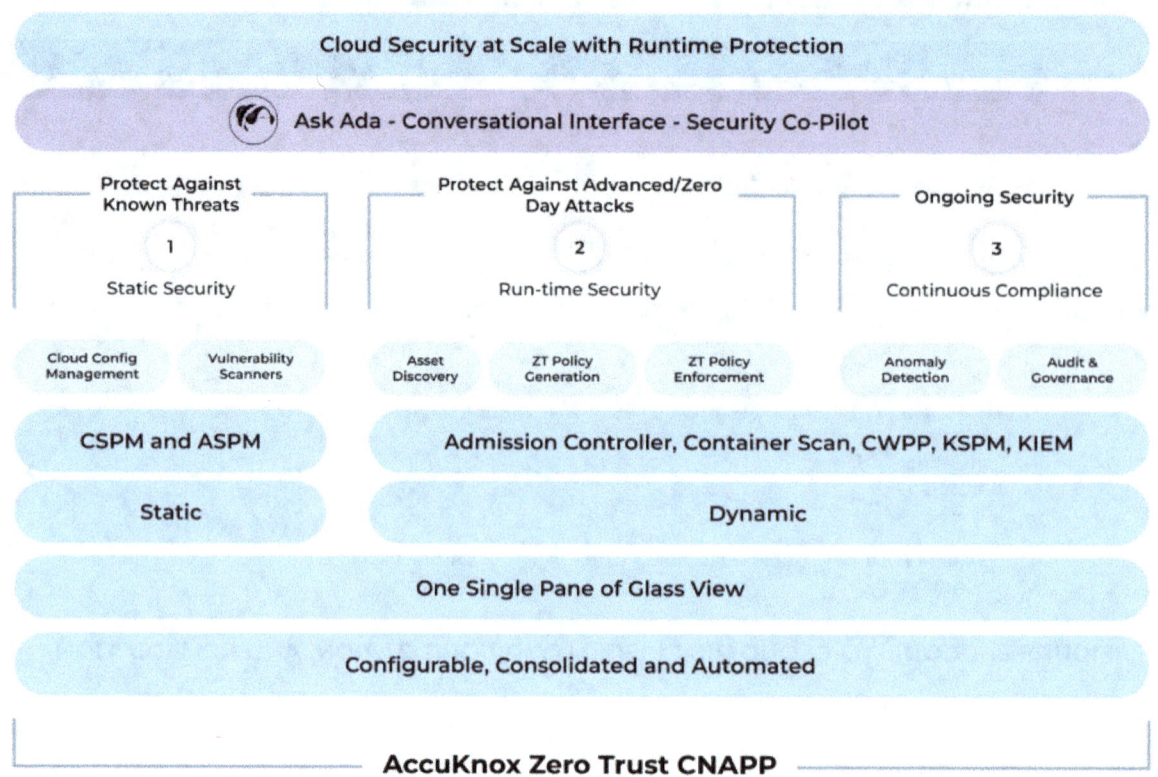

FIGURE 8. ACCUKNOX ENTERPRISE CNAPP OFFERINGS

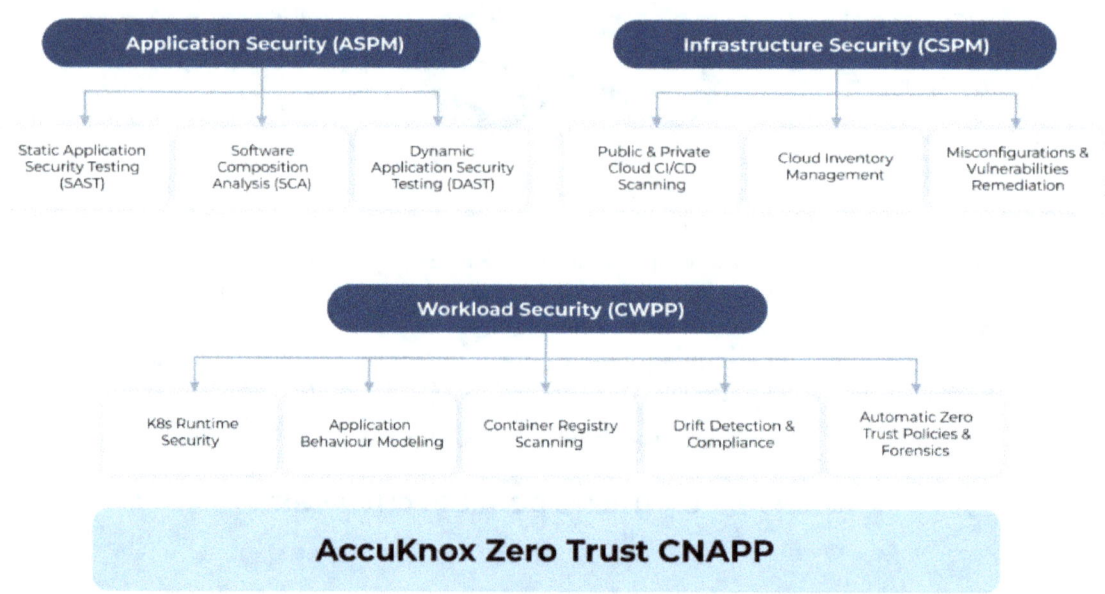

FIGURE 9. ACCUKNOX ALL-IN-ONE CNAPP SUITE

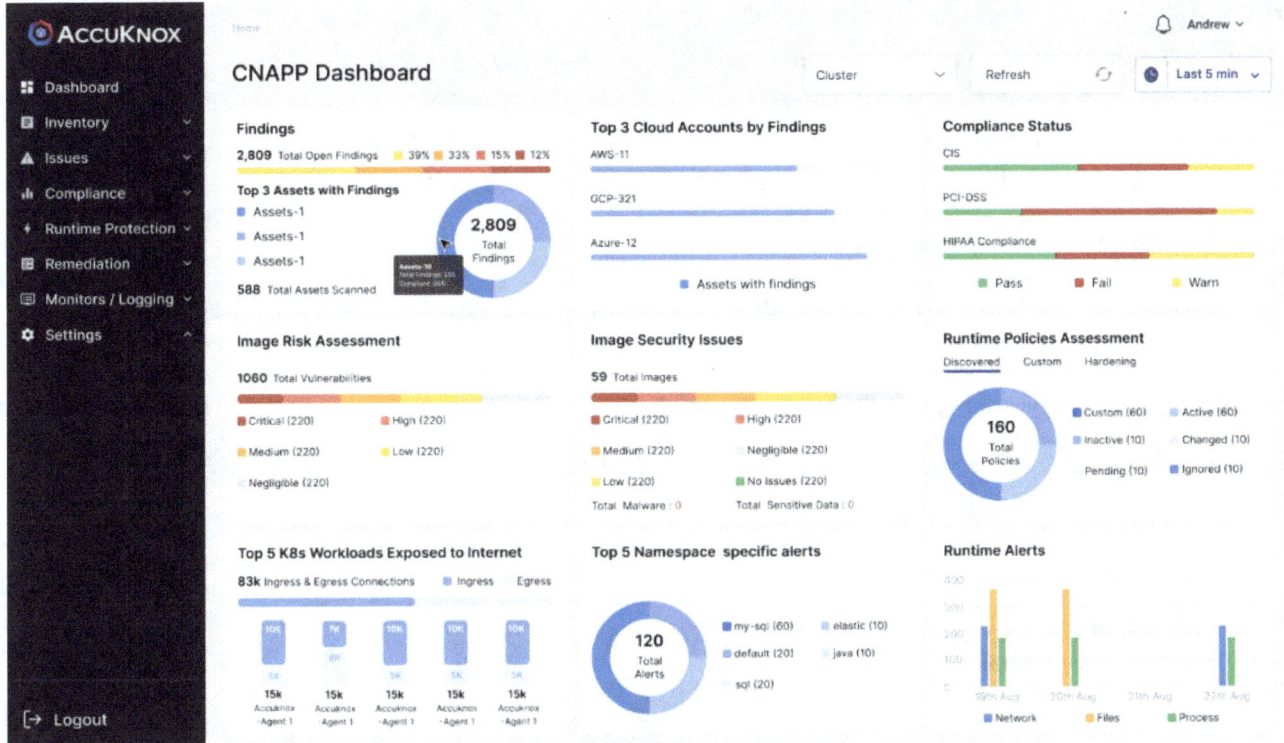

FIGURE 10. ACCUKNOX ENTERPRISE CNAPP DASHBOARD

Section 4.1.   ASPM (Application Security Posture Management)

Application Security Posture Management (ASPM) is a holistic approach to identifying and mitigating security vulnerabilities in applications throughout their entire lifecycle. It combines various security testing techniques, including Static Application Security Testing (SAST), Dynamic Application Security Testing (DAST), Software Composition Analysis (SCA), and Infrastructure as Code (IaC) scanning, to provide a holistic view of an application's security posture.

What is ASPM?

ASPM is a set of tools, processes, and best practices that enable organizations to proactively identify and remediate security vulnerabilities in their applications. It encompasses different security testing techniques, each with its strengths and weaknesses, to provide a comprehensive view of an application's security posture.

Why is ASPM important?

AccuKnox CNAPP Definitive Guide

In today's rapidly evolving threat landscape, applications are a prime target for attackers seeking to exploit vulnerabilities and gain unauthorized access to sensitive data or systems. ASPM plays a crucial role in ensuring the security and compliance of applications by identifying and addressing vulnerabilities early in the development lifecycle, reducing the risk of successful attacks and associated costs.

How is ASPM accomplished?

ASPM is achieved through the integration and orchestration of various security testing techniques, including:

Static Application Security Testing (SAST)

- **Definition**: Analyzes source code for potential security vulnerabilities without running the application.
- **Used at**: During development.
- **Advantages**: Ability to fail a build in the CI/CD pipeline; identifying vulnerabilities early in the development cycle.
- **Disadvantages**: Prone to false positives, lacks runtime context.
- **Cost**: Significant investment in tools and expertise.
- **Use-cases**: Finding common CVEs, coding errors, and security best practice violations.

Dynamic Application Security Testing (DAST) / API Security

- **Definition**: Simulates attack scenarios on a running application to identify vulnerabilities.
- **Used at** Post-development (test or production environments).
- **Advantages**: Identifies vulnerabilities in the running environment, accounting for runtime context.
- **Disadvantages**: May miss some vulnerabilities, prone to false positives, and can slow down the application.
- **Cost**: Significant investment in tools and expertise.
- **Use-cases**: Finding common CVEs, coding errors, and security best practice violations.

Software Composition Analysis (SCA)

- **Definition**: Analyzes third-party dependencies and libraries used in open-source components for known vulnerabilities.
- **Used at:** Continuous integration and deployment pipelines.
- **Advantages**: Identifies vulnerabilities in third-party components, enabling proactive remediation.
- **Disadvantages**: Reliance on accurate and up-to-date vulnerability databases.
- **Cost**: Moderate investment in tools and processes.
- **Use-cases**: Identifying known vulnerabilities in open-source components; ensuring compliance with software supply chain security best practices.

Infrastructure as Code (IaC) Scanning

- **Definition**: Analyzes Infrastructure as Code (IaC) templates, such as Terraform and Dockerfiles, for potential security misconfigurations and vulnerabilities.
- **Used at** Continuous integration and deployment pipelines.
- **Advantages**: Identifies security issues in infrastructure configurations before deployment, enabling early remediation.
- **Disadvantages**: Limited to the scope of the IaC templates analyzed.
- **Cost**: Moderate investment in tools and processes.
- **Use-cases**: Identifying misconfigurations, insecure practices, and vulnerabilities in infrastructure configurations, ensuring compliance with security best practices.

Architecture

ASPM typically follows a centralized architecture, with a single pane of glass view that integrates and orchestrates the various security testing techniques. This architecture allows for efficient management, reporting, and prioritization of identified vulnerabilities.

In this architecture, the ASPM platform integrates with the organization's CI/CD pipelines, source code repositories, and infrastructure provisioning tools. It orchestrates the execution of SAST, DAST, SCA, and IaC scanning tools, consolidating their findings into a centralized dashboard.

Key Differentiators

FIGURE 11. ACCUKNOX ASPM SUPPORTS A VARIETY OF TOOLS WITH MORE TO COME

Leverage a wide range of tools for SCA, SAST, DAST, and IaC with a single pane of glass view

AccuKnox integrates with a variety of industry-leading security testing tools, providing a unified view of an application's security posture across multiple testing techniques. This ensures that vulnerabilities are identified and addressed from all angles, reducing the risk of overlooking critical security issues.

Prioritize vulnerabilities based on exposure at runtime, exploitability, environmental factors, and others

AccuKnox is powered by advanced vulnerability prioritization algorithms that consider factors such as exposure at runtime, exploitability, environmental factors, and business criticality. This prioritization helps organizations focus their remediation efforts on the most critical vulnerabilities, optimizing resource allocation and reducing overall risk.

Flexibility and Expandability

AccuKnox is designed to be flexible and expandable, allowing organizations to integrate new security testing tools or adapt to changing requirements. This flexibility ensures that the ASPM solution remains relevant and effective as an organization's security needs evolve.

Key Takeaways

- ASPM provides a comprehensive approach to identifying and mitigating security vulnerabilities in applications throughout their entire lifecycle.
- It combines various security testing techniques, including SAST, DAST, SCA, and IaC scanning, to provide a holistic view of an application's security posture.
- AccuKnox has a single pane of glass view, enabling efficient management, reporting, and prioritization of identified vulnerabilities.

AccuKnox CNAPP Definitive Guide

- Key Differentiators include leveraging a wide range of security testing tools, prioritizing vulnerabilities based on multiple factors, and offering flexibility and expandability.

- Adopting ASPM is crucial for organizations seeking to proactively identify and remediate security vulnerabilities, ensuring the security and compliance of their applications, and reducing the risk of successful attacks.

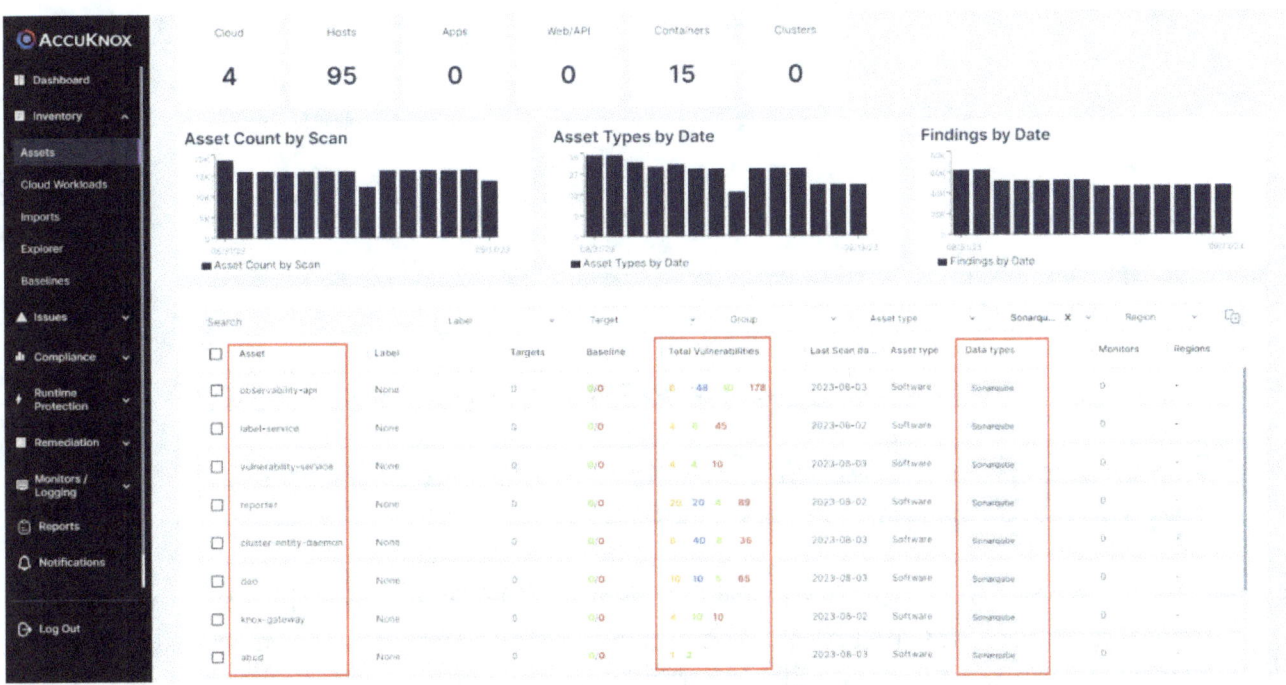

FIGURE 12. ACCUKNOX DASHBOARD VIEW OF ASSET INVENTORY

FIGURE 13. ASSET VISIBILITY AND THREAT BREAKDOWN

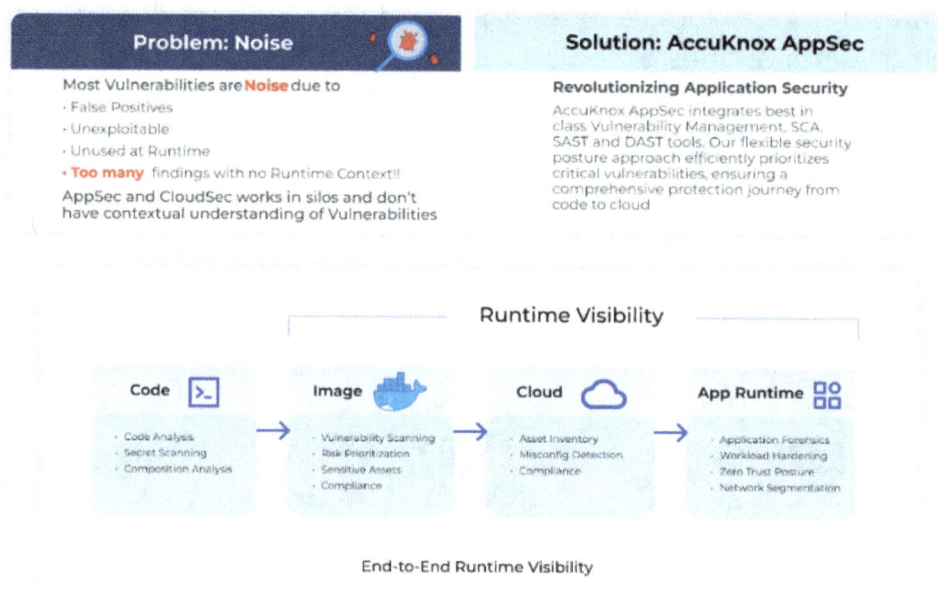

FIGURE 14. ACCUKNOX ACHIEVES APPSEC WITH RUNTIME VISIBILITY

Section 4.2. CSPM (Cloud Security Posture Management)

AccuKnox Cloud Security Posture Management (CSPM) is an agentless technology that proactively identifies and prioritizes vulnerabilities, and provides a seamless orchestration and management platform for cloud security.

What is CSPM?

Cloud Security Posture Management (CSPM) is defined by Gartner as "a continuous process of cloud security improvement and adaptation to reduce the likelihood of a successful attack."

Why is this important?

With the increasing adoption of cloud services, it is crucial to continuously monitor and improve the security posture of cloud environments to mitigate risks and prevent successful attacks.

How is this accomplished?

AccuKnox CSPM leverages agentless technology and native APIs to discover cloud resources, assess their configurations, and detect misconfigurations and vulnerabilities. It continuously monitors the environment for changes and deviations from established baselines or security frameworks (e.g., CIS, NIST, HIPAA).

Key features of AccuKnox CSPM include:

1. Cloud Continuous Compliance
2. Asset Inventory
3. Misconfiguration Detection
4. Baseline and Drift Detection
5. Reporting and Governance
6. DevOps Integrations

Architecture

AccuKnox CSPM follows architectural guidelines that align with best practices for Zero Trust Cloud Security, as outlined by the US Department of Defense NSA, CNCF, GSA, and Gartner. It integrates with various security tools, CI/CD pipelines, and SIEM solutions.

Feature	Description
Cloud Continuous Compliance	Review cloud infrastructure health and compliance posture against frameworks like STIG, CIS, NIST CSF, HIPAA, and MITRE.
Asset Inventory	Identify assets and provide visibility across multi-cloud infrastructure, categorize resources, and associate misconfigurations and vulnerabilities.
Misconfiguration Detection	Unified view of misconfigurations and vulnerabilities across multi-cloud environments.
Baseline and Drift Detection	Establish custom baselines and receive alerts when security controls are breached or configurations change.
Reporting and Governance	Generate detailed reports for sensitive assets, compliance audits, and third-party audits (3PAO).
DevOps Integrations	Integrate with various tools, including scanners, ticketing systems, notification channels, SIEM, and registries.

AccuKnox CNAPP Definitive Guide

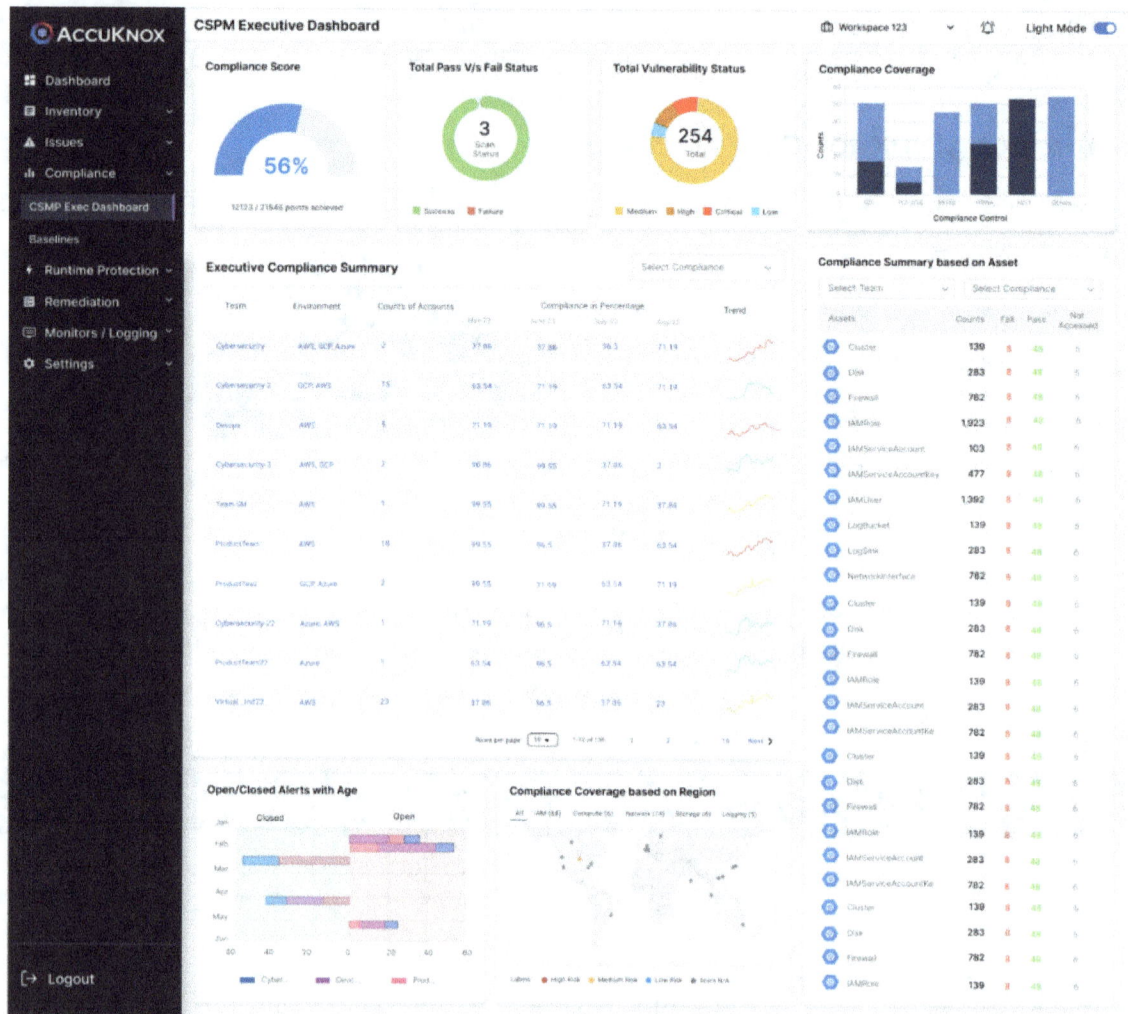

FIGURE 15. ACCUKNOX DASHBOARD WITH COMPLIANCE SUMMARY

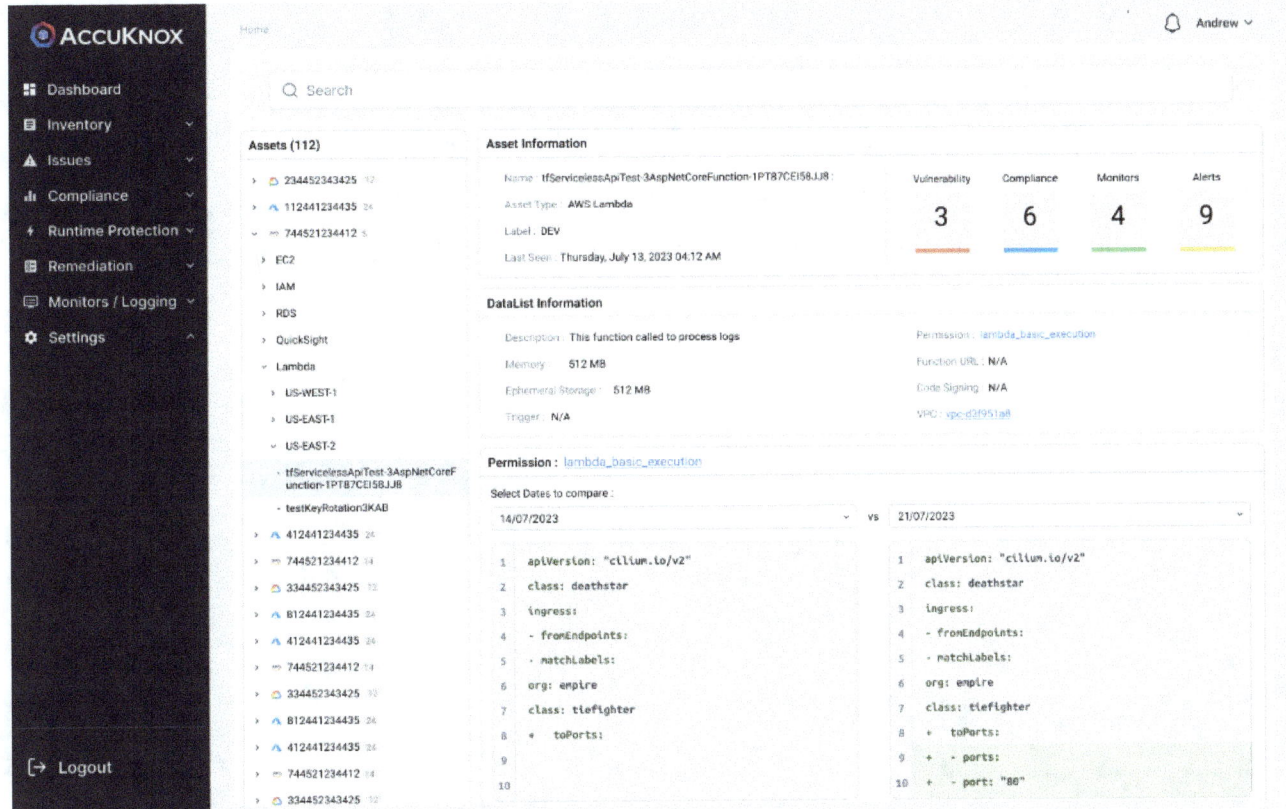

FIGURE 16. ACCUKNOX DASHBOARD WITH ASSET INFORMATION AND PERMISSIONS

Key Differentiators

Automated Security & Compliance

- Continuously monitor security posture and compliance across multi-cloud environments.
- Gain real-time insights with a customizable dashboard and in-depth reporting.
- Simplify remediation with one-click assistance and track configuration changes.
- Analyze baseline compliance for all regions and prioritize findings.

Streamlined Workflows

- Review security policies and findings without granting full console access.
- Monitor asset changes and trigger re-reviews when needed.
- Correlate findings from various sources for comprehensive analysis.
- Generate reports by real-world structures for easy understanding.

- Demonstrate security activity to regulators and auditors.

Actionable Threat Management

- Manage the entire security lifecycle, from identification to remediation.
- Act on findings with automated ticketing for faster resolution.
- Establish baselines and track progress for improved security posture.

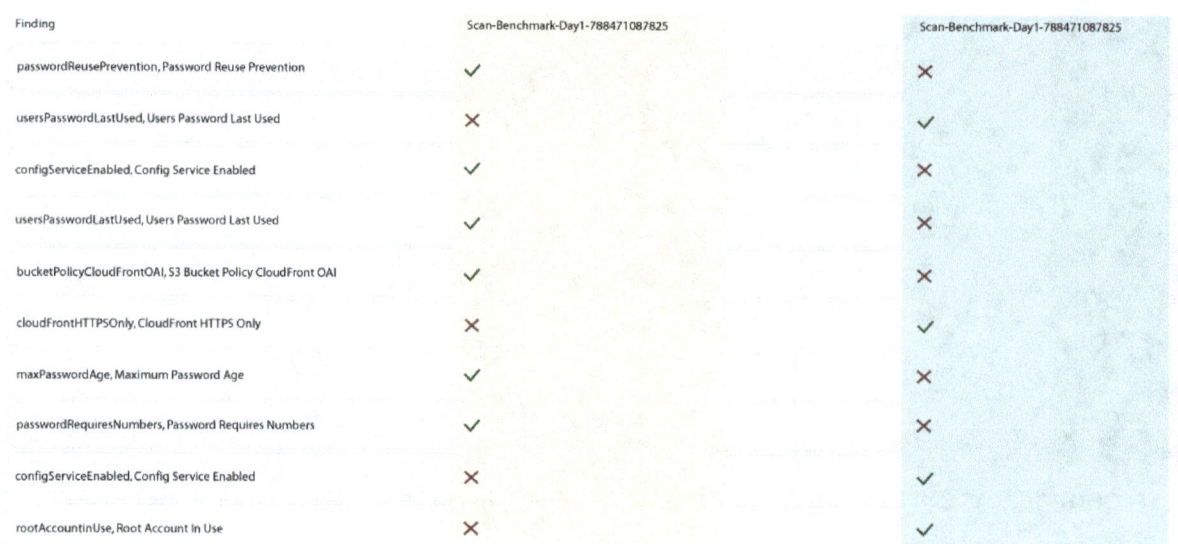

FIGURE 17. ACCUKNOX DASHBOARD WITH SCAN COMPARISONS

Key Takeaways

AccuKnox CSPM

- is an agentless tool that enhances cloud security by actively identifying and prioritizing vulnerabilities.
- simplifies achieving compliance with various regulations.
- facilitates tight integration with SIEM/SOAR platforms.
- provides asset discovery, mapping of misconfigurations and vulnerabilities to assets, critical asset grouping, and proactive monitoring for configuration changes across multi-cloud environments.
- supports full scans, baselining infrastructure based on controls (CIS, PCI-DSS, etc.), and delta difference reporting over time.

- offers proactive monitoring instead of point-in-time snapshots.
- identifies publicly accessible S3 buckets as an "Exposed Treasure" example.

Section 4.3. KSPM (Kubernetes Security Posture Management)

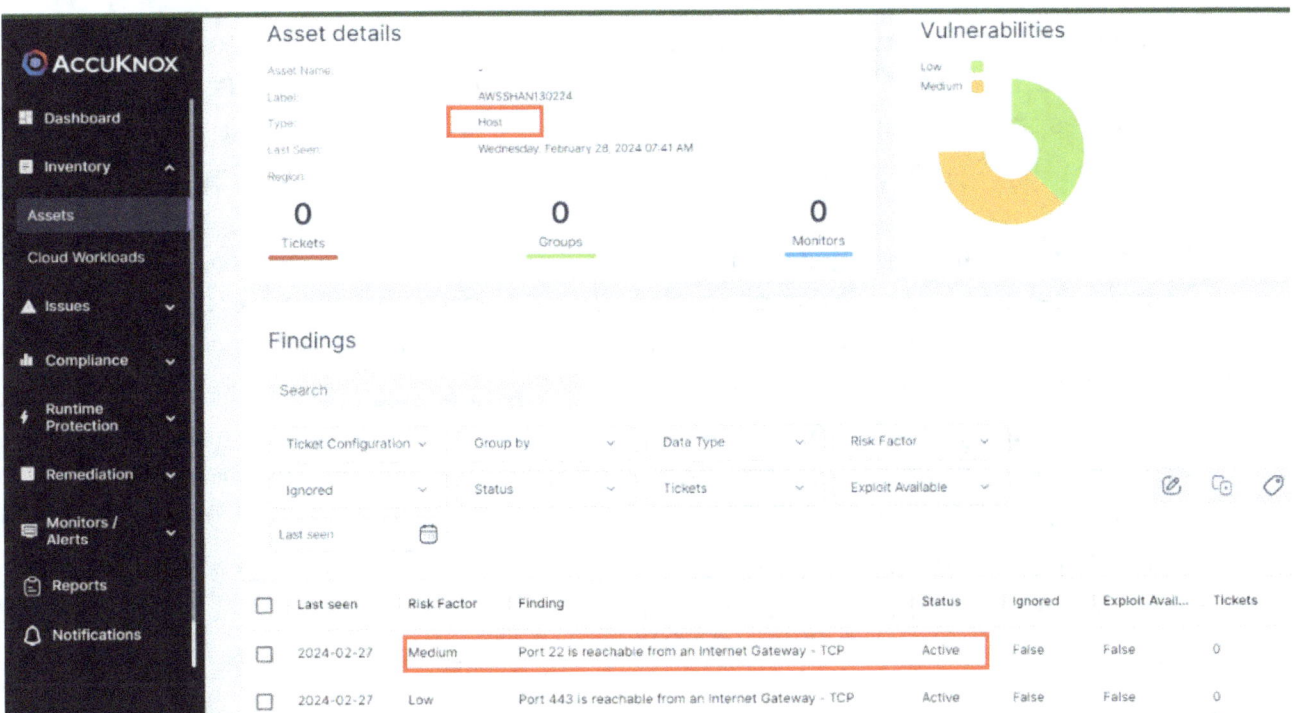

FIGURE 18. ACCUKNOX DASHBOARD WITH ASSETS VIEW SHOWING GRANULAR DETAILS WITH FILTER/SEARCH FUNCTIONALITY

AccuKnox KSPM allows DevSecOps teams to gain complete control over their Kubernetes environments. It delivers a centralized view of all Kubernetes resources, including containers, workloads, identities, and network configurations, enabling security teams to effectively manage and secure their cloud-native infrastructure.

Why is Kubernetes Security important?

As organizations continue to embrace Kubernetes for their cloud-native applications, the complexity of managing and securing these environments has grown exponentially. AccuKnox KSPM addresses this challenge by providing a comprehensive set of features that help organizations identify and mitigate risks, ensure compliance, and maintain a robust security posture for their Kubernetes deployments.

How is this accomplished?

1. **Unified Kubernetes Inventory**: A centralized view of all Kubernetes resources, including containers, images, workloads, identities, and network configurations, across multiple cloud environments allows security teams to have a complete understanding of their Kubernetes landscape.
2. **Risk Prioritization and Remediation**: The platform analyzes the Kubernetes environment for misconfigurations, security issues, and other risks, and prioritizes them based on factors like network exposure, permission levels, and security characteristics. It then provides guided remediation steps to address these issues.
3. **Kubernetes RBAC Analysis:** The platform provides an in-depth analysis of Kubernetes Role-Based Access Control (RBAC) configurations, detecting misconfigurations, overprivileged, and risky permissions, and providing actionable insights to improve access control.
4. **Network Configuration Analysis**: Analyzes the network configuration of Kubernetes pods and resources, revealing risky API access and other insecure network configurations, allowing security teams to address these vulnerabilities.
5. **Compliance Controls**: Scans for compliance with CIS Kubernetes benchmarks, as well as a wide range of industry standards and best practices, helping organizations maintain a secure and compliant Kubernetes environment.

Architecture

AccuKnox KSPM follows a multi-layered architecture that ensures comprehensive visibility, risk assessment, and compliance management for Kubernetes environments. The platform consists of the following key components:

1. **Data Collectors**: These agents are deployed in the Kubernetes clusters to gather configuration data from various sources, such as the Kubernetes API, cloud provider APIs, and container images.
2. **Data Processing and Analysis**: The collected data is processed and analyzed by the AccuKnox KSPM platform, which uses advanced algorithms and machine learning techniques to identify risks, misconfigurations, and compliance issues.
3. **Reporting and Remediation**: The platform provides intuitive dashboards, reports, and guided remediation steps to help security teams understand the security posture of their Kubernetes environments and take necessary actions to address the identified issues.

AccuKnox CNAPP Definitive Guide

4. **Integration and Automation**: AccuKnox KSPM seamlessly integrates with other security and DevOps tools, allowing for automated workflows and integration with existing security processes.

Feature	Description
Kubernetes Inventory	Centralized visibility into all Kubernetes resources, including containers, images, workloads, identities, and network configurations.
Risk Prioritization	Analyzes Kubernetes environments for misconfigurations and security issues, and prioritizes them based on risk factors.
RBAC Analysis	Provides in-depth analysis of Kubernetes RBAC configurations, detecting misconfigurations and risky permissions.
Network Configuration Analysis	Analyzes the network configuration of Kubernetes pods and resources, revealing insecure configurations.
Compliance Controls	Scans for compliance with CIS Kubernetes benchmarks and other industry standards.
Guided Remediation	Provides step-by-step guidance to address the identified issues and improve the security posture.
Automation and Integration	Seamlessly integrates with other security and DevOps tools for automated workflows and enhanced security processes.

FIGURE 19. FILTER ASSETS TO REDUCE INFORMATION DELUGE AND ZONE-IN ON WHAT MATTERS

Key Differentiators

1. **Comprehensive Kubernetes Security**: AccuKnox KSPM offers a holistic approach to Kubernetes security, addressing challenges across inventory, identity and access management, network configurations, and compliance.
2. **Intuitive User Experience**: The platform provides an easy-to-use interface with intuitive features that enable security and Kubernetes teams to quickly understand the security posture of their Kubernetes environments and take appropriate actions.
3. **Seamless Integration**: AccuKnox KSPM seamlessly integrates with other security and DevOps tools, allowing for automated workflows and enhanced security processes.
4. **Compliance and Governance**: The platform offers comprehensive compliance mapping, scoring, and reporting against industry standards and best practices, helping organizations maintain a secure and compliant Kubernetes environment.
5. **Shift-Left Approach**: AccuKnox KSPM enables security teams to identify and remediate Kubernetes misconfigurations and vulnerabilities at the source by integrating with Infrastructure as Code (IaC) processes.

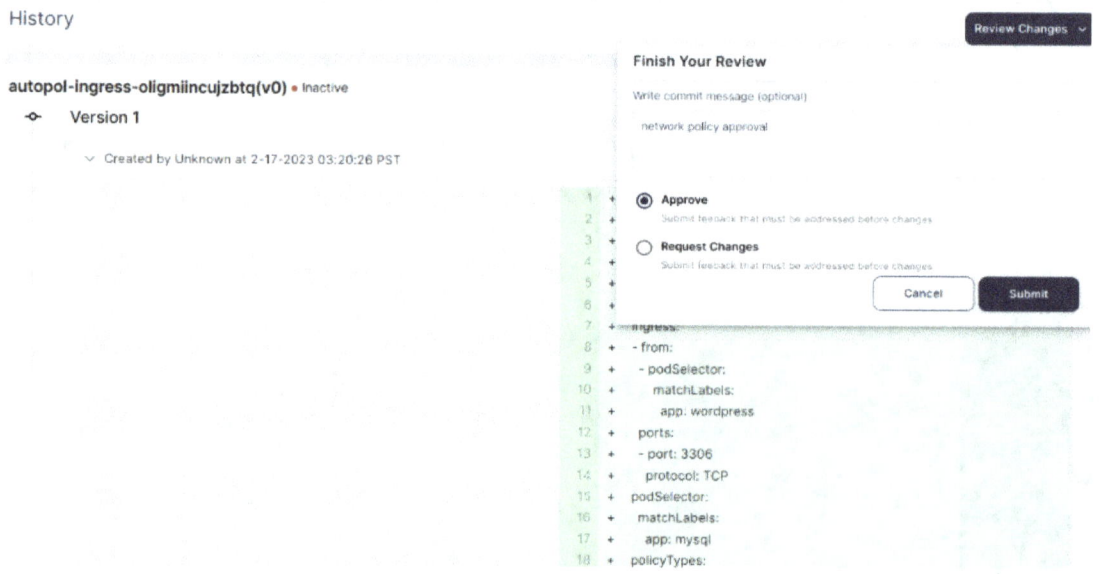

FIGURE 20. CONFIGURATION OF SECURITY POLICIES WITH ACCUKNOX

Key Takeaways

1. AccuKnox KSPM provides a centralized and comprehensive view of Kubernetes environments, enabling security teams to effectively manage and secure their cloud-native infrastructure.

2. The platform's risk prioritization and remediation features help organizations identify and address security issues, misconfigurations, and compliance gaps in their Kubernetes deployments.

3. AccuKnox KSPM's Kubernetes RBAC analysis and network configuration analysis capabilities ensure that organizations maintain robust access control and secure network posture for their Kubernetes environments.

4. The platform's compliance controls, guided remediation, and integration with other security and DevOps tools make it a powerful solution for organizations looking to enhance their Kubernetes security and compliance posture.

5. AccuKnox KSPM's shift-left approach and comprehensive capabilities make it a valuable addition to organizations' cloud-native security strategies, helping them secure their Kubernetes environments from the ground up.

Section 4.4. Alert Fatigue & Prioritizing Vulnerabilities with AccuKnox

AccuKnox helps prioritize vulnerabilities across container image scans, secret information, sensitive data, or malware through runtime context and agentless risk scanning for an ideal workload security posture.

What is it?

AccuKnox's Cloud-Native Application Protection Platform (CNAPP) brings together multiple security and protection capabilities into a single platform focused on identifying and prioritizing excessive risk of the entire cloud-native application and its associated infrastructure. Thus, a priority-based filtering/tagging and assessment is necessary to avoid "alert deluge"; and inefficient; and ineffective security operations caused by fragmented and disjointed approaches.

How is this accomplished?

AccuKnox is powered by the KubeArmor Discovery Engine, which simplifies policy management for effective, metadata-driven security solutions. Granular security policies are enforced at the system level with real-time monitoring for prompt alerts.

Alerts are generated based on audit, block, drift detection, operations, severity, and pods.

FIGURE 21. DASHBOARD ALERTS BASED ON OPERATIONS AND SEVERITY

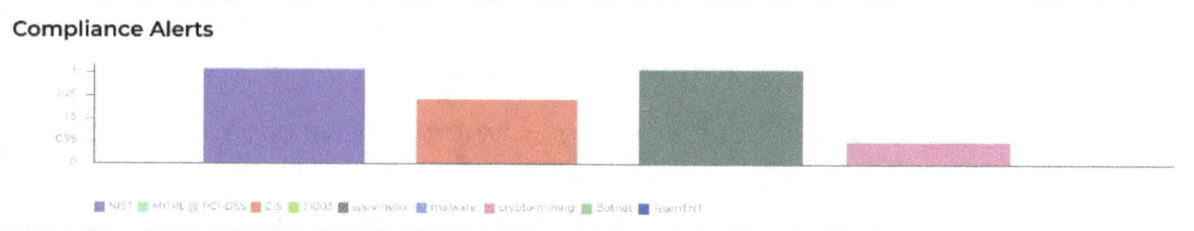

FIGURE 22. ACCUKNOX DASHBOARD WITH COMPLIANCE ALERTS

Alerts Summary

Total Alerts Generated
477363
Alerts

Total Blocked Alerts
418967
Blocked Alerts

Total Audited Alerts
58395
Audited Alerts

FIGURE 23. ACCUKNOX ALERTS DASHBOARD WITH REAL-TIME UPDATES AND NOTIFICATIONS

Key Differentiators

- Agentless risk scanning
- Runtime context for prioritizing vulnerabilities
- Unified CNAPP Dashboard with end-to-end tooling to suit all personas
- KubeArmor Discovery Engine for policy management

- Granular system-level security policy enforcement
- Real-time monitoring and prompt alerts
- Audit-based alerts
- Block-based alerts
- Drift detection alerts
- Operation and severity-based alerts
- Pod alerts
- Compliance summary and alerts for MITRE, NIST, CIS, PCI-DSS

Key Takeaways

- AccuKnox prioritizes vulnerabilities across various aspects of cloud-native applications and infrastructure through agentless scanning and runtime context.
- It provides a comprehensive CNAPP platform that identifies and prioritizes excessive risk, avoiding alert deluge and inefficient security operations.
- The KubeArmor Discovery Engine simplifies policy management, enforces granular security policies, and provides real-time monitoring and prompt alerts based on various criteria, including audit, block, drift detection, operations, severity, and pods.
- Compliance summaries and alerts are generated for industry standards like MITRE, NIST, CIS, and PCI-DSS.

Section 4.5. KIEM (Kubernetes Identity and Entitlement Management)

AccuKnox KIEM simplifies Kubernetes Role-Based Access Control (RBAC) management with powerful analytics and visualization, being the first CNAPP Cloud Security Tool to provide Kubernetes Identity Entitlement Management (KIEM) out of the box.

What is it?

KIEM is a solution that provides full-text search across RBAC entities; interactive graph visualization of connections between users, permissions, and resources; predefined queries to highlight critical issues; custom filtering; and change history monitoring for Kubernetes access configurations.

AccuKnox CNAPP Definitive Guide

Why is this important?

Managing access control and permissions in Kubernetes is complex, with over 65% of Kubernetes admins struggling with properly configuring and analyzing RBAC policies. The default RBAC implementation in Kubernetes quickly becomes difficult to monitor and secure due to the web of interdependent entities and relationships.

How is this accomplished?

KIEM works by installing agents to index Kubernetes audit data, defining admin users and access credentials for the KIEM console; reviewing pre-built dashboards, relationship graphs, and risk queries; customizing searches and alerts tailored to deployments; and receiving notifications when risky changes or configurations are detected.

Key Differentiators

Full-text search across all RBAC entities like service accounts and role bindings	
Interactive graph visualization of connections between users, permissions, and resources	

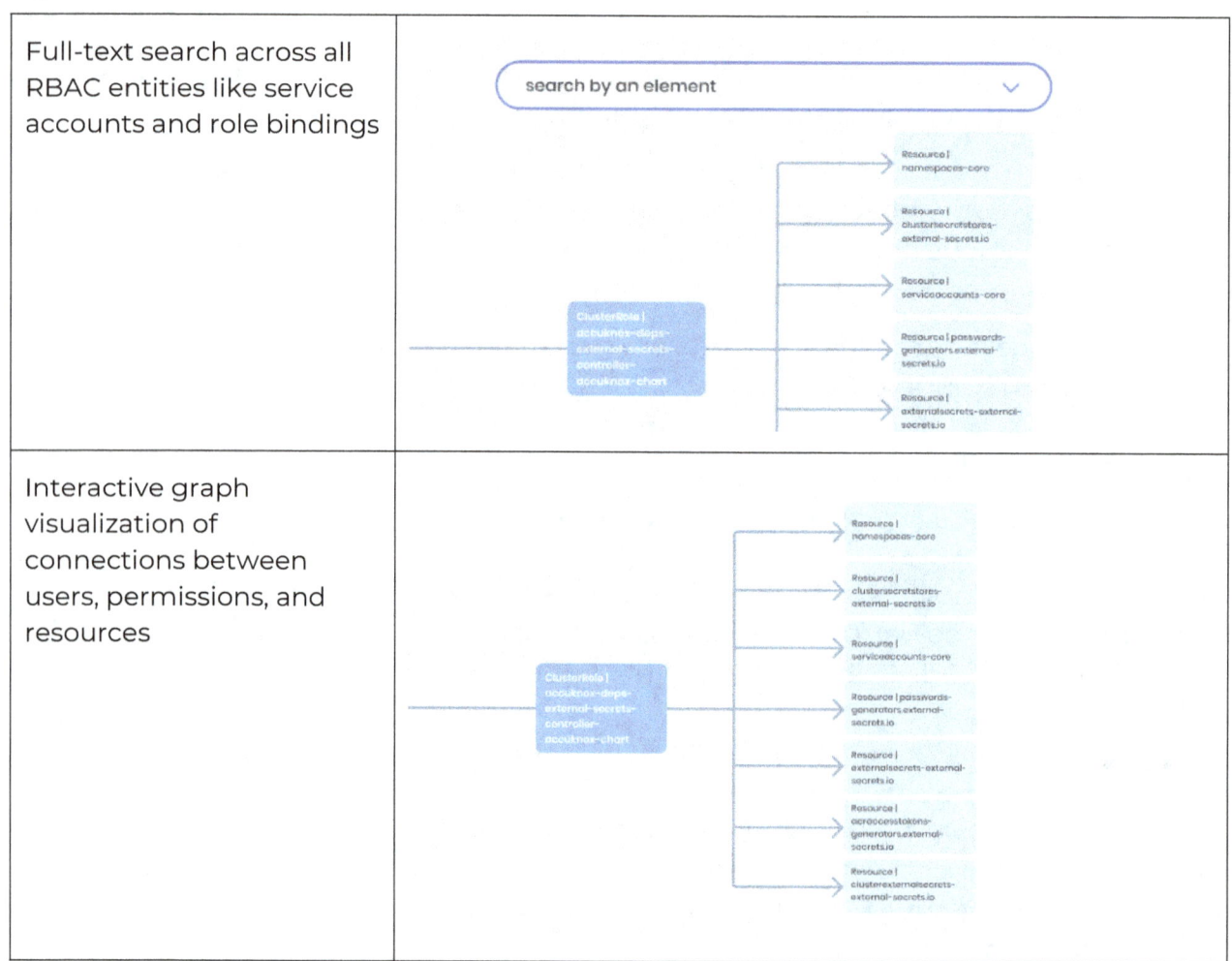

AccuKnox CNAPP Definitive Guide

Predefined queries that highlight critical issues like unnecessary privileges	
Custom filtering to continuously monitor access configurations and changes	
Change history review to identify risky modifications	

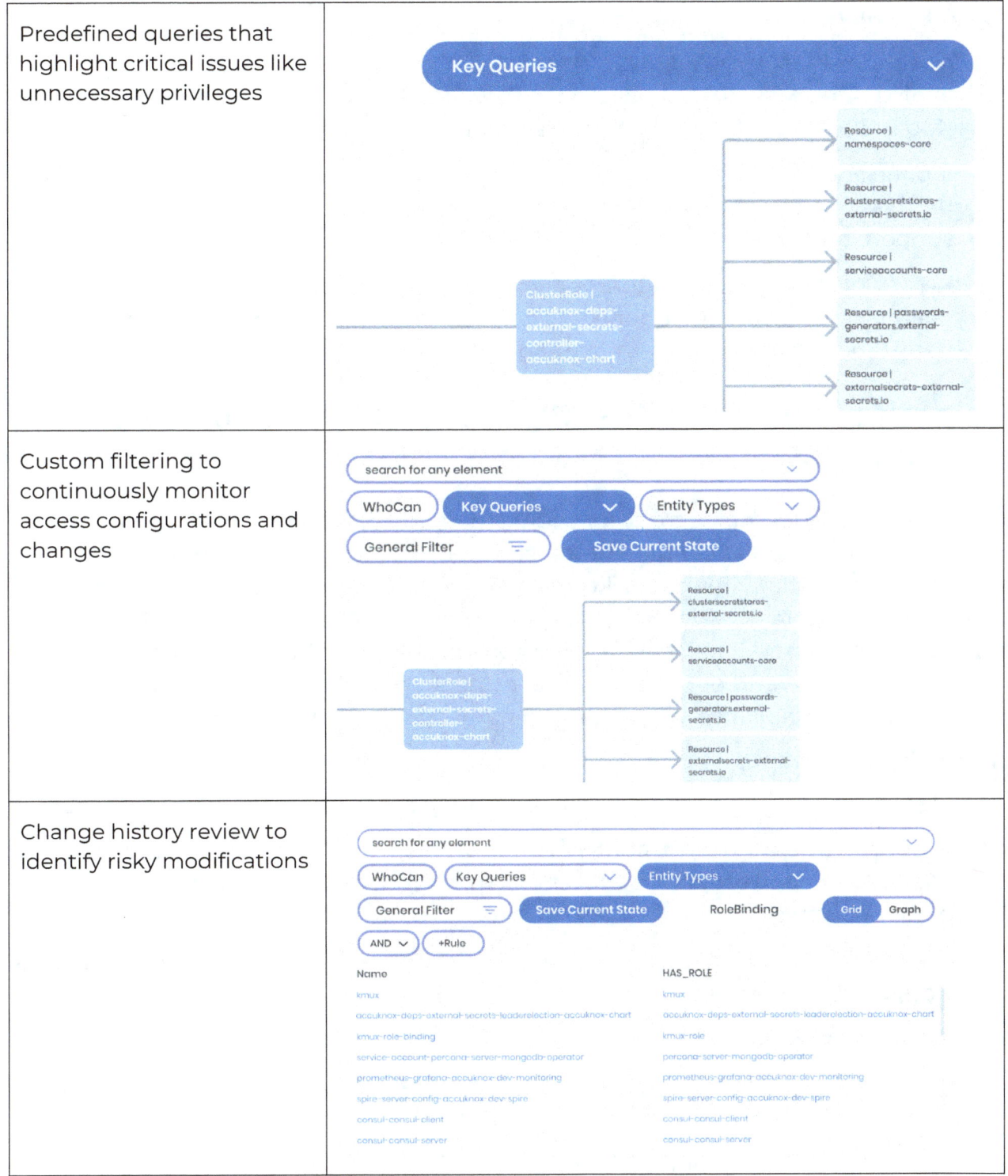

Key Takeaways

- AccuKnox KIEM simplifies Kubernetes RBAC management with powerful analytics and visualization, being the first CNAPP Cloud Security Tool to provide Kubernetes Identity Entitlement Management (KIEM) out of the box.

- It offers increased visibility into access policies, detection of unnecessary or risky permissions, easier RBAC management and troubleshooting, compliance support, and safeguarding of sensitive resources and data.

- KIEM works by indexing Kubernetes audit data; providing pre-built dashboards, relationship graphs, risk queries, customizable searches and alerts, and notification of risky changes or configurations.

Section 4.6. CWPP (Cloud Workload Protection Platform)

AccuKnox CWPP delivers security for multi-cloud and on-premise environments. It includes features such as container forensics, container drift detection, workload hardening, application firewalling, kernel hardening, and preemptive mitigation against zero-day attacks. AccuKnox integrates with CI/CD pipelines and SIEM tools like Jira, Slack, Splunk, and Rsyslog for a robust security system. The platform follows a zero-trust approach and provides runtime protection through various widgets like alert summary, compliance summary, and namespace severity.

Why is this important?

- Cloud security is crucial to protect applications and data from various threats.

- AccuKnox's data-driven security solution works well for cloud workloads, ensuring the protection of applications throughout the development and production stages.

- The platform offers features that help detect and mitigate vulnerabilities, secure workloads, and prevent attacks.

How is this accomplished?

- AccuKnox uses a lightweight industry-standard sensor agent based on eBPF (extended Berkeley Packet Filter) for workload protection.

- It follows a zero-trust approach, which means that it does not trust any user or workload by default and verifies every access request.

AccuKnox CNAPP Definitive Guide

- The platform provides container forensics to analyze containers and detect any malicious activity or unauthorized changes.
- It offers container drift detection to identify any configuration changes or deviations from the desired state.
- AccuKnox allows for workload hardening based on various industry standards such as MITRE, NIST, CIS, PCI, and HIPAA.
- It includes an application firewall to protect against application layer attacks.
- The platform also focuses on kernel hardening to secure the underlying operating system.
- AccuKnox integrates with various tools and services such as SIEM tools, notification tools, AppSec tools, and registries.

Architecture

- AccuKnox follows a cloud-native architecture, leveraging microservices for static and dynamic security measures.
- It securely stores data in S3 buckets for reliable and scalable storage.
- The platform integrates with CI/CD pipelines to ensure security throughout the development lifecycle.
- AccuKnox also integrates with SIEM tools like Jira, Slack, Splunk, and Rsyslog for centralized monitoring and alerting.

Feature	Description
Container Forensics	Analyzes containers to detect malicious activity or unauthorized changes
Container Drift Detection	Identifies configuration changes or deviations from the desired state
Workload Hardening	Implements security measures based on industry standards such as MITRE, NIST, CIS, PCI, and HIPAA
Application Firewalling	Protects against application layer attacks
Kernel Hardening	Focuses on securing the underlying operating system
Pre-emptive Mitigation	Provides proactive mitigation against zero-day attacks

Integration with CI/CD	Ensures security throughout the development lifecycle by integrating with CI/CD pipelines

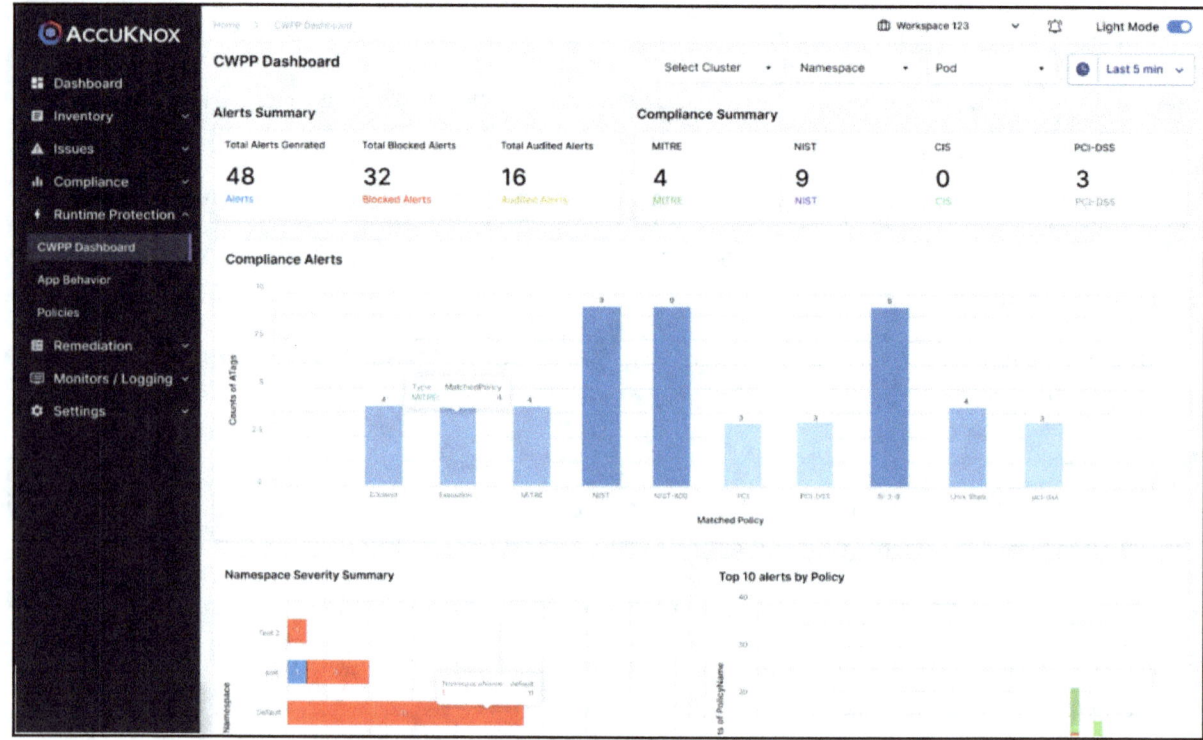

FIGURE 24. ACCUKNOX CWPP DASHBOARD

Auto Discovered Zero Trust Policy	Automatically Generated Hardening Policies Based on Standard Compliance Framework. Our system has the capability to suggest hardening policies based on common compliance frameworks such as MITRE, NIST, PCI-DSS, and CIS.
Custom Zero Trust Policy	Using the Policy Editor Tool to Personalize Policy Creation
Inline Remediation	Ensuring Application Uptime and Zero Trust Posture with Inline Remediation, With a robust, declarative policy in place, it's possible to execute inline remediation against runtime attacks like APT vulnerability and log4j. This approach helps to maintain the uptime and zero trust posture of your applications, ensuring their continued protection.
Network Microsegmentation	Isolating Workloads and Restricting Traffic to Prevent Malicious Lateral Movements is simplified. To prevent malicious lateral movements, it is important to have the ability to isolate workloads and restrict traffic.

FIGURE 25. ACCUKNOX ZERO TRUST CWPP FEATURES

FIGURE 26. ACCUKNOX CWPP INTEGRATIONS

Registry: CWPP provides container image scanning capabilities by integrating with various registries like ECR, ACR, Docker Hub, Nexus, and Harbor. Users can onboard registries, initiate scans, and view scan results within the CWPP dashboard.

The Registry Scan feature allows users to:

- view scan progress in the Scan Queue.
- access scan findings, including vulnerabilities classified by severity, for each repository and image.
- get detailed information about vulnerabilities, resources, sensitive data, and layers in a comprehensive view.

Remediation: CWPP offers remediation capabilities to address identified vulnerabilities and issues. Users can leverage the Risk-Based Prioritization view to see vulnerabilities prioritized based on environment and risk factors.

For efficient remediation, CWPP provides:

Feature	Description
View All Images	View vulnerabilities for specific images in the Inventory → Assets section.
View Image Vulnerabilities	Access a list of vulnerabilities for selected images in the Issues → Vulnerabilities section.
Ticket Creation	Automatically create tickets for selected vulnerabilities by integrating with ticketing systems like Jira, FreshService, and ConnectWise.

With this combination of vulnerability scanning, prioritization, and ticketing integration, CWPP streamlines the remediation process, ensuring efficient and timely mitigation of identified risks.

Key Differentiators

- **Inline Mitigation with KubeArmor**: AccuKnox uses KubeArmor (an open-source project) and Linux Security Modules to prevent attacks before execution.
- **eBPF Integration**: Extends kernel capabilities with eBPF without modifying kernel source code, enabling modern workload protection.
- **Centralized Dashboard**: Get an overarching view of runtime protection through various widgets and visualizations.
- **Unique Combination of Technologies**: Combines advanced technologies for proactive security, inline remediation, and efficient kernel capability extension.

Key Takeaways

- CWPP is a comprehensive Zero Trust security solution for cloud-native applications, offering runtime protection, workload hardening, and compliance across multiple environments.
- It leverages open-source projects like KubeArmor and cutting-edge technologies like eBPF and Linux Security Modules for efficient security enforcement.
- CWPP's unique combination of features, including application behaviour discovery, network micro-segmentation, auto-discovered policies, inline remediation, and integrations, sets it apart from traditional security solutions.
- With its centralized dashboard and visualizations, CWPP provides a clear view of runtime protection and compliance status, enabling organizations to proactively mitigate risks and maintain a secure posture.

Layered Security

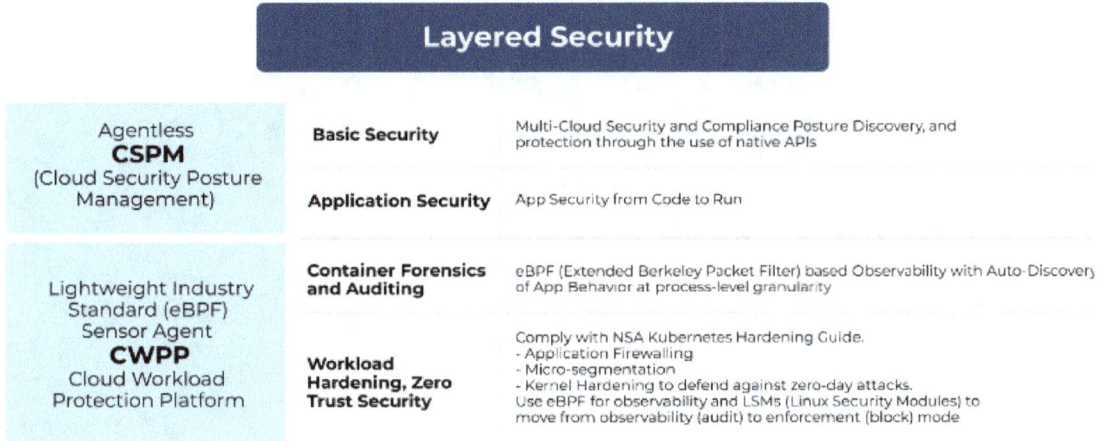

Section 4.7.   Inline Mitigation vs. Post-Attack Remediation

Inline Remediation is a proactive approach to security that aims to prevent and mitigate threats in real-time, as they occur, within the system's runtime environment. In contrast, Post-Attack Mitigation is a reactive approach that focuses on responding to and recovering from security incidents after they have already occurred.

What is it?

Inline Remediation, also known as Inline Security or Inline Mitigation, is a security approach that involves detecting and neutralizing threats within the runtime environment of an application or system, preventing malicious activities from executing or causing harm. It operates proactively, monitoring and enforcing security policies at the application level, rather than relying solely on perimeter defenses.

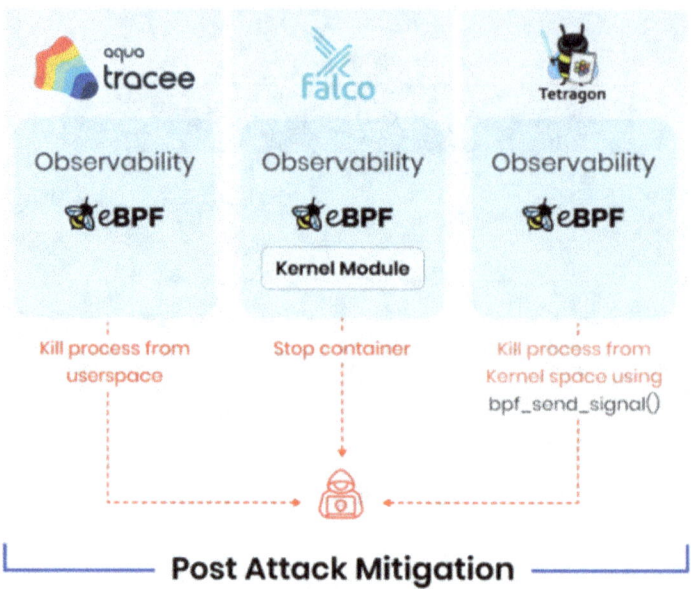

FIGURE 27. HOW POST ATTACK MITIGATION IS A FLAWED STRATEGY

Post-Attack Mitigation, on the other hand, refers to the process of implementing security measures and remediation steps after a security incident has occurred. It involves analyzing the incident, identifying the root causes, and implementing fixes or countermeasures to prevent similar incidents from happening in the future. It is a confined strategy.

Why is this important?

1. **Real-time Protection**: Traditional Post-Attack Mitigation approaches may be too slow to effectively counter rapidly evolving threats, such as zero-day exploits, supply chain attacks, or advanced persistent threats (APTs). Inline Remediation provides real-time protection by intercepting and neutralizing threats as they occur, minimizing the potential for damage.

2. **Attack Surface Reduction**: By proactively enforcing security policies at the application level, Inline Remediation reduces the attack surface by limiting the potential entry points and vectors for threats. This approach aligns with the principles of the Zero Trust security model, which advocates for least-privileged access and a more granular approach to security.

3. **Continuous Visibility and Monitoring**: Inline Remediation tools often incorporate continuous monitoring and observability capabilities, providing visibility into the runtime behavior of applications and their interactions with other components. This visibility helps in detecting anomalies and potential threats more effectively.

4. **Minimal Disruption**: Inline Remediation aims to prevent and mitigate threats without disrupting the normal operations of the application or system. By surgically neutralizing malicious activities, it avoids the need for complete system shutdowns or restarts, ensuring business continuity.

How is this accomplished?

Inline Remediation is typically accomplished through a combination of advanced security technologies and techniques, such as:

1. **Runtime Application Self-Protection (RASP)**: RASP solutions integrate security capabilities directly into the application runtime, allowing for real-time monitoring, analysis, and enforcement of security policies within the application context.

2. **eBPF (Extended Berkeley Packet Filter)**: eBPF is a powerful kernel technology that enables efficient and safe execution of user-defined programs within the kernel space. It provides a secure and efficient way to monitor and enforce security policies at the system level without modifying the kernel code.

3. **Linux Security Modules (LSMs)**: LSMs are kernel modules that allow for the implementation of mandatory access control (MAC) policies within the Linux kernel. They provide a way to enforce security policies at a low level, enabling fine-grained control over system resources and actions.

4. **Container Security**: In the context of cloud-native applications, Inline Remediation often involves the use of container security solutions, such as container runtime security tools, network micro-segmentation, and application-level firewalling.

5. **Behavior Analysis and Anomaly Detection**: Advanced machine learning and anomaly detection techniques are employed to establish baselines of normal application behavior and detect deviations that may indicate potential threats or malicious activities.

Architecture

The architecture of an Inline Remediation solution typically involves the following components:

1. **Sensor or Agent**: This component is responsible for collecting runtime data and monitoring the application or system behavior. It can be implemented as an agent within the application runtime or as a kernel module or eBPF program.

2. **Policy Engine**: The policy engine defines the security policies and rules that govern the acceptable behavior of the application or system. These policies can be defined based on industry best practices, compliance requirements, or specific organizational needs.

3. **Analysis and Detection**: This component analyzes the collected runtime data and applies anomaly detection algorithms, machine learning models, or rule-based engines to identify potential threats or violations of security policies.

4. **Enforcement and Mitigation**: When a threat or policy violation is detected, this component takes appropriate actions to mitigate or neutralize the threat. These actions can include blocking malicious activities, terminating malicious processes, or implementing compensating controls.

5. **Management and Reporting**: A centralized management console or dashboard provides visibility into the security posture, alerts, and reports, enabling security teams to monitor and respond to incidents effectively.

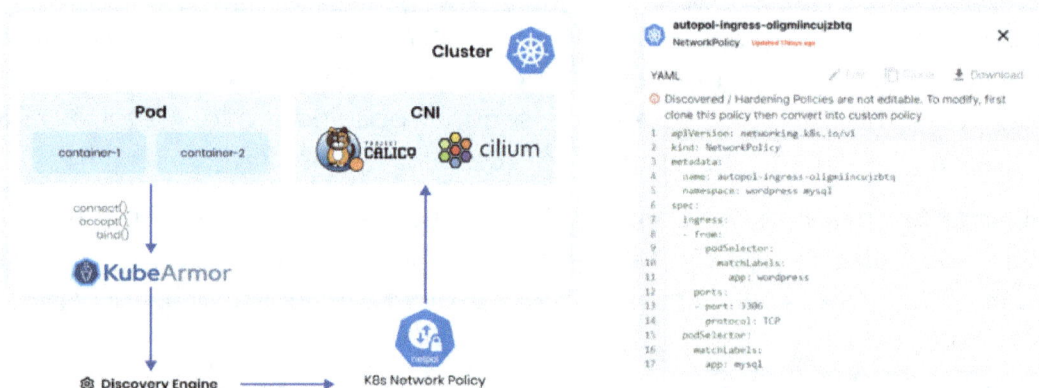

FIGURE 28. KUBEARMOR DISCOVERY ENGINE POWERS ACCUKNOX CNAPP FOR NETWORK POLICY MANAGEMENT

Feature	Inline Remediation	Post-Attack Mitigation
Approach	Proactive	Reactive
Focus	Threat prevention and real-time mitigation	Incident response and remediation
Timing	Real-time, within the application runtime	After a security incident has occurred

Feature	Inline Remediation	Post-Attack Mitigation
Attack Surface	Reduced by enforcing security policies at the application level	Unchanged or potentially increased until remediation is complete
Visibility	Continuous monitoring and observability of application behavior	Relies on forensic analysis and incident data
Disruption	Minimal, aims to prevent disruption to normal operations	Potentially disruptive, depending on the extent of the incident
Effectiveness	Highly effective against known and unknown threats	Limited effectiveness against evolving or advanced threats

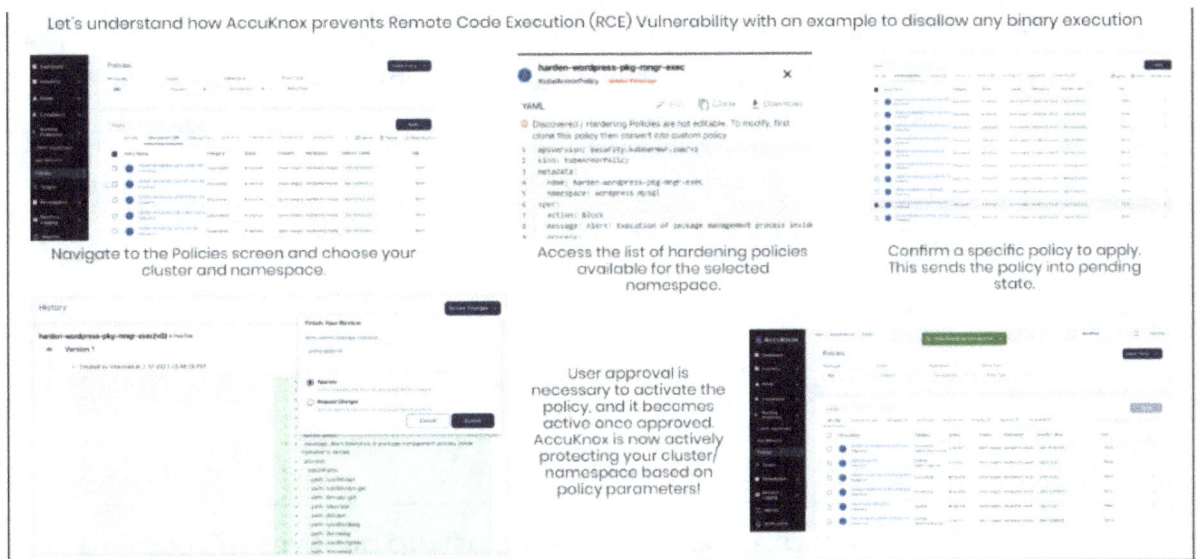

FIGURE 29. RUNTIME APPLICATION HARDENING AND FORENSICS WITH ACCUKNOX

Key Differentiators

Inline Remediation sets itself apart from traditional Post-Attack Mitigation approaches in several ways:

1. **Proactive Approach**: Inline Remediation is proactive, focusing on preventing threats from executing or causing harm, rather than reacting after the fact.

2. **Real-Time Protection**: By operating within the application runtime, Inline Remediation solutions can detect and mitigate threats in real-time, minimizing the potential for damage and data breaches.

3. **Attack Surface Reduction**: Enforcing security policies at the application level reduces the attack surface and limits potential entry points for threats, aligning with the principles of the Zero Trust security model.

4. **Continuous Visibility and Monitoring**: Inline Remediation solutions provide continuous visibility into the runtime behavior of applications, enabling more effective threat detection and response.

5. **Minimal Disruption**: Inline Remediation aims to neutralize threats without disrupting normal operations, ensuring business continuity and minimizing the impact on productivity.

6. **Effectiveness Against Advanced Threats**: By combining advanced technologies like eBPF, LSMs, and machine learning, Inline Remediation solutions can effectively detect and mitigate both known and unknown threats, including zero-day exploits and advanced persistent threats (APTs).

Features	AccuKnox	Brand A	Brand B	Brand C	Brand X
Design Approach	Zero Trust Enforcement + Observability	Observability + Add-on Enforcement	Observability + Add-on Enforcement	Observability + Add-on Enforcement	Observability + Add-on Enforcement
Enforcement Method	Inline Mitigation Any LSM	Post-execution Stop container	Post-execution Kill Proc from user space	Post-execution Kill Proc from kernel space	Replaces runC. Shim layer added before runC
Reliability	Stable. Only stops malicious actions. App keeps working.	Potential service impact	Potential service impact	Potential service impact	Generally Reliable but the app will experience downtimes
Policy Creation	Auto-discovered policies	Auto-discovered policies		manual rules	Predefined Policies

FIGURE 30. ACCUKNOX COMPETITOR ANALYSIS AND DIFFERENTIATORS

Key Takeaways

- Inline Remediation is a proactive approach to security that operates within the application runtime, detecting and mitigating threats in real-time, while Post-Attack Mitigation is a reactive approach focused on incident response and recovery.

- Inline Remediation is crucial for providing real-time protection against modern cyber threats, reducing the attack surface, and ensuring continuous visibility and monitoring of application behavior.

- It leverages advanced technologies like RASP, eBPF, LSMs, and machine learning to enforce security policies, detect anomalies, and neutralize threats without disrupting normal operations.

- Inline Remediation sets itself apart by offering a proactive approach, real-time protection, attack surface reduction, continuous visibility, minimal disruption, and effectiveness against advanced threats, aligning with the principles of the Zero Trust security model.

- Adopting Inline Remediation solutions is essential for organizations to stay ahead of evolving cyber threats and protect their cloud-native applications and critical systems in real time, ensuring business continuity and minimizing the potential for data breaches and reputational damage.

Section 4.8. GRC (Governance, Risk, and Compliance)

AccuKnox provides a comprehensive Governance, Risk, and Compliance (GRC) platform allowing you to define and enforce security policies, monitor and audit compliance, and automate remediation across cloud, Kubernetes, and traditional workloads. We have multi-tenancy, RBAC controls, and risk-based prioritization, ensuring secure and compliant digital transformation.

What is it?

The AccuKnox GRC platform is a comprehensive solution designed to help organizations maintain governance, manage risks, and ensure compliance across their IT infrastructure and applications. It provides a unified platform to define and enforce security policies, continuously monitor and audit compliance, and proactively remediate violations and vulnerabilities.

Why is this important?

In today's digital landscape, organizations face an increasing number of security threats, regulatory requirements, and compliance mandates. Failure to maintain governance, manage risks, and ensure compliance can result in severe consequences, including financial penalties, reputational damage, and operational disruptions. The AccuKnox GRC platform addresses these challenges by providing a comprehensive solution that streamlines and automates GRC processes, reducing the risk of non-compliance and security breaches.

How is this accomplished?

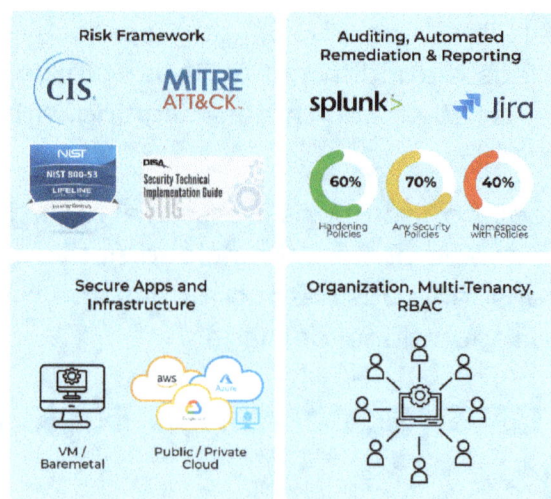

FIGURE 31.   ACCUKNOX GRC MATRIX

The AccuKnox GRC platform accomplishes its objectives through the following key components and features:

1. **Policy Definition and Enforcement**: Organizations can define security policies and rules based on industry standards (e.g., CIS, HIPAA, PCI-DSS, MITRE, NIST) and enforce them across their infrastructure and applications.

2. **Cloud and Kubernetes Posture Management**: The platform enables continuous monitoring and assessment of the security posture of cloud environments, Kubernetes clusters, and workloads, ensuring compliance with defined policies.

3. **Cloud Workload Protection Platform (CWPP)**: AccuKnox provides real-time monitoring and protection for cloud workloads, detecting and mitigating threats, vulnerabilities, and policy violations.

4. **Automated Remediation and Risk-Based Prioritization**: The platform prioritizes vulnerabilities and risks based on factors such as network exposure, exploitability, and runtime usage. It automates remediation processes and can block non-conforming actions.

5. **Comprehensive Reporting and Auditing**: AccuKnox generates detailed compliance reports, audit trails, and forensic data, enabling organizations to demonstrate compliance and perform root cause analysis.

6. **Multi-Tenancy and RBAC**: The platform supports multi-tenancy, role-based access control (RBAC), and organizational isolation, ensuring secure and segregated access to different teams and projects.

Architecture

FIGURE 32. RIGOROUS CLOUD SECURITY COMPLIANCE STANDARDS

The AccuKnox GRC platform follows a comprehensive architecture that covers the entire lifecycle of governance, risk management, and compliance. The key components of the architecture include:

1. **Onboarding and Auto-Discovery**: AccuKnox can automatically discover and onboard cloud infrastructure, applications, and workloads, establishing a baseline security posture.

2. **Continuous Observability**: The platform continuously monitors and assesses the security posture of cloud environments, Kubernetes clusters, and workloads, detecting any drift or deviations from defined policies.

3. **Enforcement and Remediation**: Based on the observed security posture, AccuKnox can enforce policies through various modes, such as alerting, blocking non-conforming actions, or automatically remediating violations.

AccuKnox CNAPP Definitive Guide

4. **Reporting, Analytics, and Auditing**: The platform generates comprehensive reports, provides analytics and insights, and maintains detailed audit trails for compliance and forensic purposes.

Table: AccuKnox GRC Platform

Feature	Description
Policy Definition and Enforcement	Define and enforce security policies based on industry standards
Cloud and Kubernetes Posture Management	Continuous monitoring and assessment of cloud and Kubernetes security posture
Cloud Workload Protection Platform (CWPP)	Real-time monitoring and protection for cloud workloads
Automated Remediation	Automate remediation processes and block non-conforming actions
Risk-Based Prioritization	Prioritize vulnerabilities and risks based on factors like network exposure and exploitability
Comprehensive Reporting and Auditing	Generate detailed compliance reports, audit trails, and forensic data
Multi-Tenancy and RBAC	Support for multi-tenancy, role-based access control, and organizational isolation

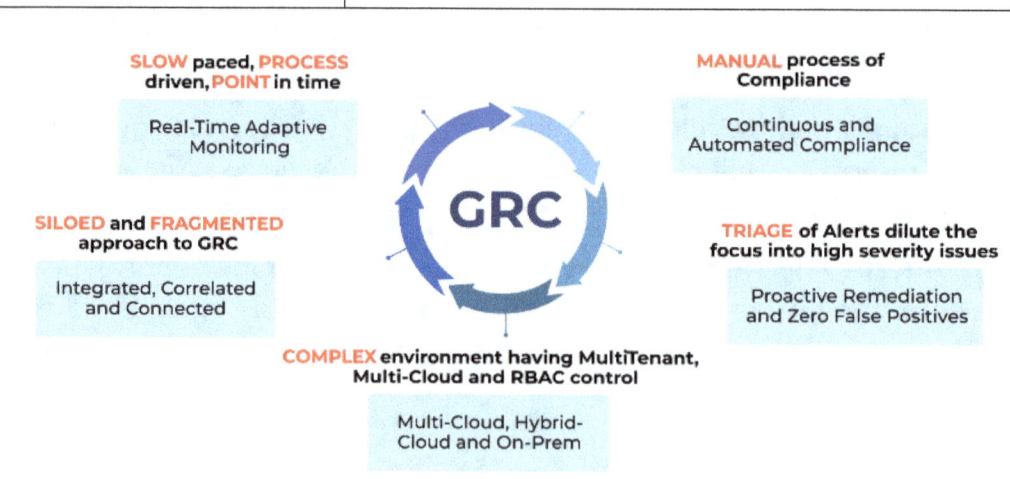

FIGURE 33. HOW ACCUKNOX FULFILLS GRC AT SCALE

Key Differentiators

1. **Zero Trust Cloud Native Application Security (CNAPP) Platform**: AccuKnox is built on a Zero Trust security model, providing comprehensive protection for cloud-native applications and workloads.

2. **Seminal Innovations from SRI (Stanford Research Institute)**: AccuKnox is developed in partnership with SRI and incorporates seminal inventions in areas such as container security, anomaly detection, and data provenance.

3. **eBPF-based Observability and Enforcement**: The platform leverages eBPF (extended Berkeley Packet Filter) technology for efficient and secure observability and enforcement of security policies.

4. **Proactive and Automated Remediation**: AccuKnox prioritizes risks and automates remediation processes, reducing the risk of non-compliance and security breaches.

5. **Multi-Cloud and Hybrid Cloud Support**: The platform supports public, private, and hybrid cloud environments, as well as on-premises deployments, ensuring consistent governance, risk management, and compliance across the organization's entire IT infrastructure.

Key Takeaways

- AccuKnox provides a comprehensive GRC platform for maintaining governance, managing risks, and ensuring compliance across cloud, Kubernetes, and traditional workloads.

- The platform offers multi-tenancy, RBAC controls, and risk-based prioritization, enabling secure and compliant digital transformation.

- AccuKnox automates policy enforcement, continuous monitoring, and remediation, reducing the risk of non-compliance and security breaches.

- The platform leverages innovative technologies, such as eBPF and seminal inventions from SRI, to provide efficient and secure observability and enforcement.

- With its multi-cloud and hybrid cloud support, AccuKnox enables consistent governance, risk management, and compliance across an organization's entire IT infrastructure.

Section 4.9. CDR (Cloud Detection & Response)

What is AccuKnox CDR?

AccuKnox Cloud Detection & Response (CDR) is a comprehensive security toolkit designed to address the unique challenges of cloud security. It offers a centralized view of an organization's multi-cloud environment, leverages advanced behavioral analytics to detect threats and enables lightning-fast automated response to contain and mitigate attacks.

Why is AccuKnox CDR important?

As organizations embrace cloud computing, they face new security blindspots and risks. Traditional security solutions often struggle to keep pace with the dynamic nature of cloud environments. AccuKnox CDR is purpose-built to address these challenges, providing organizations with the visibility, detection capabilities, and rapid response needed to secure their cloud infrastructure, workloads, identities, and data.

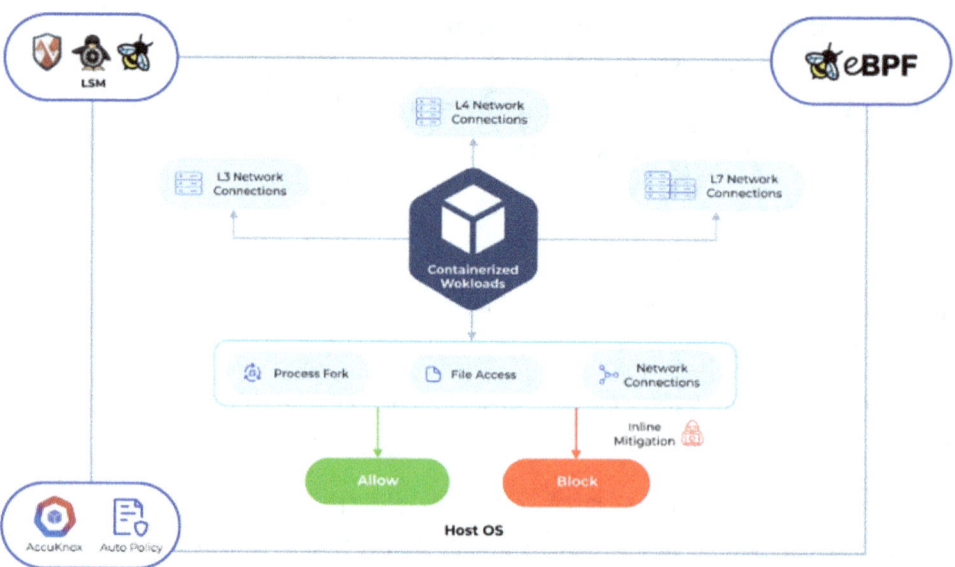

FIGURE 34. POLICY APPLICATION LEVERAGING EBPF/LSM

How is AccuKnox CDR accomplished?

AccuKnox CDR employs a multi-layered approach to monitor the entire cloud attack surface and thwart threats at machine speed. Here's how it works:

1. **Full Stack Observability**: Lightweight sensors are embedded across the cloud environment, including workloads, identities, networks, files, processes, and

storage infrastructure, achieving pervasive visibility even as the cloud footprint changes.

2. **Mapping the Threat Terrain**: Powered by an ever-updating Threat database, the AI engine has an evolving understanding of malware, suspicious behavior, and normal resource patterns. It baselines cloud-specific risks like misconfigurations while also tracing multi-stage attacks.
3. **Lightning-Fast Response**: AccuKnox CDR's automated response playbooks trigger containment measures within milliseconds against confirmed threats before they spread, while also notifying and equipping analysts to investigate.

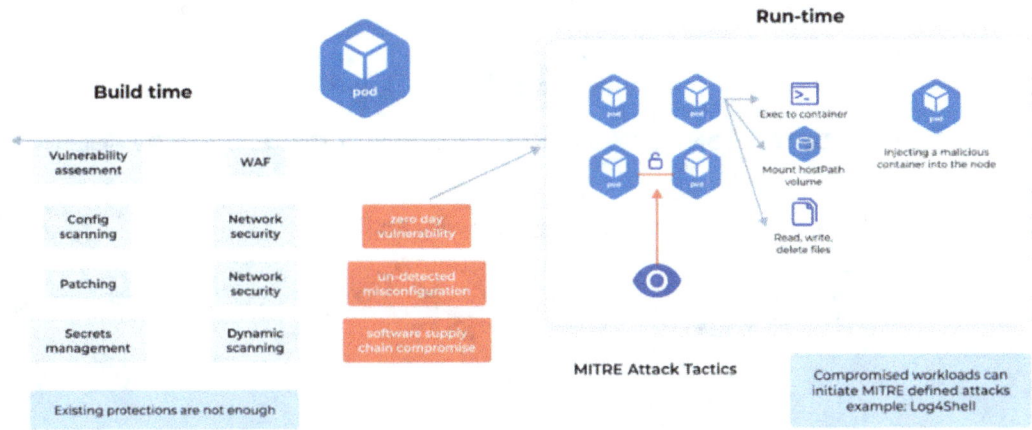

FIGURE 35. ACCUKNOX BUILD TO RUNTIME SECURITY

Key Features

Feature	Description
Unified Visibility	Integrations map cloud services, workloads, identities, and network flows into a single pane of glass.
AI Threat Hunters	Advanced behavioral analytics baseline normal activity and pinpoint anomalies in real-time.
Automated Response	Automatically respond to threats by quarantining workloads, adapting network controls, and more.
Threat Prioritization	Analyzes risks in the business context, accounts for vulnerabilities, and prioritizes critical threats.
Attack Narrative	Correlates events and audit logs to reconstruct attack narratives and follow the breadcrumbs of compromise.

AccuKnox CNAPP Definitive Guide

FIGURE 36. FROM DETECTION TO RESPONSE, ACCUKNOX COVERS EVERY SCENARIO

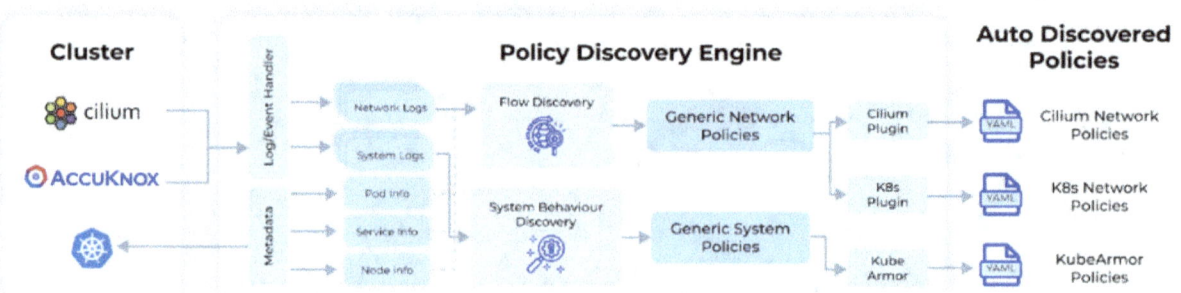

FIGURE 37. POLICY DISCOVERY ENGINE FOR ACCELERATED SECURITY

Key Differentiators

- Cloud-native architecture tailored for dynamic cloud environments
- Unified visibility across multi-cloud environments (AWS, Azure, GCP)
- Advanced behavioral analytics for cloud-specific threats
- Automated response at machine speed
- End-to-end attack narrative reconstruction

Key Takeaways

AccuKnox CDR is the analysts' choice for Cloud Workload Protection Platforms, providing organizations with unparalleled visibility, advanced threat detection, and rapid response capabilities tailored for the cloud era. By addressing the unique challenges of cloud security, AccuKnox CDR empowers enterprises to secure their cloud infrastructure, workloads, identities, and data while enabling them to take full advantage of the agility and scalability of the cloud.

Section 4.10. IaC (Infrastructure as Code) Security

What is AccuKnox IaC Security?

AccuKnox IaC Security is a holistic solution designed to address the unique security challenges associated with managing cloud infrastructure through code. It encompasses a range of tools, techniques, and best practices to mitigate risks, enforce compliance, and maintain the security posture of cloud environments. AccuKnox's Infrastructure as Code (IaC) Security solution provides a comprehensive suite of tools and best practices to secure cloud infrastructure throughout its lifecycle, ensuring confidentiality, integrity, and availability of resources.

Why is AccuKnox IaC Security important?

Template misconfigurations pose a significant security risk for IaC. It potentially allows skilled attackers to exploit system security or unintentionally undermine system security. As organizations increasingly adopt IaC for provisioning and managing cloud infrastructure, securing these code-driven environments becomes critical. IaC introduces new security risks, such as misconfigurations, unauthorized access, outdated dependencies, and malicious code injections. AccuKnox IaC Security helps organizations address these risks, ensuring the confidentiality, integrity, and availability of cloud infrastructure resources.

How AccuKnox Achieves IaC?

AccuKnox IaC Security leverages a multi-layered approach to secure cloud infrastructure throughout its lifecycle:

1. **Static Code Analysis**: Tools like Checkov, tfsec, and Terrascan perform static code analysis on IaC templates, detecting potential security vulnerabilities, misconfigurations, and compliance violations.
2. **Dynamic Security Testing**: Runtime security testing evaluates the actual state of cloud infrastructure resources, identifying and remediating security issues in a production-like environment.
3. **Continuous Monitoring and Logging**: Tools like AWS CloudTrail, Azure Monitor, and Google Cloud's Operations Suite provide comprehensive monitoring and logging capabilities, enabling real-time visibility into infrastructure changes and potential security incidents.

AccuKnox CNAPP Definitive Guide

4. **Policy as Code (PaC):** AccuKnox integrates Open Policy Agent (OPA), a powerful policy engine that automates the enforcement of security and compliance best practices through declarative policies.
5. **Security-First Mindset**: AccuKnox promotes a security-first mindset by fostering collaboration between security and development teams, providing security training, using secure architecture templates, and conducting regular security reviews and audits.

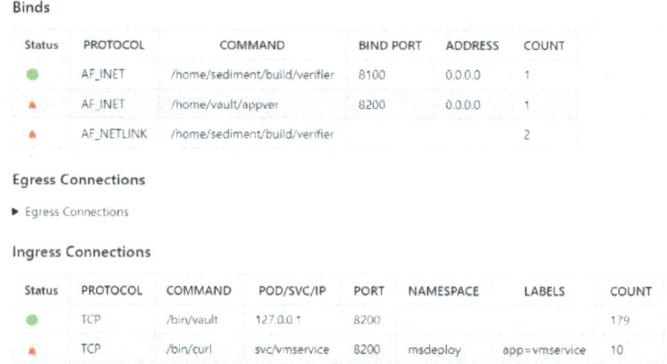

FIGURE 38. NETWORK BEHAVIOR SUMMARY

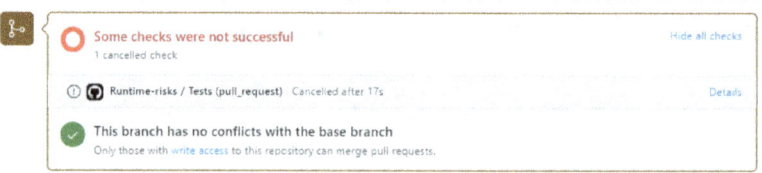

FIGURE 39. SIMPLIFIED CI/CD BASED INTEGRATIONS

Architecture

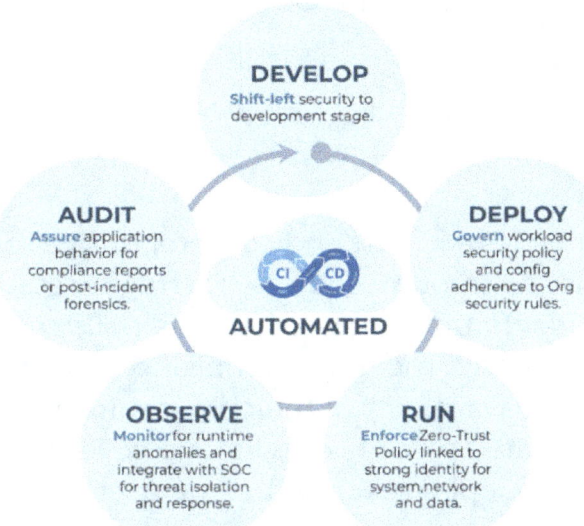

FIGURE 40. DEVSECOPS WORKFLOWS

AccuKnox IaC Security leverages a centralized platform that integrates seamlessly with existing DevOps toolchains and cloud environments. Its architecture includes the following key components:

Feature	Description
Unified Security Management	Centralized platform for managing IaC security across multiple cloud providers and environments.
Automated Security Checks	Automated security scanning and validation of IaC templates during development and deployment.
Policy Enforcement	Automated enforcement of security and compliance policies through Policy as Code (PaC).
Continuous Monitoring	Real-time monitoring and logging of infrastructure changes and security events.
Collaboration and Visibility	Collaboration tools and visual dashboards for improved visibility and communication between security and development teams.

Key Differentiators

- Comprehensive IaC security solution covering the entire infrastructure lifecycle
- Native integration with leading cloud providers and DevOps tools

- Automated policy enforcement and compliance checks
- Real-time monitoring and logging capabilities
- Centralized management and visibility across multi-cloud environments

Key Takeaways

AccuKnox IaC Security provides a robust and comprehensive solution for securing cloud infrastructure managed through code. By leveraging static code analysis, dynamic security testing, continuous monitoring, and policy enforcement, AccuKnox helps organizations mitigate risks, maintain compliance, and ensure the confidentiality, integrity, and availability of their cloud infrastructure resources. With its centralized platform, automated security checks, and collaboration tools, AccuKnox empowers organizations to adopt a security-first mindset and seamlessly integrate security into their IaC practices.

Section 4.11.   Capturing Forensics

AccuKnox is a robust container security and forensics solution that leverages KubeArmor's continuous monitoring and policy enforcement capabilities. It provides detailed insights, real-time alerts, and an audit trail for proactive identification and mitigation of security threats within Kubernetes environments.

What is AccuKnox Forensics? AccuKnox Forensics is a comprehensive forensic analysis and incident response component of the AccuKnox platform. It enables security teams to investigate and respond to security incidents within their Kubernetes clusters by providing detailed logs, audit trails, and forensic evidence.

Why is AccuKnox Forensics important? In today's rapidly evolving threat landscape, organizations need to be proactive in detecting and responding to security incidents within their cloud-native environments. AccuKnox Forensics plays a crucial role in enabling security teams to:

1. Identify and investigate security breaches promptly.
2. Determine the scope and impact of an incident.
3. Gather forensic evidence for root cause analysis and legal proceedings.
4. Implement appropriate remediation measures to secure the compromised environment.
5. Learn from security incidents and improve overall security posture.

How is AccuKnox Forensics accomplished? AccuKnox Forensics leverages several key capabilities to provide comprehensive forensic analysis and incident response:

1. **Continuous Monitoring**: AccuKnox continuously monitors the Kubernetes environment, aggregating logs and triggering alerts for any suspicious activities or policy violations.
2. **Aggregated Logging**: Logs from various pods across the cluster are aggregated and monitored for deviations from expected behavior, indicating potential security breaches.
3. **Policy Enforcement**: KubeArmor's policy enforcement capabilities ensure that any unauthorized activities, such as unauthorized file access, network connections, or process execution, are detected and logged.
4. **Forensic Analysis**: Security analysts or forensic experts can analyze the aggregated logs and triggered alerts to identify the attacker's actions, determine the extent of the compromise, and assess the potential impact on the cluster's security.
5. **Incident Response**: Based on the forensic analysis, the security team can investigate alerts, isolate compromised pods, apply necessary security patches, or roll back affected pods to a secure state.

Architecture

The AccuKnox Forensics architecture consists of the following key components:

1. **KubeArmor**: A Kubernetes security enforcement system that continuously monitors and enforces security policies within the cluster.
2. **Log Aggregation**: A centralized log aggregation system that collects and stores logs from all pods across the cluster.
3. **Forensic Analysis Engine**: A powerful forensic analysis engine that processes the aggregated logs, correlates events and provides detailed insights for incident investigation and response.
4. **Alert Management**: A comprehensive alert management system that generates real-time alerts for any policy violations or suspicious activities detected within the cluster.
5. **Incident Response Module**: A dedicated module that facilitates incident response actions, such as isolating compromised pods, applying security patches, or rolling back affected pods to a secure state.

Table: Key Forensic Capabilities of AccuKnox

AccuKnox CNAPP Definitive Guide

Capability	Description
File Access Monitoring	Logs and alerts for unauthorized file access attempts across the cluster.
Network Activity Monitoring	Monitors and logs network connections and network reconnaissance activities.
Process Monitoring	Logs and alerts for unauthorized process execution or command execution within pods.
Audit Trail	Provides a detailed audit trail of all activities within the cluster for forensic analysis.
Real-Time Alerting	Generates real-time alerts for any policy violations or suspicious activities.

Process forensics

Get granular details of all the executed processes within the target workloads.

File forensics

Get granular details of all the accessed files within the target workloads.

Network forensics

Get granular details of all the network accesses within the target workloads.

Syscall forensics

Get granular details of all the security sensitive system calls within the target workloads.

Sensitive Asset audit

Audit any (read/write) accesses to sensitive assets.

FIGURE 41. ACCUKNOX SUPPORTS PROCESS, FILE, NETWORK FORENSICS AND ASSET AUDITS

Process Forensics

```
apiVersion: security.kubearmor.com/v1
kind: KubeArmorPolicy
metadata:
```

```yaml
  name: ksp-discovery-process-discovery
  namespace: wordpress-mysql
spec:
  tags: ["MITRE", "Discovery"]
  message: "Someone accessed running process"
  selector:
    matchLabels:
      app: wordpress
  process:
    matchPaths:
    - path: /bin/ps
    - path: /usr/bin/ps
    - path: /usr/bin/pgrep
    - path: /usr/bin/top
    - path: /usr/bin/htop
  action: Audit
  severity: 5
```

Simulation

```
kubectl exec -it wordpress-7c966b5d85-wvtln -n wordpress-mysql -- bash
root@wordpress-7c966b5d85-wvtln:/var/www/html# ps -A
    PID TTY          TIME CMD
      1 ?        00:00:08 apache2
    189 ?        00:00:00 apache2
    190 ?        00:00:00 apache2
    191 ?        00:00:00 apache2
    192 ?        00:00:00 apache2
    193 ?        00:00:00 apache2
    245 pts/0    00:00:00 bash
```

Expected Alert

```
ClusterName: default
HostName: gke-cluster-1-default-pool-37f4c896-8cn6
NamespaceName: wordpress-mysql
PodName: wordpress-7c966b5d85-wvtln
Labels: app=wordpress
ContainerName: wordpress
ContainerID: 6d09394a988c5cf6b9fe260d28fdd57d6ff281618869a173965ecd94a3efac44
ContainerImage: docker.io/library/wordpress:4.8-apache@sha256:6216f64ab88fc51d311e38c7f69ca3f9aaba621492b4f1fa93ddf63093768845
Type: MatchedPolicy
```

```
PolicyName: ksp-discovery-process-discovery
Severity: 5
Message: Someone accessed running process
Source: /bin/bash
Resource: /bin/ps -A
Operation: Process
Action: Audit
Data: syscall=SYS_EXECVE
Enforcer: eBPF Monitor
Result: Passed
ATags: [MITRE Discovery]
HostPID: 1.252488e+06
HostPPID: 1.250979e+06
Owner: map[Name:wordpress Namespace:wordpress-mysql Ref:Deployment]
PID: 288
PPID: 281
ParentProcessName: /bin/bash
ProcessName: /bin/ps
Tags: MITRE,Discovery
```

Key Differentiators of AccuKnox Forensics

1. **Comprehensive Monitoring**: AccuKnox Forensics provides comprehensive monitoring of file access, network activity, and process execution within Kubernetes clusters, ensuring complete visibility into potential security threats.

2. **Aggregated Logging**: By aggregating logs from all pods across the cluster, AccuKnox Forensics provides a centralized view of all activities, enabling efficient forensic analysis.

3. **Policy Enforcement Integration**: The integration with KubeArmor's policy enforcement capabilities ensures that any unauthorized activities are promptly detected and logged, providing valuable forensic evidence.

4. **Real-Time Alerting**: Real-time alerts enable security teams to respond swiftly to potential security incidents, minimizing the potential impact.

5. **Incident Response Capabilities**: AccuKnox Forensics provides dedicated incident response capabilities, enabling security teams to isolate compromised pods, apply security patches, or roll back affected pods to a secure state.

Key Takeaways

- AccuKnox Forensics is a powerful solution for container security and forensics within Kubernetes environments.

- It provides detailed insights, real-time alerts, and an audit trail for proactive identification and mitigation of security threats.
- The solution leverages continuous monitoring, policy enforcement, and aggregated logging to detect and investigate security incidents.
- AccuKnox Forensics enables security teams to perform comprehensive forensic analysis, determine the scope and impact of incidents, and implement appropriate remediation measures.
- With its robust architecture and key differentiators, AccuKnox Forensics empowers organizations to enhance their overall security posture and effectively respond to security incidents within their cloud-native environments.

Section 4.12. Enterprise Integration

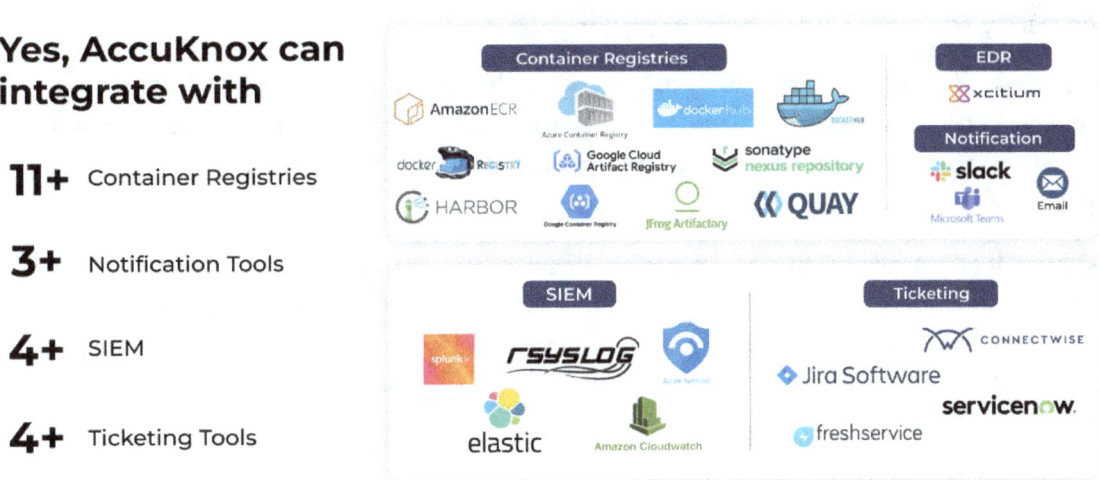

FIGURE 42. ACCUKNOX ENTERPRISE INTEGRATION ACROSS REGISTRIES AND TOOLS

AccuKnox is one of the industry's most comprehensive and integrated Cloud Native Application Protection Platform (CNAPP) solutions. It brings together multiple security modules to deliver a holistic Zero Trust security approach for networks, applications (Kubernetes, VMs), and data across cloud environments. The Enterprise edition offers advanced features and capabilities for robust security, visibility, and control over cloud-native applications.

What is AccuKnox Enterprise CNAPP? AccuKnox Enterprise CNAPP is a feature-rich, enterprise-grade security solution designed to provide comprehensive protection for cloud-native applications and workloads. It combines various security modules, including Cloud Security Posture Management (CSPM), Cloud Workload Protection

Platform (CWPP), and Identity and Access Management (IAM), into a single, integrated platform.

Why is AccuKnox Enterprise CNAPP important? In today's cloud-native landscape, organizations face numerous security challenges, including the complexity of managing diverse workloads, the threat of zero-day attacks, and the need for continuous compliance. AccuKnox Enterprise CNAPP addresses these challenges by providing:

1. **Comprehensive Security**: It offers a holistic approach to cloud security, covering all aspects of cloud-native applications, from static code analysis to runtime protection and identity management.

2. **Real-Time Defense**: With its advanced capabilities, AccuKnox Enterprise CNAPP enables real-time defense against zero-day attacks, ensuring proactive security for cloud-native environments.

3. **Unified Visibility and Control**: By consolidating multiple security modules into a single platform, AccuKnox Enterprise CNAPP provides unified visibility and control over the entire cloud-native stack, simplifying security operations and reducing alert fatigue.

4. **Compliance and Governance**: The solution incorporates industry-standard compliance frameworks (e.g., MITRE, NIST, PCI-DSS, CIS) and offers robust governance capabilities, such as policy lifecycle management and version control, ensuring adherence to security best practices

AccuKnox CNAPP Definitive Guide

FIGURE 43. ACCUKNOX CAN ONBOARD FOR A VARIETY OF USE CASES - FROM ON-PREM TO PUBLIC AND PRIVATE CLOUDS

How is AccuKnox Enterprise CNAPP accomplished?

AccuKnox Enterprise CNAPP leverages a comprehensive set of features and capabilities to deliver robust security for cloud-native applications:

1. **Shift Left Defense**: AccuKnox embraces a proactive "Shift Left" approach, thwarting advanced zero-day attacks through a combination of static and runtime security measures.

2. **Static Security**: The solution integrates Cloud Security Posture Management (CSPM) capabilities to assess and remediate misconfigurations and vulnerabilities in cloud infrastructure and resources.

3. **Runtime Security**: AccuKnox incorporates a powerful Cloud Workload Protection Platform (CWPP) to monitor and protect applications during runtime, leveraging auto-discovered behavioral policies and network micro segmentation.

4. **Integrated Testing**: AccuKnox seamlessly integrates with various testing tools, including Static Application Security Testing (SAST), Software Composition Analysis (SCA), and Dynamic Application Security Testing (DAST), enabling comprehensive application security testing.

5. **Identity Management**: The solution offers Kubernetes Identity and Entitlement Management (KIEM) capabilities, ensuring proper access control and identity governance across cloud and Kubernetes environments.

6. **Observability and Visibility**: AccuKnox provides granular observability into workloads, including network graph views, inventory views, and telemetry aggregation (process execution, file access, network connections), enabling deep visibility into application behavior.

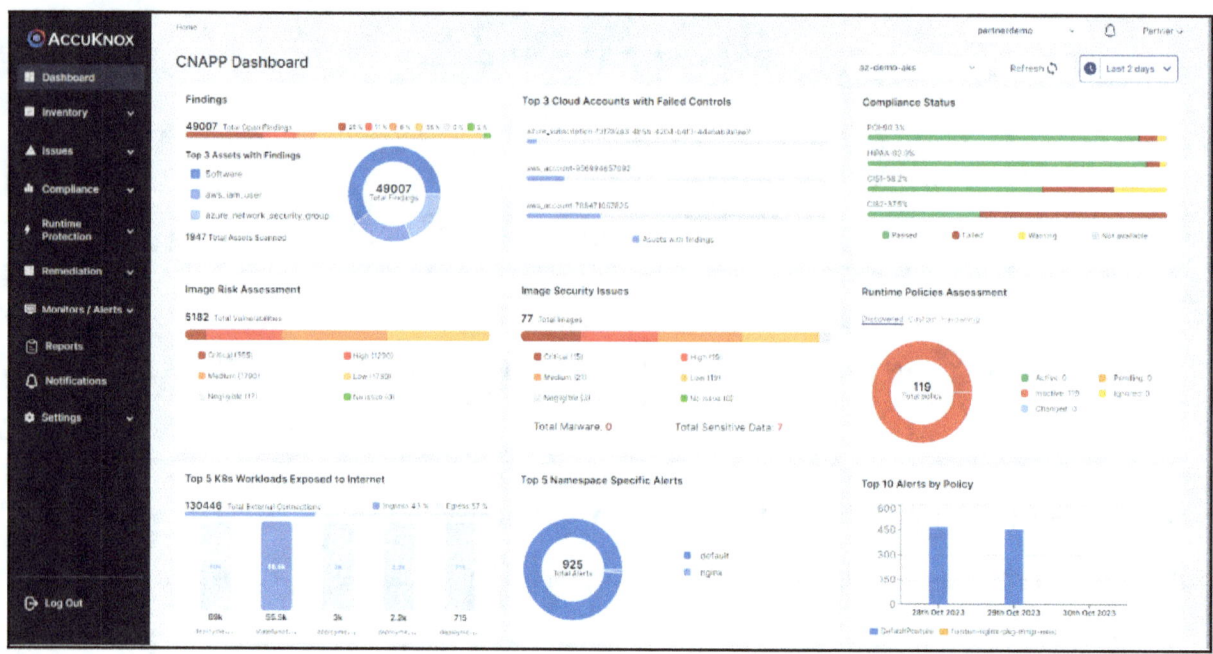

FIGURE 44. ACCUKNOX CNAPP DASHBOARD

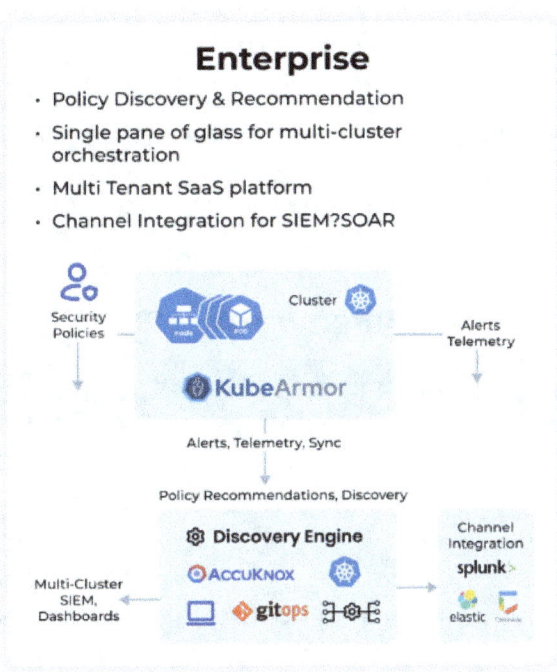

FIGURE 45. ACCUKNOX ENTERPRISE CNAPP OFFERINGS

Architecture

1. **Security Orchestration and Analytics Layer**: This layer serves as the central control plane, orchestrating and coordinating security operations across various modules. It includes the policy management engine, analytics engine, and incident response capabilities.

2. **Cloud Security Posture Management (CSPM)**: This module assesses and remediates misconfigurations and vulnerabilities in cloud infrastructure and resources, ensuring compliance with industry standards.

3. **Cloud Workload Protection Platform (CWPP)**: This module monitors and protects applications during runtime, leveraging auto-discovered behavioral policies, network micro segmentation, and real-time threat detection and response capabilities.

4. **Identity and Access Management (IAM):** This module encompasses Cloud Identity and Entitlement Management (CIEM) and Kubernetes Identity and Entitlement Management (KIEM), providing robust identity governance and access control across cloud and Kubernetes environments.

AccuKnox CNAPP Definitive Guide

5. **Integration Layer**: AccuKnox integrates with various third-party tools and services, including SAST, SCA, DAST, SIEM, notification tools, and container registries, enabling seamless integration into existing security workflows.
6. **Data and Telemetry Layer**: This layer collects and aggregates telemetry data, such as process execution, file access, and network connections, from workloads across different environments (Kubernetes, VMs, bare metal), providing deep observability and visibility into application behavior.

Table: Key Features of AccuKnox Enterprise CNAPP

Feature	Description
Cloud Security Posture Management (CSPM)	Assess and remediate misconfigurations and vulnerabilities in cloud infrastructure and resources.
Cloud Workload Protection Platform (CWPP)	Monitor and protect applications during runtime, leveraging auto-discovered behavioral policies and network microsegmentation.
Identity and Access Management (IAM)	Cloud Identity and Entitlement Management (CIEM) and Kubernetes Identity and Entitlement Management (KIEM) for robust identity governance and access control.
Integrated Testing	Integration with SAST, SCA, and DAST tools for comprehensive application security testing.
Policy Lifecycle Management	GitOps-based version control and lifecycle management for security policies governing application behavior.
Real-Time Threat Detection and Response	Real-time detection and inline remediation capabilities for zero-day attacks.
Observability and Visibility	Granular observability into workloads, including network graph views, inventory views, and telemetry aggregation.

Key Differentiators of AccuKnox Enterprise CNAPP

1. **Comprehensive and Integrated Platform**: AccuKnox Enterprise CNAPP consolidates multiple security modules, including CSPM, CWPP, and IAM, into a

single, integrated platform, providing a holistic approach to cloud-native security.
2. **Real-Time Defense**: With its advanced capabilities, AccuKnox enables real-time defense against zero-day attacks, ensuring proactive security for cloud-native environments.
3. **Unified Visibility and Control**: The solution provides unified visibility and control over the entire cloud-native stack, simplifying security operations and reducing alert fatigue.
4. **Robust Policy Management**: AccuKnox offers robust policy management capabilities, including auto-discovered behavioral policies, policy lifecycle management, and version control, ensuring consistent and compliant application behavior.
5. **Seamless Integration**: The solution seamlessly integrates with various testing tools, SIEM, notification tools, and container registries, enabling seamless integration into existing security workflows.

Key Takeaways
- AccuKnox Enterprise CNAPP is a comprehensive and integrated Cloud Native Application Protection Platform, offering robust security, visibility, and control for cloud-native applications and workloads.
- It combines multiple security modules, including CSPM, CWPP, and IAM, into a single platform, delivering a holistic Zero Trust security approach.
- AccuKnox Enterprise CNAPP embraces a "Shift Left" approach, thwarting advanced zero-day attacks through a combination of static and runtime security measures.
- The solution provides granular observability into workloads, integrated testing capabilities, robust policy management, and seamless integration with existing security tools and workflows.

With its advanced features and capabilities, AccuKnox Enterprise CNAPP empowers organizations to achieve comprehensive security, compliance, and governance for their cloud-native applications.

Section 4.13. EDR (Endpoint Detection and Response) Integration

AccuKnox Endpoint Detection and Response (EDR) is a robust endpoint security solution that continuously monitors end-user devices to detect and respond to cyber threats. It provides real-time visibility, threat intelligence integration, proactive threat hunting, and fast incident response capabilities, empowering organizations to defend against advanced threats like ransomware and malware.

What is AccuKnox Endpoint Detection and Response (EDR)? AccuKnox EDR is an advanced endpoint security solution that combines continuous monitoring, threat detection, investigation, and response capabilities into a single platform. It is designed to provide comprehensive visibility into endpoint activities, enabling organizations to detect and mitigate cyber threats in real-time.

Why is AccuKnox EDR important? In today's threat landscape, traditional prevention-based security measures are no longer sufficient. Adversaries are becoming increasingly sophisticated and persistent, often evading detection and remaining within networks for extended periods. AccuKnox EDR addresses these challenges by providing:

1. **Comprehensive Visibility**: EDR acts as a "digital video recorder" on the endpoint, recording and analyzing all relevant activities for both real-time monitoring and historical analysis, ensuring no threats go unnoticed.
2. **Advanced Threat Detection**: By leveraging threat intelligence integration, behavioral analysis, and machine learning, AccuKnox EDR can detect known and unknown threats, including advanced persistent threats (APTs), file-less attacks, and zero-day exploits.
3. **Accelerated Investigations**: AccuKnox EDR stores endpoint data in the cloud and provides rapid context through a powerful graph database, enabling security teams to investigate and respond to incidents quickly and efficiently.
4. **Proactive Threat Hunting**: AccuKnox EDR facilitates proactive threat hunting, empowering security teams to actively search for and identify potential threats within their environment before they can cause harm.
5. **Rapid Incident Response**: With its containment and remediation capabilities, AccuKnox EDR enables swift and decisive action against compromised hosts, minimizing the impact of security incidents without disrupting ongoing operations.

How is AccuKnox EDR accomplished?

AccuKnox EDR leverages a robust set of capabilities to provide comprehensive endpoint security:

1. **Continuous Monitoring**: AccuKnox EDR continuously monitors end-user devices, recording and analyzing all relevant activities, including process execution, file access, network connections, and system changes.
2. **Threat Intelligence Integration**: AccuKnox EDR integrates with threat intelligence sources, providing contextualized information about known and emerging threats, enabling more accurate and timely threat detection.
3. **Behavioral Analysis**: AccuKnox EDR employs advanced behavioral analysis techniques, including machine learning, to identify anomalous activities and detect threats based on their behavior rather than relying solely on signatures.
4. **Incident Data Search**: AccuKnox EDR provides powerful search capabilities, allowing security teams to quickly locate and analyze relevant endpoint data during investigations.
5. **Automated Response and Containment**: Upon detecting a threat, AccuKnox EDR can automatically initiate containment and remediation actions, such as isolating compromised hosts, terminating malicious processes, and blocking malicious network connections.
6. **Threat Hunting: AccuKnox EDR** enables proactive threat hunting by providing security analysts with the tools and data needed to actively search for and identify potential threats within their environment.

Architecture

The AccuKnox EDR architecture consists of the following key components:

1. **Endpoint Sensors**: Lightweight agents deployed on end-user devices collect and transmit endpoint data to the central management platform.
2. **Data Collection and Processing**: This component receives and processes the endpoint data, performing data normalization, enrichment, and correlation.
3. **Threat Intelligence Integration**: AccuKnox EDR integrates with various threat intelligence sources to enhance its detection capabilities.
4. **Behavioral Analysis Engine**: Utilizing machine learning and behavioral analysis techniques, this engine identifies anomalous activities and potential threats.

5. **Incident Response and Containment**: This component enables security teams to investigate, respond to, and contain security incidents through a centralized console.
6. **Cloud-based Data Storage**: Endpoint data is securely stored in the cloud, enabling rapid access and analysis during investigations.
7. **Threat Hunting and Analytics**: AccuKnox EDR provides advanced analytics and threat hunting capabilities, empowering security teams to proactively identify and investigate potential threats.

Key Capabilities of AccuKnox EDR

Capabilities	Description
Continuous Monitoring	Continuous monitoring of end-user devices for comprehensive visibility.
Advanced Threat Detection	Leverages threat intelligence, behavioral analysis, and machine learning for threat detection.
Incident Data Search	Powerful search capabilities for locating and analyzing relevant endpoint data.
Automated Response and Containment	Automated containment and remediation actions for detected threats.
Proactive Threat Hunting	Enables security teams to actively search for and identify potential threats.
Cloud-based Data Storage	Secure cloud-based storage for endpoint data, enabling rapid access and analysis.
Integration with Threat Intelligence	Integration with threat intelligence sources for enhanced detection capabilities.

Key Differentiators of AccuKnox EDR

1. **Comprehensive Visibility**: AccuKnox EDR provides unparalleled visibility into endpoint activities, ensuring no threats go unnoticed.
2. **Advanced Threat Detection**: By combining threat intelligence, behavioral analysis, and machine learning, AccuKnox EDR can detect even the most advanced and elusive threats.

3. **Proactive Threat Hunting**: AccuKnox EDR empowers security teams to take a proactive approach to threat detection and investigation, reducing the risk of undetected threats.
4. **Rapid Incident Response**: With its automated response and containment capabilities, AccuKnox EDR enables swift and decisive action against security incidents, minimizing potential damage.
5. **Cloud-based Architecture**: AccuKnox EDR's cloud-based architecture ensures scalability, rapid access to endpoint data, and seamless integration with other security tools.

Key Takeaways

- AccuKnox Endpoint Detection and Response (EDR) is a powerful endpoint security solution that provides continuous monitoring, advanced threat detection, and rapid incident response capabilities.
- It addresses the limitations of traditional prevention-based security measures by offering comprehensive visibility, proactive threat hunting, and integrated threat intelligence.
- AccuKnox EDR's robust architecture, featuring cloud-based data storage, behavioral analysis engines, and automated response capabilities, enables organizations to defend against advanced threats effectively.
- With its advanced capabilities and unique differentiators, AccuKnox EDR empowers security teams to stay ahead of cyber threats, ensuring the protection of their critical assets and minimizing the impact of security incidents.

Section 4.14.   SIEM (Security Information and Event Management) Integration

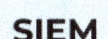

Users can use the Feeder service agent to pass the logs to other SIEM tools like Splunk, ELK, Rsyslog, etc.., Users can also forward the logs from AccuKnox SaaS using the channel integration option to these SIEM tools. Users can integrate with various SIEM and ticketing tools like Splunk, Rsyslog, AWS CloudWatch, Elastic Search, Slack and Jira.

Splunk Integration

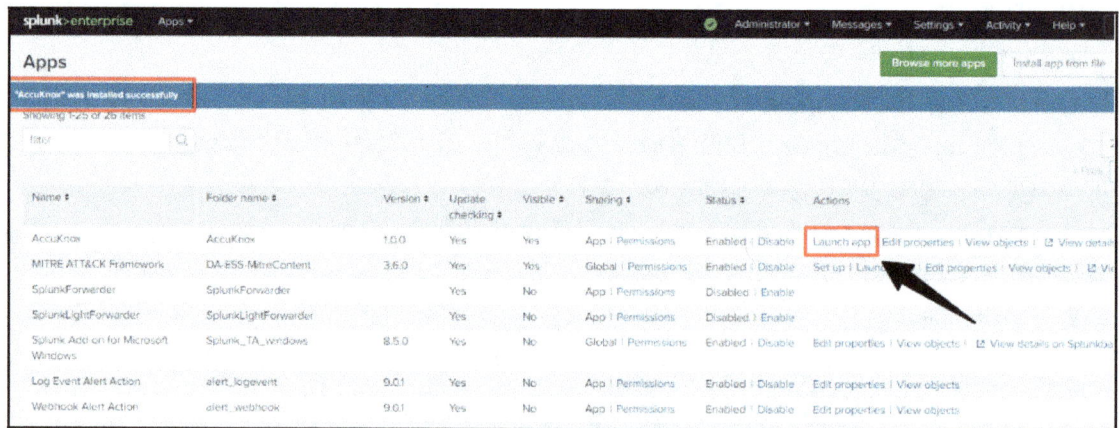

FIGURE 46. LAUNCHING ACCUKNOX VIA SPLUNK

AccuKnox integrates with Splunk, a powerful software platform for searching, analyzing, and visualizing machine-generated data. This integration allows AccuKnox to monitor assets and send alerts for issues such as misconfigurations and security risks directly to Splunk. The integration process involves setting up the Splunk HTTP Event Collector (HEC) and obtaining the necessary HEC URL and Token. Once configured, organizations can leverage Splunk's robust analytics and visualization capabilities to gain insights from AccuKnox's security data.

AccuKnox Splunk App

In addition to the integration, AccuKnox offers a dedicated Splunk App that provides operational reporting and configurable dashboards for real-time alerts in Kubernetes clusters. This app offers features like real-time alert tracking, data models with pivots, and the ability to filter alerts based on various parameters. The installation process for the AccuKnox Splunk App involves prerequisites such as a running Kubernetes cluster with AccuKnox agents and access to a Splunk deployment. AccuKnox supports multiple installation methods, including file upload, SplunkBase, or GitHub cloning.

AWS CloudWatch Integration

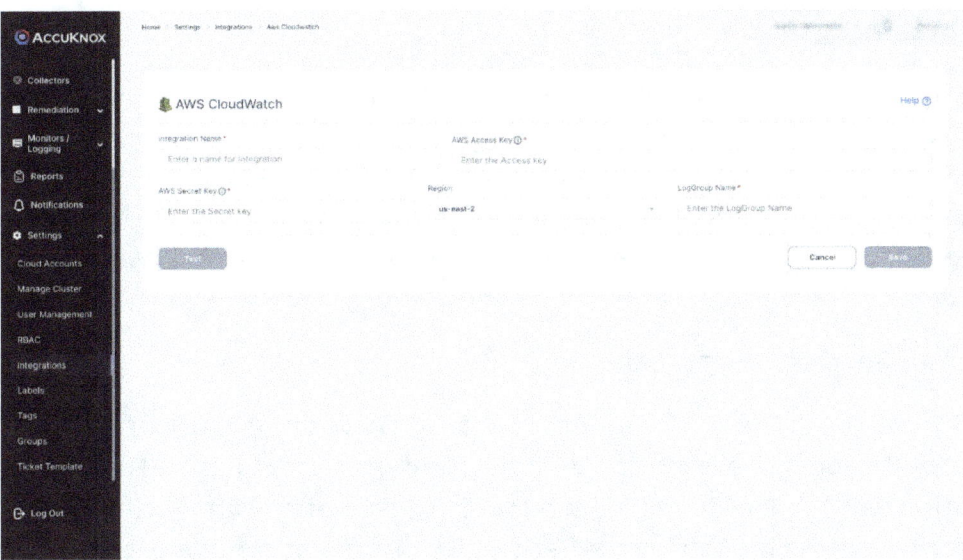

FIGURE 47. STEPS TO GET STARTED WITH AWS CLOUDWATCH ON ACCUKNOX CNAPP DASHBOARD

AccuKnox can integrate with Amazon CloudWatch, enabling organizations to leverage the powerful monitoring and logging capabilities of AWS. The integration requires an AWS Access Key and an AWS Secret Key. Configuration involves naming the Alert Trigger, specifying trigger frequency and severity, and selecting AWS CloudWatch as the integration channel. AccuKnox logs are forwarded to CloudWatch based on the configured trigger frequency, with the Rule Engine matching real-time logs against created triggers.

Rsyslog Integration

For organizations using the Rsyslog server for log management, AccuKnox provides a dedicated integration option. The integration requires a running Rsyslog server and specific setup steps, including providing the hostname/IP, port number, and transport type (TCP or UDP). Once configured, AccuKnox can send alerts and logs directly to the Rsyslog server, enabling centralized log management and analysis.

Rsyslog Feeder Integration

AccuKnox also supports forwarding syslogs to various destinations through the Rsyslog Feeder Integration. This integration offers high-performance log processing, security features, and a modular design. Prerequisites include a running Rsyslog server and configuration of hostname/IP, port number, and transport type (TCP or UDP). Configuration involves setting environment variables that dictate the behavior of the Feeder-Service-Agent, enabling the forwarding of logs and alerts to the Rsyslog server.

Azure Sentinel Integration

AccuKnox integrates with Azure Sentinel, a cloud-native SIEM solution by Microsoft. The integration process involves having an Azure Logic App webhook and an Azure Sentinel Subscription. Organizations can configure the integration by providing the necessary details, such as the Integration Name, Webhook URL, Group Name, and Group Value. Testing the integration is possible by sending a test message to verify functionality.

Azure Sentinel Feeder Integration

In addition to the direct integration, AccuKnox supports forwarding logs and alerts to Azure Sentinel through the Feeder Service running on the client's Kubernetes cluster. This integration leverages Azure Logic Apps to create automated workflows and webhooks for receiving logs in Azure Sentinel. Configuration involves setting environment variables that control the forwarding of alerts and logs to Azure Sentinel.

KubeArmor Splunk Integration

AccuKnox also offers a dedicated integration between KubeArmor and Splunk. The AccuKnox Splunk App provides operational reporting and a customizable dashboard for real-time alerts from Kubernetes clusters. This integration offers features like alert tracking, data models for easy data access and visualization, and the ability to filter alerts based on various criteria. The installation process involves prerequisites such as a Kubernetes cluster with Feeder-Service and KubeArmor, along with an active Splunk deployment.

Section 4.15. Ticketing Systems

What is AccuKnox Ticketing? AccuKnox Ticketing is a feature that enables seamless integration with popular ticketing systems, allowing organizations to automate the process of generating tickets based on security alerts and findings from AccuKnox. This integration streamlines the existing security workflow and enhances collaboration between security teams and other stakeholders.

Why is AccuKnox Ticketing important? Ticketing integration is crucial for several reasons:

1. **Efficient Incident Management**: By automatically generating tickets for security alerts and findings, AccuKnox Ticketing ensures that incidents are promptly addressed and resolved, minimizing the risk of overlooking critical issues.

2. **Centralized Workflow**: Integrating with existing ticketing systems allows security teams to work within a familiar environment, reducing the need for context switching and enhancing productivity.
3. **Improved Collaboration**: Ticketing integration facilitates better collaboration between security teams and other stakeholders, such as IT operations, development teams, and management, by providing a centralized platform for tracking and managing security issues.
4. **Audit Trail and Reporting**: Tickets generated by AccuKnox provide a comprehensive audit trail, enabling organizations to demonstrate compliance with security policies and regulatory requirements.

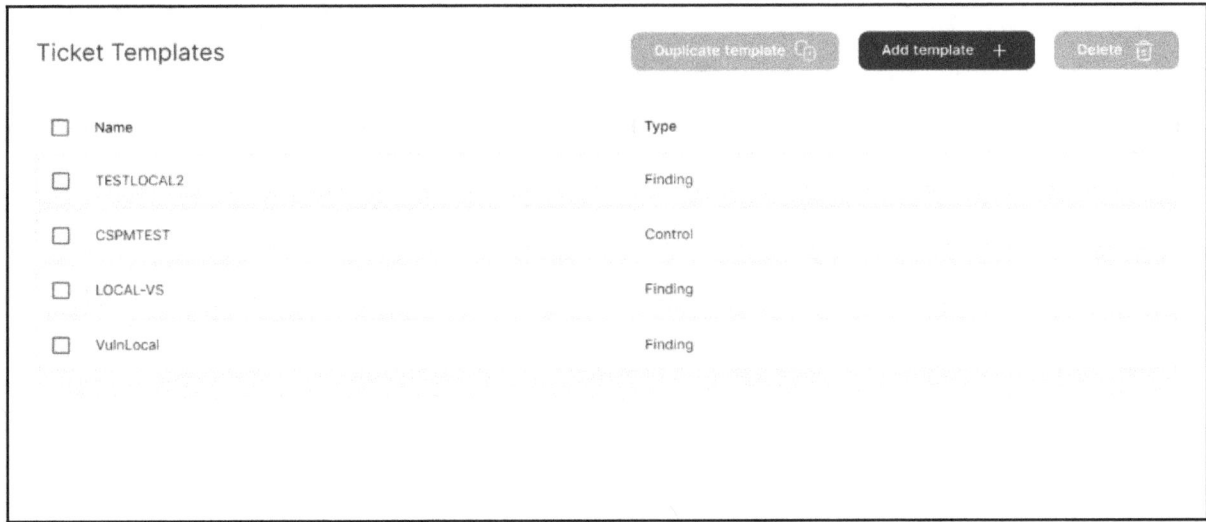

FIGURE 48. TICKETING TEMPLATES

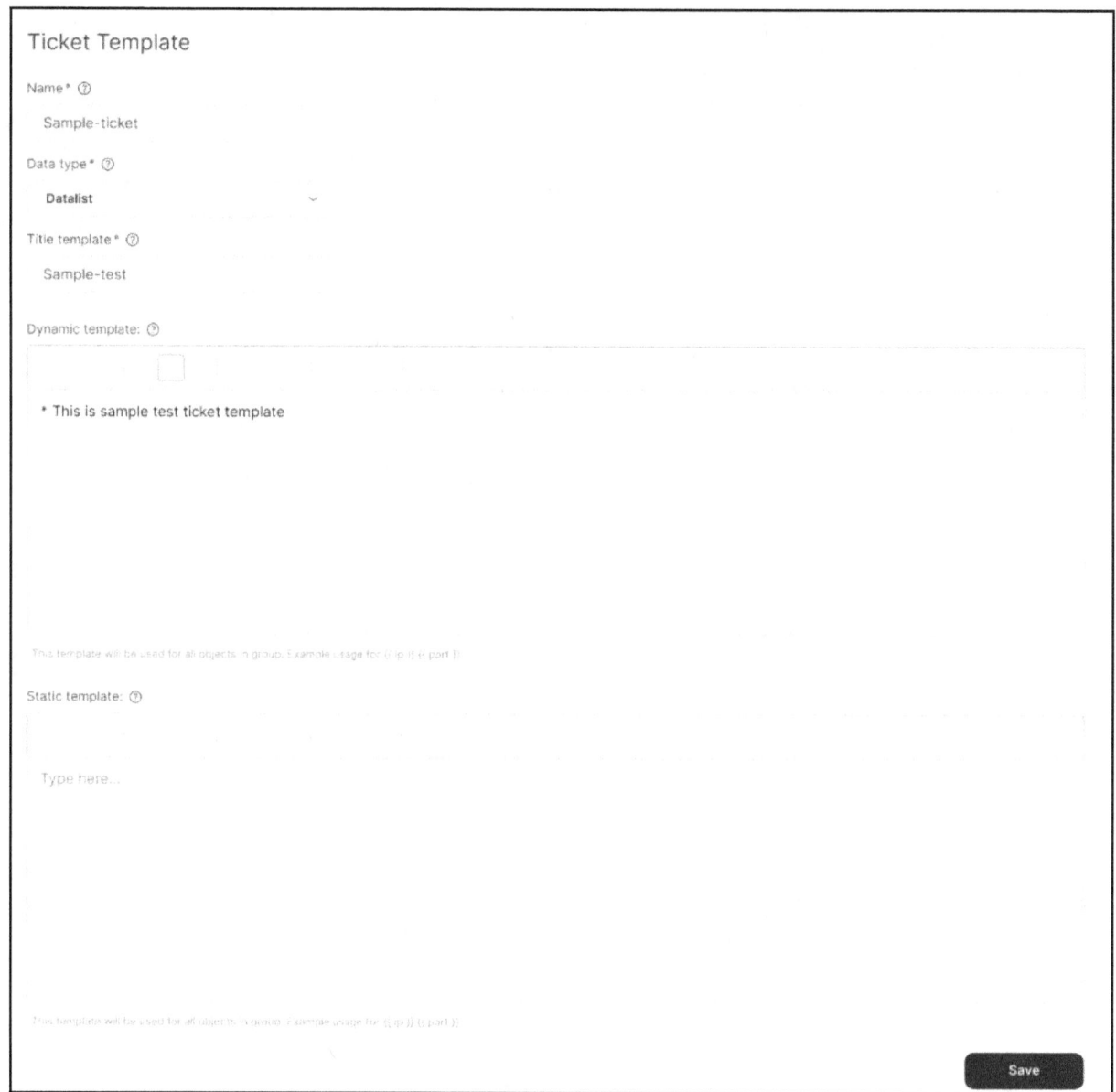

FIGURE 49. CUSTOMIZING AND CREATING NEW TICKET TEMPLATES

How is AccuKnox Ticketing accomplished?

AccuKnox offers integration with several popular ticketing systems, including Jira, ConnectWise, FreshService, and ServiceNow. The integration process typically involves the following steps:

1. **Gathering Prerequisites**: Obtain the necessary credentials, URLs, and API keys required for integration with the chosen ticketing system.

2. **Configuration**: In the AccuKnox platform, navigate to the "Channel Integration" section and select the desired ticketing system. Enter the required integration details, such as the integration name, service desk URL, username, and API keys.

3. **Ticket Configuration**: After configuring the integration, users can set up ticketing backends by specifying the configuration name, default template, project or company name, issue type, and priority mapping.

4. **Trigger Configuration**: Finally, users can configure alert triggers to automatically generate tickets in the integrated ticketing system based on specific criteria, such as threat severity or frequency.

Ticketing Provisions from AccuKnox:

Jira Integration: AccuKnox integrates with Jira, allowing users to receive AccuKnox alert notifications in their Jira accounts. This integration automates the process of generating Jira tickets based on existing security workflows.

Prerequisites:

- Jira Site URL
- Email
- User ID
- API token (generated from https://id.atlassian.com/manage-profile/security/api-tokens
- Project key

Integration Steps:

1. Go to the "**Channel Integration**" section in AccuKnox and select the "CWPP" or "CSPM" tab.

2. Click "**Add Connector**" and select "Jira Server".

3. Enter the integration details (Integration Name, Service Desk URL, Username, Secret/API token).

4. Click on **the Jira ticketing backend** and provide the configuration details (Configuration name, Default template, Project name, Issue Type, Priority mapping).

5. Save the configuration.

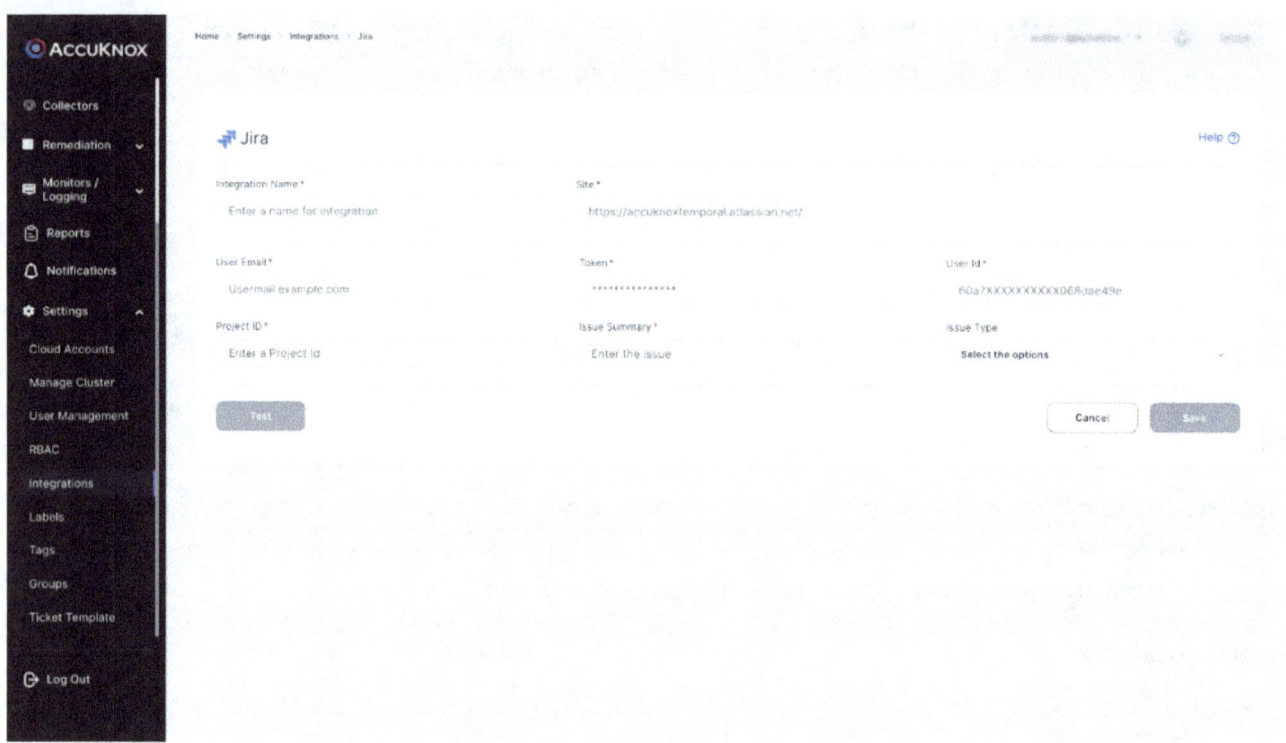

FIGURE 50. CONFIGURE ALERT TRIGGERS FOR JIRA NOTIFICATIONS

ConnectWise Integration: AccuKnox can integrate with ConnectWise, enabling users to receive AccuKnox alert notifications in their ConnectWise account. This integration automates the process of generating ConnectWise tickets based on existing security workflows.

Prerequisites:
- Service Desk URL
- Company ID
- Public key
- Private key
- Client ID (obtained from https://developer.connectwise.com/ClientID)

Integration Steps:
1. Go to the "Channel Integration" section in AccuKnox and select the "CSPM" tab.
2. Click "Add Connector" and select "ConnectWise".
3. Enter the integration details (Integration Name, Service Desk URL, Company ID, Public key, Private key, and Client ID).

4. Click on the ConnectWise ticketing backend and provide the configuration details (Configuration name, Default template, Companies, Issue Type, Priority mapping).
5. Save the configuration.
6. Configure alert triggers for ConnectWise notifications.

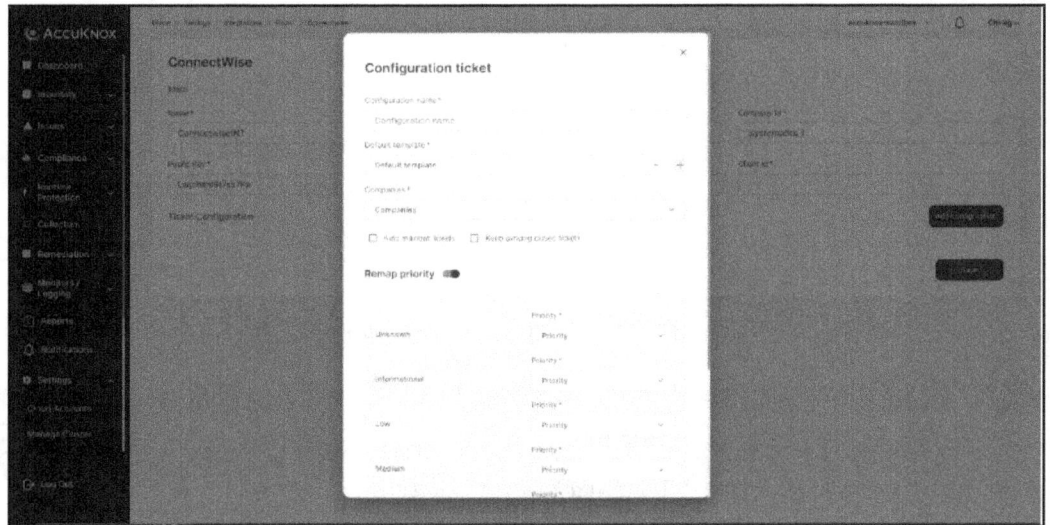

FIGURE 51. CONNECTWISE INTEGRATION NOTIFICATION TICKET SAMPLE

FreshService Integration: AccuKnox integrates with FreshService, allowing users to receive AccuKnox alert notifications in their FreshService accounts. This integration automates the process of generating FreshService "Problem alerts" based on existing security workflows.

Prerequisites:
- Company domain
- Email
- API key (secret)

Integration Steps:
1. Go to the "Channel Integration" section in AccuKnox and select the "CSPM" tab.
2. Click "Add Connector" and select "FreshService".
3. Enter the integration details (Integration Name, Domain Name, User Email, Secret/API key).
4. Click on the FreshService ticketing backend and provide the configuration details (Configuration name, Default template, Issue Type, Priority mapping).

5. Save the configuration.
6. Configure alert triggers for FreshService notifications.

ServiceNow Integration: AccuKnox can integrate with ServiceNow, enabling users to receive AccuKnox alert notifications in their ServiceNow account. This integration automates the process of generating ServiceNow tickets based on existing security workflows.

Prerequisites:
- Instance URL
- Instance Username
- Instance Password

Integration Steps:
1. Go to the "Channel Integration" section in AccuKnox and select the "CSPM" tab.
2. Click "Add Connector" and select "ServiceNow".
3. Enter the integration details (Integration Name, ServiceNow Instance URL, Instance Username, Secret/Instance Password).
4. Click on the ServiceNow ticketing backend and provide the configuration details (Configuration name, Default template, Issue Type, Priority mapping).
5. Save the configuration.
6. Configure alert triggers for ServiceNow notifications.

Ticket Template: AccuKnox provides the option to create Jira ticket templates related to vulnerability findings, particular assets, and particular scan results. Users can create new ticket templates by following these steps:
1. Navigate to the Ticket Template section.
2. Click on the "Add Template" option.
3. Fill in the required details, such as the template name, and click "Save" to create the new ticket template.

Key Takeaways:

AccuKnox CNAPP Definitive Guide

- AccuKnox Ticketing enables seamless integration with popular ticketing systems, automating the process of generating tickets based on security alerts and findings.
- This integration streamlines incident management, improves collaboration, and provides a centralized platform for tracking and managing security issues.
- AccuKnox offers integration with Jira, ConnectWise , Freshservice, and ServiceNow, with specific prerequisites and configuration steps for each system.
- Users can create custom ticket templates and configure alert triggers to automatically generate tickets based on specific criteria.
- Ticketing integration enhances security workflows, improves productivity, and facilitates better collaboration between security teams and other stakeholders.

Chapter 5   Zero Trust CNAPP Use Cases

Section 5.1.   Application Firewalling

AccuKnox Application Firewalling is a vital component of modern cybersecurity strategies, offering robust protection for cloud-based and on-premise infrastructures. It defends against a variety of cyber threats, safeguarding sensitive data and ensuring compliance with regulatory requirements.

What is AccuKnox Application Firewalling?

AccuKnox Application Firewalling is a comprehensive security solution designed to protect web applications from various cyber threats such as SQL injection, cross-site scripting (XSS), and unauthorized access attempts. It employs advanced techniques like behavioral analysis and intelligent traffic filtering to detect and mitigate potential risks in real time.

Why is this important?

Application firewalling is crucial in today's digital landscape where web applications serve as primary targets for cyber attacks. By implementing AccuKnox Application Firewalling, organizations can fortify their defenses, prevent data breaches, and maintain the integrity of their systems and data.

How is this accomplished?

AccuKnox Application Firewalling achieves its objectives through a multi-layered approach that includes:

- **Traffic filtering**: Examining incoming traffic using various parameters such as source IP addresses and URLs to block suspicious activities.
- **Security rules**: Defining rules to control access based on user agents, geolocation, or specific patterns in HTTP requests.
- **Rate limiting**: Limiting the number of requests a user can make within a certain timeframe to prevent denial-of-service (DoS) attacks.
- **Bot management**: Distinguishing between legitimate human traffic and automated bots to mitigate spam threats.
- **DDoS protection**: Detecting and mitigating abnormal traffic patterns to ensure uninterrupted service for legitimate users.

- **SSL/TLS encryption**: Encrypting sensitive data in transit to prevent interception and eavesdropping.

Architecture

AccuKnox Application Firewalling architecture consists of:

- **Core components**: Traffic filtering engine, rule engine, rate limiting module, bot management system, DDoS detection and mitigation module, and SSL/TLS encryption module.
- **Integration points**: APIs for seamless integration with other security products such as DDoS protection and endpoint security solutions.
- **Scalability**: Designed to scale horizontally to accommodate growing traffic and evolving security needs.

Application Firewalling Features

Feature	Description
Traffic Filtering	Examines incoming traffic to block suspicious activities based on source IP addresses and URLs.
Security Rules	Defines rules to control access based on user agents, geolocation, or specific patterns in HTTP requests.
Rate Limiting	Limits the number of requests a user can make within a certain timeframe to prevent DoS attacks.
Bot Management	Distinguishes between legitimate human traffic and automated bots to mitigate spam threats.
DDoS Protection	Detects and mitigates abnormal traffic patterns to ensure uninterrupted service for legitimate users.
SSL/TLS Encryption	Encrypts sensitive data in transit to prevent interception and eavesdropping.

Web Application Firewalling (WAF)

A WAF protects web applications by targeting HTTP traffic. This differs from a standard firewall, which provides a barrier between external and internal network traffic. A WAF sits between external users and web applications to analyze all HTTP communication.

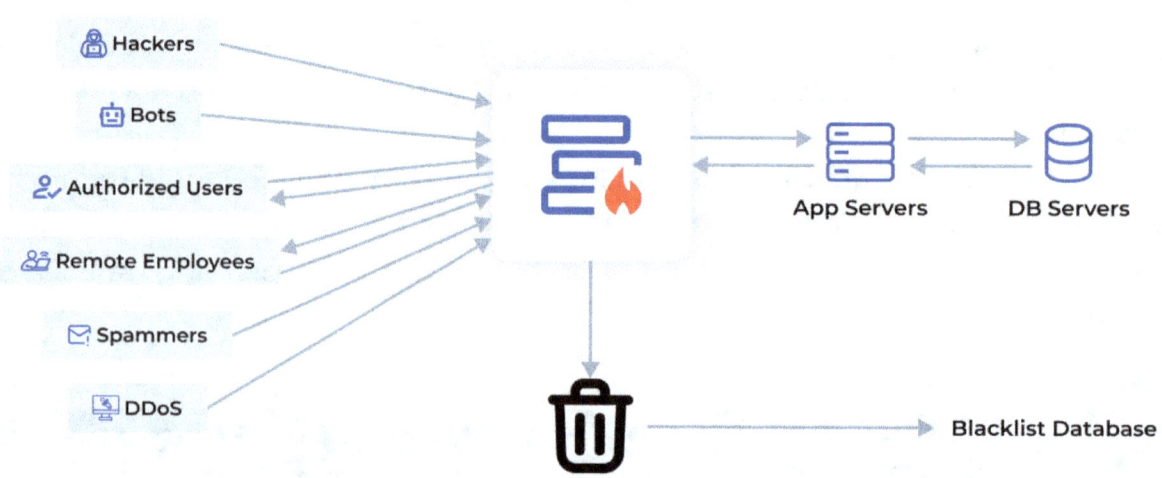

FIGURE 52. HOW WEB APPLICATION FIREWALLING WORKS

Key Differentiators

- AccuKnox Application Firewalling uses **advanced behavioral analysis** techniques to detect and mitigate emerging threats in real-time.
- It **seamlessly integrates with other platforms and tooling**, enabling organizations to build a holistic security ecosystem.
- Scalability: Designed to scale horizontally, AccuKnox Application Firewalling can accommodate growing traffic and evolving security needs without compromising performance.
- By following guidelines like HIPPA, NIST and more, it helps organizations **comply with regulatory requirements** by providing comprehensive application security and access controls.

Key Takeaways

AccuKnox Application Firewalling is a powerful security solution that offers robust protection for web applications against a wide range of cyber threats. By leveraging advanced techniques such as behavioral analysis and intelligent traffic filtering, organizations can fortify their defenses, prevent data breaches, and maintain regulatory compliance. With its seamless integration capabilities and scalability,

AccuKnox Application Firewalling is the ideal choice for organizations looking to enhance their cybersecurity posture in today's evolving threat landscape.

Section 5.2. Microsegmentation

Microsegmentation is a cutting-edge network security strategy that enhances data protection and reduces cyber risks by dividing network infrastructure into smaller, isolated segments. This guide provides an overview of micro-segmentation, its importance, implementation methods, architecture, key differentiators, and summary takeaways.

What is Microsegmentation?

Microsegmentation is a network security approach that divides a network into small, isolated segments, enabling organizations to establish granular control over network traffic and access. Unlike traditional network security measures, which rely on perimeter defences, microsegmentation focuses on securing individual workloads or applications within the network.

Why is Microsegmentation Important?

Microsegmentation is crucial for modern cybersecurity because it addresses the limitations of traditional perimeter-based security measures. By creating virtual boundaries around each workload or application, micro-segmentation reduces the attack surface, limits the lateral movement of attackers, and enhances visibility and control over network traffic. This approach is especially valuable in cloud environments, where dynamic workloads and distributed architectures require robust security measures.

How is Microsegmentation Accomplished?

Microsegmentation is typically implemented using software-defined networking (SDN) technologies and security policies enforced at the workload level. By leveraging SDN, organizations can create virtual network overlays that segment traffic and apply access controls based on predefined policies. This allows for fine-grained control over network communication, ensuring that only authorized connections are allowed.

Architecture: Microsegmentation architecture consists of three main components:

1. **Controller**: Manages and orchestrates network policies and configurations.
2. **Enforcement Points**: Implemented as software agents or virtual appliances on network endpoints to enforce security policies.

3. **Policy Engine**: Defines and enforces access control policies based on application requirements and security policies.

Component	Description
Controller	Centralized management of security policies
Enforcement Points	Agents or virtual appliances on network endpoints
Policy Engine	Defines and enforces access control policies

Key Differentiators

- Microsegmentation enables organizations to define security policies at the workload level, providing granular control over network traffic.
- By isolating workloads and applications, micro-segmentation reduces the attack surface and limits the impact of cyber attacks.
- Microsegmentation adapts to changing network environments and application requirements, ensuring continuous protection against evolving threats.
- Microsegmentation provides detailed insights into network traffic patterns and communication flows. It facilitates threat detection and incident response.

Key Takeaways

- Microsegmentation enhances network security by dividing infrastructure into isolated segments.
- It reduces the attack surface, limits the lateral movement of attackers, and provides granular control over network traffic.
- Implementation involves SDN technologies, security policies, and centralized management.
- Key benefits include reduced cyber risks, improved visibility, and dynamic adaptability to changing environments.
- Organizations should consider microsegmentation as a fundamental component of their cybersecurity strategy to protect against modern threats.

Section 5.3. Network Firewalling

Network firewalling is a crucial security measure that controls incoming and outgoing traffic in your cloud environment, allowing authorized communication while blocking unauthorized access and defending against network-based attacks.

What is it?

Network firewalling is a security mechanism that enforces access control policies by analyzing and filtering network traffic based on predefined rules. It acts as a gatekeeper, allowing legitimate traffic to pass through while blocking unauthorized or malicious traffic, and protecting your cloud resources from potential threats.

Why is this important?

Network firewalling is essential for securing your cloud environment for several reasons:

1. It keeps unauthorized entities out of your network, enforcing access control policies and preventing unauthorized access.
2. It controls incoming traffic, analyzing and filtering network packets based on predefined rules, allowing authorized traffic while blocking potential threats.
3. It manages outgoing traffic, preventing data exfiltration attempts from compromised systems within your network.
4. It thwarts network-based attacks, such as DDoS attacks, port scanning attempts, and intrusion efforts, by recognizing and blocking malicious traffic patterns.

How is this accomplished?

AccuKnox delivers advanced network firewalling solutions designed specifically for securing cloud environments. These solutions combine robust firewall capabilities with cloud-native features:

1. **Robust firewall capabilities**: AccuKnox provides powerful firewall features, offering granular management for incoming and outgoing traffic in your cloud environment.
2. **Cloud-native features**: The solutions are tailored to the unique requirements of cloud environments, ensuring seamless integration and optimal performance. AccuKnox offers bleeding-edge network firewalling solutions that combine robust capabilities with cloud-native features, ensuring you never compromise on control.

Architecture

The architecture of AccuKnox's network firewalling solution is designed to seamlessly integrate with cloud environments, providing a robust and scalable security layer. It includes components such as a centralized management console, distributed firewalls, and integration with cloud infrastructure APIs for automated provisioning and configuration.

Network Firewalling Pros

Benefits	Description
Mitigating DDoS attacks	Network firewalls detect and block massive traffic floods from many sources, minimizing the impact of DDoS attacks and improving the availability of cloud services.
Preventing malware infections	By blocking suspicious incoming traffic and unauthorized communication, network firewalls act as a frontline defense against malware infections.
Blocking unauthorized access attempts	Firewalls prevent unauthorized access, such as brute-force attacks and unauthorized login attempts, reducing the risk of unauthorized data breaches.

Key Differentiators

AccuKnox's network firewalling solutions are designed specifically for cloud environments, offering seamless integration, optimal performance, and robust security features. Furthermore, AccuKnox provides firewalling solutions for on-premises air-gapped or VM/Bare metal environments, ensuring comprehensive protection for your cloud infrastructure and associated applications.

Key Takeaways

- Network firewalling is a crucial security measure that controls incoming and outgoing traffic in your cloud environment, preventing unauthorized access and defending against network-based attacks.
- AccuKnox offers advanced network firewalling solutions tailored for cloud environments, combining robust firewall capabilities with cloud-native features for seamless integration and optimal performance.
- AccuKnox's solutions provide granular control over network traffic, mitigate DDoS attacks, prevent malware infections, and block unauthorized access attempts, ensuring comprehensive protection for your cloud infrastructure and applications.
- The architecture is designed for seamless integration with cloud environments, providing a robust and scalable security layer.

- AccuKnox's network firewalling solutions are not limited to cloud environments; they also cater to on-premises air-gapped or VM/Bare metal environments, ensuring comprehensive protection across various deployment scenarios.

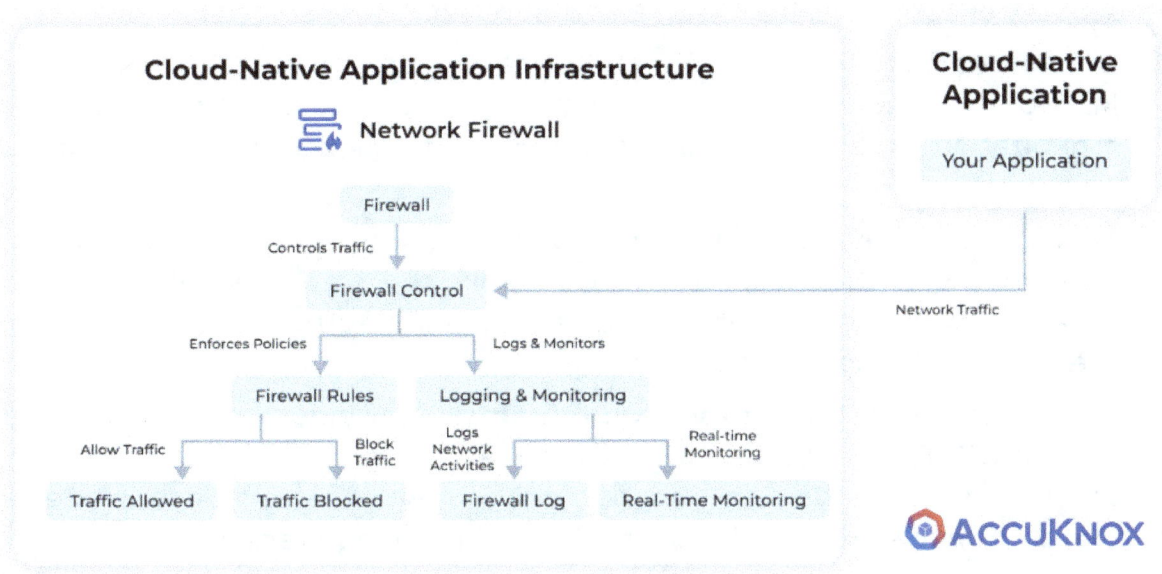

FIGURE 53. ACCUKNOX NETWORK FIREWALLING ARCHITECTURE

Section 5.4. Securing Secrets

AccuKnox provides a robust solution for securing Secrets Managers like HashiCorp Vault and CyberArk Conjur, preventing unauthorized access and ransomware attacks. It leverages KubeArmor, an open-source Cloud-Native Application Protection Platform (CNAPP), to enforce granular security policies, restrict access to sensitive file systems, and achieve zero trust security.

What is Securing Secrets Manager?

Securing Secrets Manager refers to the process of protecting and hardening the systems responsible for managing and storing sensitive information, such as passwords, API keys, and other secrets, within an organization. These Secrets Managers, like HashiCorp Vault and CyberArk Conjur, are critical components that ensure the confidentiality and integrity of sensitive data. However, if compromised, they can become entry points for attackers to gain unauthorized access or encrypt data, leading to ransomware attacks and data breaches.

Why is Securing Secrets Manager important?

1. **Protect Sensitive Data**: Secrets Managers store and manage critical information like encryption keys, passwords, and API credentials. A breach in these systems can lead to the exposure of sensitive data, compromising the security of applications and services that rely on these secrets.

2. **Prevent Ransomware Attacks**: If an attacker gains access to a Secrets Manager, they can potentially encrypt the stored secrets and hold the organization for ransom, resulting in significant financial and operational impacts.

3. **Maintain Confidentiality and Integrity**: Ensuring the confidentiality and integrity of secrets is essential for maintaining the overall security posture of an organization. Compromised secrets can lead to unauthorized access, data breaches, and other security incidents.

4. **Compliance and Regulatory Requirements**: Many industries and regulations, such as GDPR, PCI-DSS, and HIPAA, mandate strict measures for protecting sensitive data, including the secure management of secrets. Securing Secrets Managers helps organizations comply with these requirements.

How is Securing Secrets Manager accomplished with AccuKnox?

AccuKnox provides a comprehensive solution for securing Secrets Managers by leveraging KubeArmor, an open-source Cloud-Native Application Protection Platform (CNAPP). The key steps involved in securing Secrets Managers with AccuKnox include:

1. **Continuous Monitoring**: AccuKnox continuously monitors the workloads and activities within Kubernetes clusters, including the Secrets Manager pods and containers, providing visibility into potential security threats.

2. **Behavioral Analysis**: KubeArmor employs advanced behavioral analysis techniques, including machine learning, to identify anomalous activities and detect threats based on their behavior rather than relying solely on signatures.

3. **Policy Enforcement**: AccuKnox allows the creation and enforcement of granular security policies that restrict access to sensitive file system paths, limit process execution, and regulate network communication, ensuring that only authorized processes can access secrets.

4. **Process Whitelisting**: KubeArmor supports process whitelisting, allowing only known and trusted binaries to execute within the target pods or containers, preventing unauthorized processes from accessing or tampering with secrets.

5. **Inline Remediation**: Upon detecting a threat or policy violation, AccuKnox can automatically initiate containment and remediation actions, such as terminating malicious processes, blocking network connections, or isolating compromised pods, preventing further damage and protecting the Secrets Manager.

Architecture

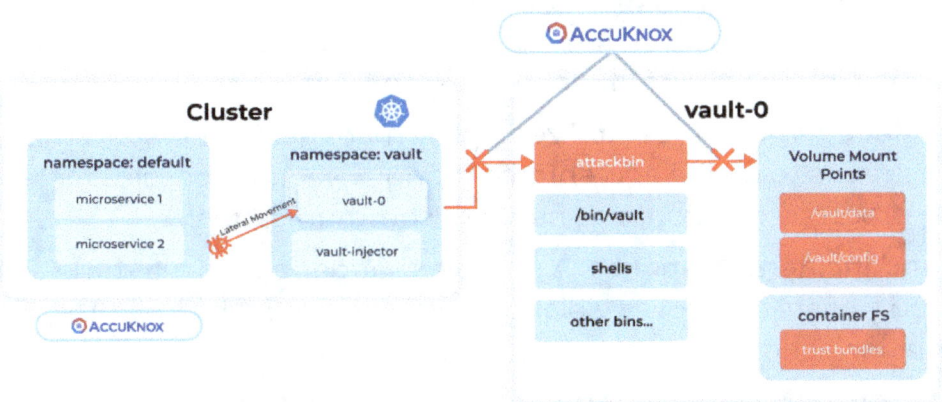

FIGURE 54. HASHICORP VAULT HARDENING

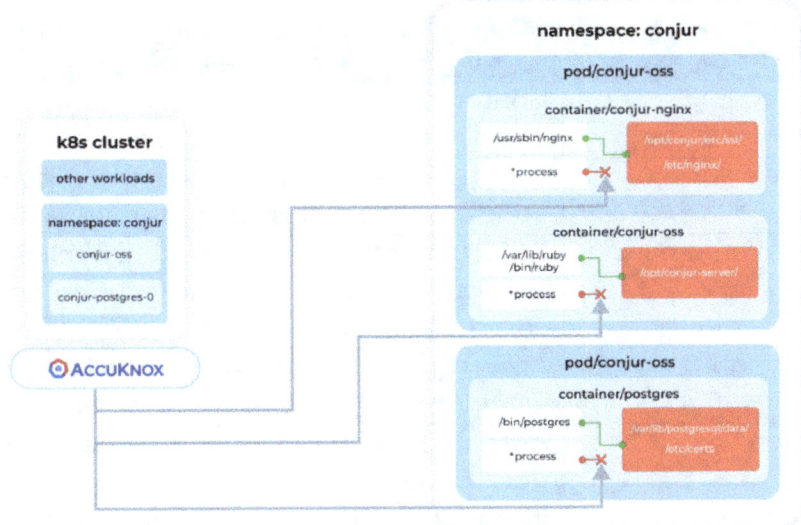

FIGURE 55. CYBERARK CONJUR HARDENING

The AccuKnox solution for securing Secrets Managers is built upon the following architectural components:

AccuKnox CNAPP Definitive Guide

1. **KubeArmor:** An open-source Cloud-Native Application Protection Platform (CNAPP) that provides continuous monitoring, behavioral analysis, and policy enforcement capabilities for Kubernetes clusters.
2. **AccuKnox SaaS Platform**: A cloud-based platform that facilitates the management, configuration, and monitoring of KubeArmor deployments across multiple clusters.
3. **Behavioral Analysis Engine**: A component that leverages machine learning and other advanced techniques to identify anomalous activities and potential threats within the Secrets Manager environment.
4. **Policy Management**: A centralized policy management system that allows administrators to define and enforce granular security policies for restricting access, process execution, and network communication.
5. **Alert and Incident Response**: A module that generates real-time alerts for detected threats and policy violations, enabling rapid incident response and remediation actions.
6. **Integration with Secrets Managers**: AccuKnox integrates with popular Secrets Managers like HashiCorp Vault and CyberArk Conjur, providing specialized security policies and monitoring capabilities tailored to these systems.

Feature	Description
Continuous Monitoring	Continuous monitoring of Secrets Manager workloads and activities within Kubernetes clusters.
Behavioral Analysis	Advanced behavioral analysis techniques to detect anomalous activities and potential threats.
Granular Policy Enforcement	Enforcement of granular security policies for restricting access, process execution, and network communication.
Process Whitelisting	Allowing only known and trusted binaries to execute within the target pods or containers.
Inline Remediation	Automatic containment and remediation actions upon detecting threats or policy violations.
Seamless Integration	Integration with popular Secrets Managers like HashiCorp Vault and CyberArk Conjur.

Key Differentiators of AccuKnox for Securing Secrets Managers

1. **Granular Policy Enforcement**: AccuKnox allows the creation and enforcement of highly granular security policies, ensuring that only authorized processes can access sensitive file system paths and execute specific binaries, effectively protecting the Secrets Manager.

2. **Inline Remediation**: With its inline remediation capabilities, AccuKnox can automatically contain and mitigate threats in real-time, preventing further damage and protecting the Secrets Manager from ransomware attacks or unauthorized access attempts.

3. **Seamless Integration**: AccuKnox seamlessly integrates with popular Secrets Managers like HashiCorp Vault and CyberArk Conjur, providing specialized security policies and monitoring capabilities tailored to these systems.

4. **Behavioral Analysis**: AccuKnox employs advanced behavioral analysis techniques, including machine learning, to detect anomalous activities and potential threats within the Secrets Manager environment, enhancing overall security posture.

5. **Centralized Management**: The AccuKnox SaaS platform provides a centralized management interface for configuring, monitoring, and enforcing security policies across multiple clusters, simplifying the management of Secrets Managers at scale.

Key Takeaways

- Securing Secrets Managers is crucial for protecting sensitive data, preventing ransomware attacks, maintaining confidentiality and integrity, and ensuring compliance with regulatory requirements.
- AccuKnox provides a comprehensive solution for securing Secrets Managers by leveraging KubeArmor, an open-source Cloud-Native Application Protection Platform (CNAPP).
- Key features include continuous monitoring, behavioral analysis, granular policy enforcement, process whitelisting, inline remediation, and seamless integration with popular Secrets Managers.
- The solution's architecture comprises KubeArmor, the AccuKnox SaaS Platform, a Behavioral Analysis Engine, Policy Management, Alert and Incident Response, and integration with Secrets Managers.

- AccuKnox differentiates itself through granular policy enforcement, inline remediation, seamless integration, advanced behavioral analysis, and centralized management capabilities.
- By securing Secrets Managers with AccuKnox, organizations can protect their sensitive data, prevent unauthorized access and ransomware attacks, and maintain a robust security posture within their Kubernetes environments.

Section 5.5.   Securing Data Science Access

AccuKnox provides robust security solutions for Jupyter Notebook environments, ensuring protection against a range of threats, including remote command injection and unauthorized access. By leveraging KubeArmor, AccuKnox offers granular control, real-time monitoring, and preemptive defense mechanisms to safeguard data science workloads.

What is it?

AccuKnox's Jupyter Notebook security solution is designed to secure data science workloads running on Jupyter Notebooks, a popular tool for interactive computing and data analysis. It employs KubeArmor, an open-source technology, to enforce fine-grained security policies and mitigate potential threats.

Why is this important?

Data science workloads often involve sensitive data and complex computations, making them prime targets for cyber-attacks. Securing Jupyter Notebooks is crucial to prevent unauthorized access, data breaches, and malicious code execution, safeguarding the integrity and confidentiality of valuable information.

How is this accomplished?

AccuKnox achieves Jupyter Notebook security through a combination of proactive measures, real-time monitoring, and granular access controls. By leveraging KubeArmor, administrators can define security policies to restrict user actions, control binary execution, and prevent unauthorized access to critical system resources.

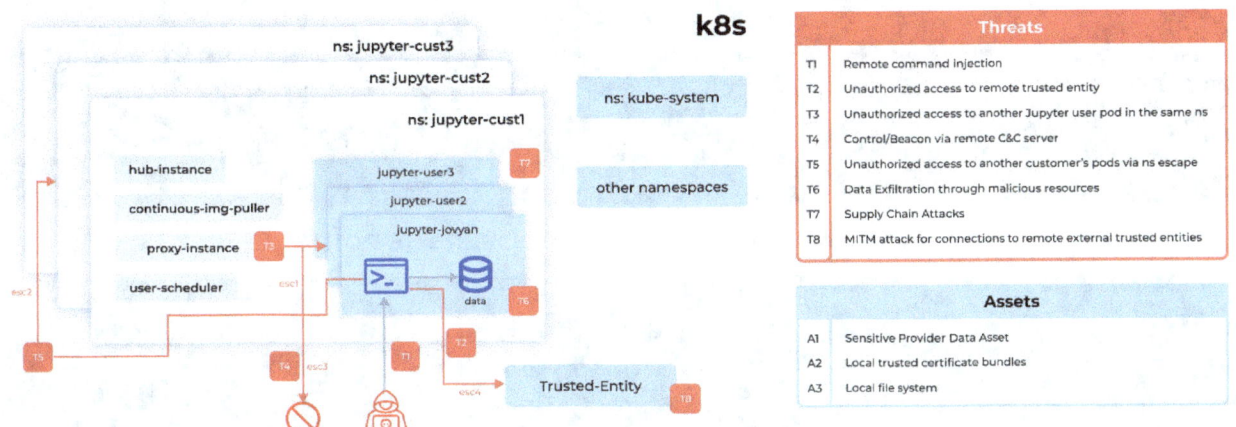

FIGURE 56. THREAT VECTORS FOR JUPYTER NOTEBOOKS AND DATA SCIENCE WORKLOADS

Architecture

AccuKnox's architecture integrates with Kubernetes clusters hosting Jupyter Notebooks, implementing security measures at both the container and system levels. KubeArmor acts as the security enforcement point, intercepting and enforcing security policies to protect against threats.

Security Measure	Description
Granular Control	Fine-grained access control over user actions
Real-time Protection	Continuous monitoring and proactive defense mechanisms
User-Friendly Configuration	Easy-to-configure security policies for administrators
Path Restriction	Restricting access to trusted paths for binary execution
Prohibit New Binaries	Preventing the creation of new binaries within critical paths
Policy Application Results	Sample threat model and KubeArmor policy for protection

```
> k -n jupyter get service proxy-public
NAME           TYPE           CLUSTER-IP     EXTERNAL-IP    PORT(S)         AGE
proxy-public   LoadBalancer   10.20.7.3      34.28.237.173  80:30420/TCP    12h
> k -n jupyter-customer2 get service proxy-public
NAME           TYPE           CLUSTER-IP     EXTERNAL-IP    PORT(S)         AGE
proxy-public   LoadBalancer   10.20.6.248    34.41.137.29   80:31066/TCP    8h
```

FIGURE 57. GRANULAR CONTROL OVER THE PORTS

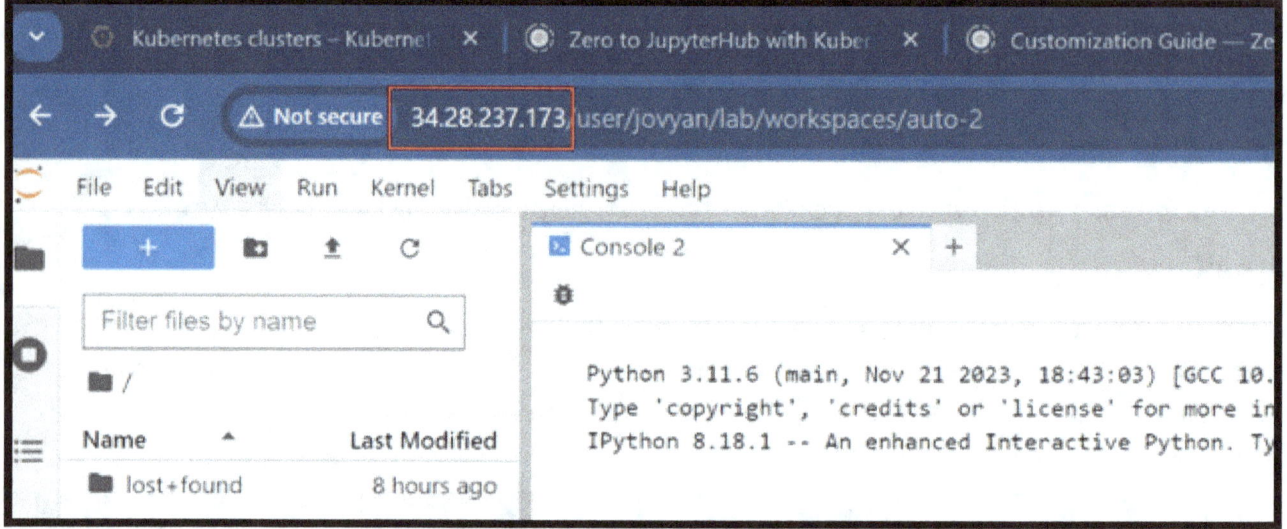

FIGURE 58. RECREATING ATTACK SCENARIOS

Granular Control & Path Restriction - KubeArmor lets admins define allowed execution paths (e.g., /usr/local/bin) for binaries within Jupyter Notebooks. This restricts unauthorized access to critical system binaries, minimizing vulnerabilities.

Prohibiting New Binaries - KubeArmor enforces rules to prevent creation of new binaries in specific paths. This proactive measure stops unknown executables from entering the system, upholding system integrity.

Policy Effectiveness - Sample threat models and KubeArmor policies showcase how it safeguard against various attack vectors. These policies ensure only authorized actions are allowed within the Jupyter Notebook environment.

Enhanced Visibility & Threat Detection - KubeArmor logs container activity and forwards it to the AccuKnox platform for analysis. This provides complete asset visibility, helps understand attack vectors, and aids in threat detection. Contextual alerts and notifications further improve troubleshooting and security posture.

Pre-emptive Security vs. Tetragon - AccuArmor utilizes LSMs and eBPF-LSM for pre-emptive security, unlike Tetragon's non-preemptive approach. This allows for inline mitigation and Zero Trust security updates with user review, making KubeArmor a superior Kubernetes policy engine.

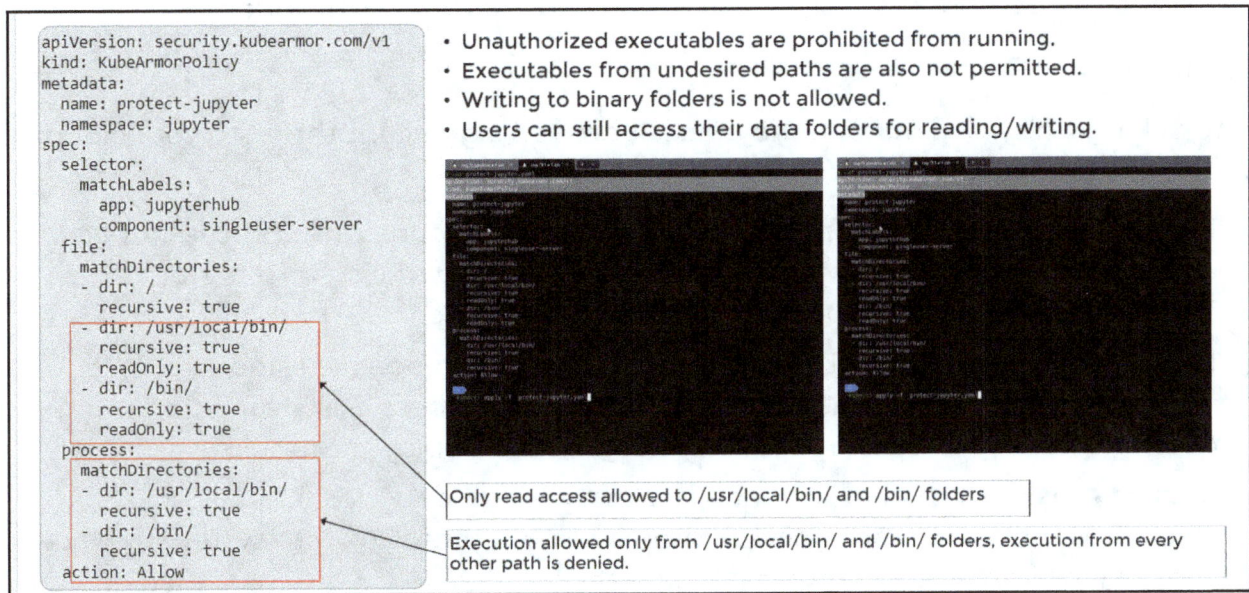

FIGURE 59. LEAST PRIVILEGE PERMISSIONS BASED ON ZERO-TRUST PRINCIPLES

Key Takeaways

- AccuKnox offers comprehensive security solutions tailored for Jupyter Notebook environments, addressing the unique challenges of data science workloads.
- By implementing pre-emptive security measures and granular access controls, AccuKnox ensures the confidentiality, integrity, and availability of sensitive data.
- Real-time monitoring and proactive defence mechanisms enable rapid response to security incidents, minimizing the impact of potential threats.
- Integration with KubeArmor provides enhanced security enforcement capabilities, strengthening protection against evolving cyber threats in Jupyter Notebook deployments.

Section 5.6.   Crypto Attacks

What is Cryptojacking?

Have you ever noticed your computer running slower than usual, fans whirring louder, or unexplained spikes in your electricity bill? These could be signs of cryptojacking.

Cryptojacking is the unauthorized use of your computing power to mine cryptocurrency, a digital form of money. Hackers infect devices with malware that secretly uses your system's resources to solve complex mathematical problems needed to generate new cryptocurrency. This process is highly intensive and can significantly impact your device's performance and energy consumption.

Why Should You Care?

Cryptojacking isn't just a minor annoyance; it poses a significant threat to your cloud environment:

- **Performance Degradation**: Cryptojacking malware consumes processing power and memory, slowing down your applications and overall system performance. This can disrupt critical workflows and user experience.
- **Increased Energy Costs**: The extra work your system does to mine cryptocurrency translates to higher electricity bills. These costs can add up quickly, especially for businesses with large cloud deployments.
- **Security Risks**: Cryptojacking malware can be a gateway for other attacks. Hackers might use it as an initial foothold to gain access to your system and steal sensitive data or deploy additional malware.

Combating Cryptojacking with AccuKnox and KubeArmor

Now that we understand the dangers of Cryptojacking in cloud environments, let's explore how AccuKnox with KubeArmor tackles this threat. AccuKnox acts as your security command center, working seamlessly with KubeArmor deployed within your Kubernetes clusters (groups of containers running applications).

KubeArmor serves as the on-ground enforcer within your Kubernetes clusters. It accomplishes this through several key functionalities:

- **Security Policy Enforcement:** Imagine KubeArmor as a security guard with a rulebook. You define security policies in AccuKnox, and KubeArmor enforces them within your clusters. These policies can restrict what applications can do, such as blocking known Cryptojacking software and preventing unauthorized access to critical resources.
- **Real-time Monitoring:** Just like a vigilant guard, KubeArmor constantly monitors your system activity for suspicious behavior that might indicate Cryptojacking. This includes unusual network traffic patterns, unauthorized processes running, or attempts to access restricted resources.
- **Isolation and Containment:** If KubeArmor detects a compromised system, it can quickly isolate it to prevent the Cryptojacking malware from spreading to other

arts of your cloud environment. This allows you to take corrective action on the infected system without jeopardizing the entire cluster.

AccuKnox with KubeArmor goes beyond basic defense mechanisms to provide a comprehensive security posture:

- **Zero-Trust Security:** Traditional security models often grant inherent privileges. AccuKnox follows a Zero-Trust approach, where no process or user has inherent access. Everything needs explicit permission through defined policies. This makes it significantly harder for cryptojackers to exploit vulnerabilities and gain a foothold in your system.
- **Pre-emptive Mitigation:** Unlike reactive security measures that wait for an attack to happen, KubeArmor takes a proactive approach. By leveraging security policies, it can block suspicious activity before it even occurs. This pre-emptive approach significantly reduces the risk of successful Cryptojacking attempts.
- **Granular Control:** AccuKnox empowers you with fine-grained control over what applications can do within your clusters. You can define policies that restrict specific actions or resources, allowing you to tailor security measures to your specific needs and applications.

Example: AccuKnox in Action Against Cryptojacking

Let's consider a scenario where a Cryptojacking malware attempts to infiltrate your Kubernetes cluster:

1. **The Attack:** The malware attempts to execute on a node within the cluster.
2. **KubeArmor Intervention:** KubeArmor, armed with the security policies defined in AccuKnox, detects the unauthorized application attempting to run.
3. **Policy Enforcement:** KubeArmor identifies the application as a known Cryptojacking tool based on the policy definitions.
4. **Blocking the Attack:** KubeArmor blocks the execution of the malware, preventing it from hijacking your system resources.
5. **Alerting and Investigation:** AccuKnox raises an alert notifying your security team about the attempted attack. This allows for further investigation and potential remediation steps.

Key Differentiators

Unlike point solutions that address specific aspects of security, AccuKnox offers a holistic approach, combining policy enforcement, real-time monitoring, and isolation capabilities to combat Cryptojacking and other threats.

- **Zero-Trust Security:** The Zero-Trust approach minimizes the attack surface and reduces the risk of unauthorized access, making it a powerful defense against Cryptojacking attempts.
- **Pre-emptive Mitigation:** By proactively blocking suspicious activity, KubeArmor prevents Cryptojacking malware from gaining a foothold in your system, minimizing potential damage.
- **Granular Control:** The ability to define fine-grained security policies allows you to tailor your defences to your specific cloud environment and applications. This policy template not only blocks the execution of known mining software but also prevents other malicious activities commonly associated with Cryptojacking attacks, such as reconnaissance tools like masscan, zgrab2, and nmap. Additionally, it restricts the execution of binaries from the /tmp/ folder, a common tactic used by cryptominers to deploy and run their malicious payloads.

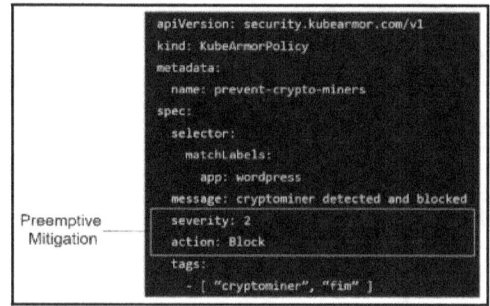
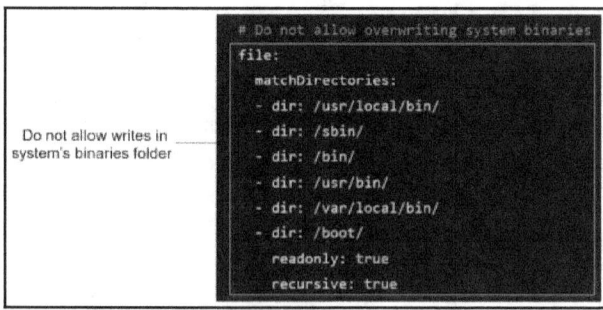

FIGURE 60. BLOCKING EXECS BEING WRITTEN FOR PRE-EMPTIVE MITIGATION

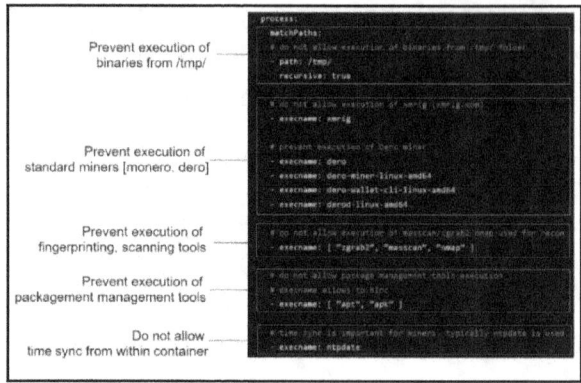

FIGURE 61. BATTLE CYRPTOJACKING VIRUSES AND THREATS WITH ACCUKNOX YAML POLICIES

Key Takeaways

Cryptojacking poses a significant threat to cloud environments, but with a proactive and layered security approach, you can effectively mitigate this risk. AccuKnox with KubeArmor provides a powerful foundation for defense, but remember, security is an ongoing process. By combining these solutions with the best practices outlined above, you can create a robust security posture that safeguards your cloud environment from Cryptojacking attacks and ensures the smooth operation of your critical applications.

Chapter 6   Kubernetes Security Best Practices

Kubernetes security refers to the practices and measures taken to protect Kubernetes clusters, the applications running on them, and the data they process from potential threats and vulnerabilities. As Kubernetes has become the de facto standard for container orchestration, ensuring its security has become paramount for organizations of all sizes.

Why is Kubernetes Security Important?

Kubernetes provides a unified platform for deploying, scaling, and managing containerized applications across hybrid cloud environments. However, the dynamic nature of Kubernetes, with its constantly changing workloads and infrastructure, introduces new security challenges. Failing to secure Kubernetes can lead to severe consequences, such as:

- Compromised applications and data
- Lateral movement of threats across the cluster
- Denial of Service (DoS) attacks
- Compliance violations
- Reputational damage and financial losses

How is Kubernetes Security Accomplished?

Kubernetes security is achieved through a combination of built-in security features, third-party tools, and best practices. AccuKnox's solutions leverage the open-source KubeArmor project, which provides inline mitigation, simplifies Linux security modules, and prevents malicious activity within Kubernetes clusters.

1. Building Small Container Images

Smaller container images have a reduced attack surface and are more efficient to pull and run, improving overall cluster performance and security. Container images are built using lightweight base images and optimized to include only the necessary dependencies and components. Use a minimal base image like Alpine Linux or Distroless, and a multi-stage build process to create smaller, optimized images.

2. Role-Based Access Control (RBAC)

RBAC is a Kubernetes feature that restricts system access based on the roles of individual users or groups, following the principle of least privilege. RBAC roles and role bindings are defined to grant specific permissions to users, groups, or service accounts. Create separate roles for developers, DevOps engineers, and cluster administrators, each with the minimum required permissions.

3. Resource Requests and Limits

Resource requests and limits ensure that Kubernetes pods have access to the required compute resources (CPU and memory) and are prevented from consuming excessive resources, which could destabilize the cluster. Resource requests and limits are specified in the pod specifications, and Kubernetes schedules pods based on available resources. Set appropriate resource requests and limits based on application requirements to ensure optimal performance and prevent resource contention.

4. Efficient Pod Termination

Proper pod termination ensures that applications shut down gracefully, preventing data corruption and enabling smooth transitions during updates or scaling operations. Kubernetes provides termination grace periods and preStop hooks to facilitate graceful termination of pods. Configure appropriate termination grace periods and implement preStop hooks to handle cleanup tasks before pod termination.

5. Fetching Updates

Keeping Kubernetes components and applications up-to-date with the latest security patches is crucial for mitigating known vulnerabilities and threats. Kubernetes supports automated updates through version upgrades, security patches, and image pulls from trusted registries. Configure automated updates for Kubernetes components and applications, and regularly scan images for vulnerabilities before deploying to production.

6. Namespaces and Labels

Namespaces provide logical isolation and segmentation within a Kubernetes cluster, while labels enable efficient organization and management of resources. Namespaces and labels are defined in Kubernetes manifests and can be used for access control, resource allocation, and monitoring. Create separate namespaces for different environments (e.g., development, staging, production) and use labels to group and filter resources.

7. Audit Logs

Audit logs provide a detailed record of activities and events within the Kubernetes cluster, enabling security monitoring, incident response, and compliance reporting. Kubernetes provides built-in auditing capabilities that can be configured to log specific events and actions. Enable and configure audit logging to capture relevant events, such as authentication attempts, resource creation/modification/deletion, and security policy changes.

8. Affinity Rules (Node/Pod)

Affinity rules control the scheduling and placement of pods on specific nodes based on various criteria, enabling better resource utilization and security isolation. Node affinity and pod affinity rules are specified in pod specifications, and Kubernetes schedules pods accordingly. Use node affinity to schedule pods on nodes with specific hardware or software requirements, and pod affinity to co-locate or avoid co-locating certain pods based on their characteristics or security requirements.

9. Probes (Liveness and Readiness)

Liveness and readiness probes help ensure the health and availability of applications running in Kubernetes pods. Liveness probes detect if a container is still running, while readiness probes determine if a container is ready to receive traffic. Implement liveness probes to restart unhealthy containers, and readiness probes to remove pods from load balancing until they are fully operational.

Key Differentiators

AccuKnox's solutions, including the integration of KubeArmor, provide several key differentiators for Kubernetes security:

- **Inline Mitigation:** KubeArmor provides inline mitigation capabilities, enabling real-time prevention of security threats and policy violations within Kubernetes clusters.
- **Simplified Linux Security Modules (LSM):** KubeArmor streamlines the complexity of LSMs, making it easier to manage and enforce security policies across diverse workloads and environments.
- **Bridging Pod Security Context Gaps:** KubeArmor fills the gaps between the BPF-LSM and native Kubernetes Pod Security Context, increasing predictability and simplifying multi-cloud compatibility.
- **Behavior Restrictions:** KubeArmor enforces behavioral restrictions on workloads, preventing malicious activities and unauthorized actions within the Kubernetes cluster.
- **Multi-Cloud Compatibility:** AccuKnox solutions are designed to work seamlessly across hybrid and multi-cloud environments, ensuring consistent security and compliance across diverse Kubernetes deployments.

- **Strict GRC Rulesets:** AccuKnox's RBAC implementation includes strict Governance, Risk, and Compliance (GRC) rulesets, ensuring that access and permissions within the Kubernetes cluster adhere to industry standards and organizational policies.

AccuKnox's solutions, including the integration of the KubeArmor project, provide additional security capabilities and simplify the management of Kubernetes security across hybrid and multi-cloud environments. With inline mitigation, streamlined LSMs, behavior restrictions, and strict GRC rulesets, AccuKnox enables organizations to proactively prevent security threats, enforce compliance, and maintain a consistent security posture across diverse Kubernetes deployments.

Key takeaways

- Embrace a comprehensive security strategy for Kubernetes, incorporating best practices and specialized tools like KubeArmor.
- Regularly assess and update your Kubernetes security posture to stay ahead of evolving threats and vulnerabilities.
- Foster a culture of security awareness and collaboration across development, operations, and security teams to ensure consistent and effective Kubernetes security practices.
- Leverage the expertise and solutions provided by trusted partners like AccuKnox to simplify and streamline Kubernetes security management while maintaining compliance and reducing risk.

Chapter 7   ADMISSION CONTROLLERS - WHERE DO THEY FIT IN

Admission Controllers are a powerful Kubernetes mechanism to enforce custom policies and validate/mutate resource requests before admission. They leverage webhooks to perform security, compliance, and governance checks on resources before deployment. Admission Controllers complement RBAC and provide fine-grained control of resource creation/updates. Tools like KubeArmor discover application behavior at runtime to generate accurate admission policies.

What are Admission Controllers?

Admission Controllers are Kubernetes plugins that validate and optionally mutate resource requests during create, update and delete operations. They act as gatekeepers enforcing semantic rules over resources before they are persisted in the cluster.

Admission controllers leverage admission webhooks, which are HTTP callbacks that receive admission requests for resources being created/updated/deleted. By intercepting these requests, admission controllers can inspect the resource objects and enforce rich, custom policies that traditional mechanisms like RBAC cannot handle.

Why are Admission Controllers Important?

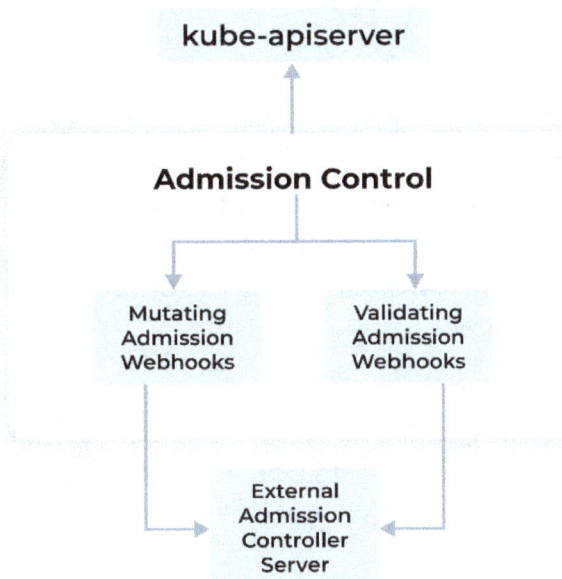

FIGURE 62. STRIPPED-DOWN VIEW OF ADMISSION CONTROLLER

While RBAC provides access controls over API resources, it does not enforce semantic constraints on the actual resource content being created. Admission Controllers fill this gap, validating the substantive content of resource objects before admitting them.

Some key use cases include:

- Ensuring resource constraints (CPU/memory limits)
- Allowing only trusted container images
- Mandating security contexts (running as non-root, read-only file system etc.)
- Policy enforcement on ingress/egress traffic, network policies etc.
- Validating proper resource labelling/annotations
- Mutation of resources by injecting sidecars, init containers etc.

Overall, Admission Controllers provide preventive governance controls over the cluster's declared state, significantly enhancing its security posture and compliance.

How are Admission Controllers Accomplished?

Admission Controllers are implemented via ValidatingAdmissionWebhooks and MutatingAdmissionWebhooks. These are Kubernetes resources configured to call webhooks hosted outside the cluster. The webhooks receive admission review requests containing the proposed resource object and can accept/reject it based on configured policies. Mutating webhooks can additionally modify object properties before acceptance.

The key components are:

1. **kube-apiserver** - The frontend for resource operations in Kubernetes
2. **Admission Webhooks** - Configure ValidatingAdmissionWebhooks and MutatingAdmissionWebhooks resources
3. **External Admission Controller** - This is the actual webhook server implementing admission policies

When a resource operation is requested, kube-apiserver executes configured admission webhooks by sending admission review requests. The admission controller server evaluates these requests against its policies and responds with admission results.

Table: Admission Controls and where they fit in

Policy Examples	Validating Admission	Mutating Admission
Resource Limits	☐	☐
Image Registry	☐	
Security Contexts	☐	
Network Policies	☐	☐
Sidecar Injection		☐

This table shows examples of policies implemented using validating and mutating admission webhooks.

Key Differentiators

While Admission Controllers provide rich policy capabilities, integrating them into a live cluster is non-trivial:

- Discovering appropriate policies based on application behavior
- Minimizing disruptions from overly restrictive policies

- Managing policy lifecycle (updating, deleting obsolete ones)

Runtime security tools like KubeArmor can help by providing visibility into the applications and generating admission policies from observed behavior. Running pre-production workloads through KubeArmor allows profiling their activities to recommend least-privileged policies.

With a gradual workflow of monitoring, generating policies and enforcing them via admission control, security posture can be systematically improved over time.

Key Takeaways

- Admission Controllers enforce custom semantic policies over K8s resources during create/update/delete operations
- They leverage ValidatingAdmissionWebhooks and MutatingAdmissionWebhooks configured to call external policy engines
- Admission Controllers provide preventive security governance that complements RBAC's access controls
- Integrating them requires understanding application behavior to generate safe, minimal policies
- Tools like KubeArmor aid in application visibility to recommend admission policies based on observed activities

Admission Controllers establish preventive guardrails around the desired cluster state and are a powerful mechanism for enhancing Kubernetes security and compliance posture when used judiciously.

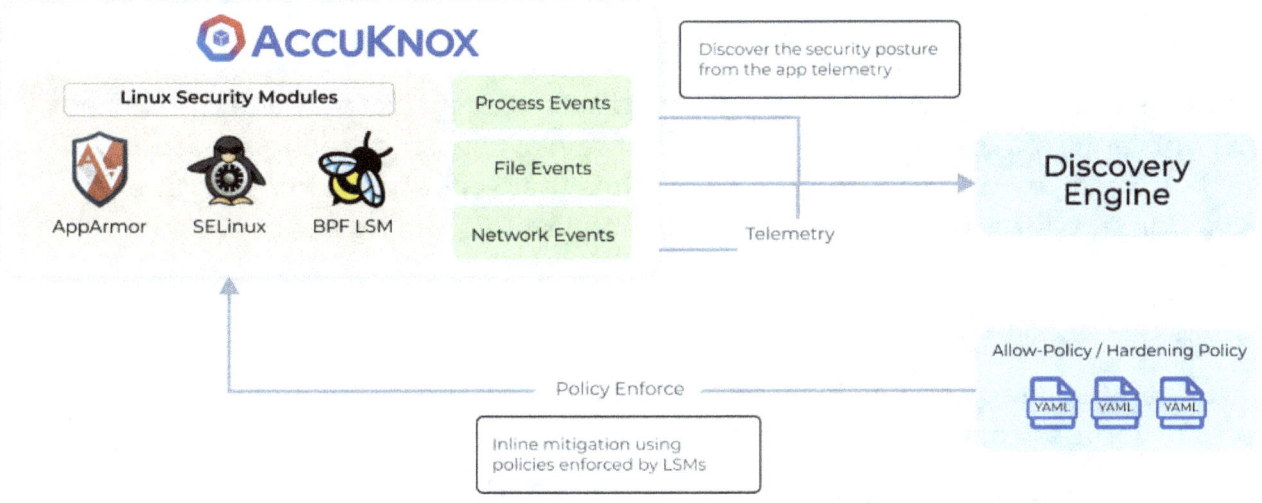

FIGURE 63. POLICY ENFORCEMENT AND TELEMETRY WITH ACCUKNOX

Chapter 8   LAYERED SECURITY

AccuKnox provides a comprehensive layered security solution for cloud-native applications, combining Cloud Security Posture Management (CSPM), Cloud Workload Protection Platform (CWPP), and Application Security. This multi-layered approach ensures end-to-end security and compliance across the entire application lifecycle, from code to runtime.

Agentless CSPM (Cloud Security Posture Management)	Basic Security	Multi-Cloud Security and Compliance Posture Discovery, and protection through the use of native APIs
	Application Security	App Security from Code to Run
Lightweight Industry Standard (eBPF) Sensor Agent CWPP Cloud Workload Protection Platform	Container Forensics and Auditing	eBPF (Extended Berkeley Packet Filter) based Observability with Auto-Discovery of App Behavior at process-level granularity
	Workload Hardening, Zero Trust Security	Comply with NSA Kubernetes Hardening Guide. - Application Firewalling - Micro-segmentation - Kernel Hardening to defend against zero-day attacks. Use eBPF for observability and LSMs (Linux Security Modules) to move from observability (audit) to enforcement (block) mode

FIGURE 64. SYNERGY OF CSPM + CWPP FOR LAYERED SECURITY

What is it?

AccuKnox's Layered Security is a holistic security solution that addresses various security aspects of cloud-native applications, including infrastructure, workloads, and applications. It combines multiple security components, such as CSPM, CWPP, and Application Security, to provide a unified and comprehensive security solution.

Why is this important?

In today's cloud-native era, applications are distributed across multiple clouds and environments, making it challenging to maintain a consistent security posture. AccuKnox's Layered Security approach ensures that security is addressed at every layer, from the infrastructure to the application level, providing a robust and comprehensive security solution.

How is this accomplished?

AccuKnox's Layered Security is accomplished through the integration of several security components, each addressing a specific security aspect:

1. **Cloud Security Posture Management (CSPM)**: This component provides visibility and control over the security posture of cloud infrastructure and

resources across multiple cloud providers. It helps identify and remediate misconfigurations, policy violations, and potential security risks.

2. **Cloud Workload Protection Platform (CWPP)**: The CWPP component focuses on securing cloud workloads, such as containers and Kubernetes clusters. It provides features like micro-segmentation, kernel hardening, and application firewalling to protect workloads from threats and vulnerabilities.

3. **Application Security**: This component addresses security concerns throughout the application lifecycle, from code to runtime. It includes features like static code analysis, dynamic application security testing (DAST), and runtime application self-protection (RASP).

Architecture

AccuKnox's Layered Security architecture consists of several components that work together to provide a comprehensive security solution:

1. **CSPM**: This component integrates with cloud providers' native APIs to discover and assess the security posture of cloud resources. It continuously monitors for misconfigurations, policy violations, and potential security risks, providing recommendations for remediation.

2. **CWPP**: The CWPP component includes an eBPF-based sensor agent that collects and analyzes workload telemetry data. It provides features like micro-segmentation, kernel hardening, and application firewalling to secure workloads at runtime.

3. **Application Security**: This component includes tools for static code analysis, DAST, and RASP. It integrates with the software development lifecycle (SDLC) to identify and mitigate security vulnerabilities throughout the application lifecycle.

4. **Centralized Management Console**: AccuKnox provides a unified management console that integrates all the security components, enabling users to manage and monitor security posture, policies, and incidents from a single pane of glass.

Table: Enterprise CNAPP Suite

Security Component	Description
Cloud Security Posture Management (CSPM)	Continuous discovery, assessment, and monitoring of cloud security posture across multiple cloud providers.

AccuKnox CNAPP Definitive Guide

Security Component	Description
Cloud Workload Protection Platform (CWPP)	Runtime protection for cloud workloads, including micro-segmentation, kernel hardening, and application firewalling.
Application Security	Identification and mitigation of security vulnerabilities throughout the application lifecycle, from code to runtime.

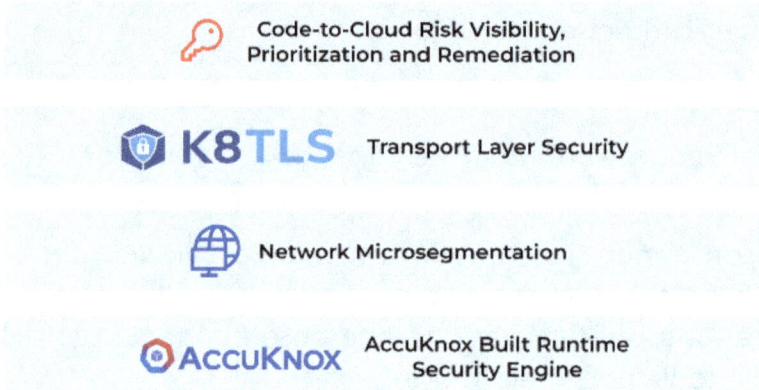

FIGURE 65. ENSURING SECURITY AT EVERY LAYER

Key Differentiators

1. **Agentless CSPM**: AccuKnox's CSPM component is agentless, leveraging cloud providers' native APIs to assess and monitor security posture, eliminating the need for additional agents or infrastructure.

2. **eBPF-based CWPP**: The CWPP component utilizes extended Berkeley Packet Filter (eBPF) technology, providing efficient and lightweight workload monitoring and protection without the overhead of traditional agents.

3. **Unified Management Console**: AccuKnox's unified management console provides a single pane of glass for managing and monitoring security posture, policies, and incidents across all security components, simplifying security operations.

4. **Multi-Cloud Support**: AccuKnox's Layered Security solution supports multiple cloud providers, enabling consistent security and compliance across hybrid and multi-cloud environments.

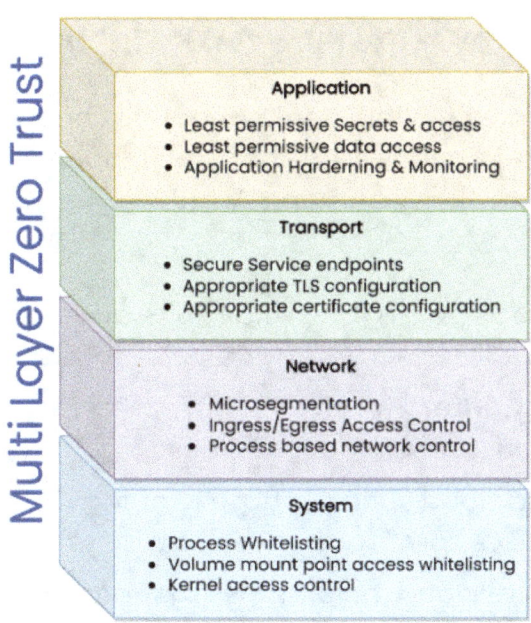

FIGURE 66. MULTI-LAYER ZERO TRUST SECURITY ARCHITECTURE

Key Takeaways

- AccuKnox's Layered Security provides a comprehensive security solution that addresses infrastructure, workload, and application security concerns.
- It combines CSPM, CWPP, and Application Security components to ensure end-to-end security and compliance across the entire application lifecycle.
- The solution leverages agentless CSPM, eBPF-based CWPP, and a unified management console for efficient and centralized security operations.
- AccuKnox's Layered Security supports multi-cloud environments, enabling consistent security and compliance across hybrid and multi-cloud deployments.
- By addressing security at every layer, AccuKnox's Layered Security solution helps organizations achieve a robust and comprehensive security posture for their cloud-native applications.

Chapter 9   Deployment Workflow

AccuKnox has one of the most flexible deployment options in the industry, catering to a wide range of infrastructure needs. Whether you're operating in the public cloud, private cloud, or a multi-cloud environment, AccuKnox has you covered.

Deployment Scenarios

1. **Hybrid/Multi-Cloud**: Secure hybrid and multi-cloud environments, ensuring consistent security policies across your diverse infrastructure.
2. **On-Premises/Data Center**: Protect your on-premises data center resources with AccuKnox's robust security capabilities.
3. **Public Cloud:** Public cloud such as those running on AWS, Azure, or Google Cloud, with AccuKnox's comprehensive security solutions.
4. **Private Cloud:** Private cloud including air-gapped and highly-sensitive environments, with AccuKnox's tailored security offerings.
5. **Edge Workloads:** Edge workloads for extending security perimeter and protection of IoT and edge computing environments.
6. **5G Workloads:** 5G workloads leverage AccuKnox's expertise to secure 5G-powered workloads, addressing the unique security challenges of this emerging technology.

Versatile Workload Support

1. **Kubernetes-Orchestrated Workloads**: KubeArmor is deployed as a Kubernetes DaemonSet, providing policy enforcement at both the pod (KubeArmorPolicy) and node (KubeArmorHostPolicy) levels.
2. **VM/Bare-Metal Workloads**: For workloads running directly on virtual machines or bare-metal servers, KubeArmor can be deployed in systemd mode, ensuring comprehensive security coverage.

The AccuKnox Advantage

- **Flexible Architecture**: AccuKnox's modular design allows for seamless integration into diverse infrastructure environments, from public and private clouds to on-premises data centers and edge/5G deployments.
- **Consistent Security Posture**: Maintain a unified security posture across your entire infrastructure, regardless of the underlying deployment model or workload type.

- **Future-Proof Solutions**: AccuKnox's roadmap includes support for emerging workloads, such as IoT/Edge and 5G, ensuring your security investments are future-proof.

Ease of Deployment: AccuKnox's streamlined deployment process simplifies the implementation of comprehensive security measures, reducing the burden on your IT and security teams.

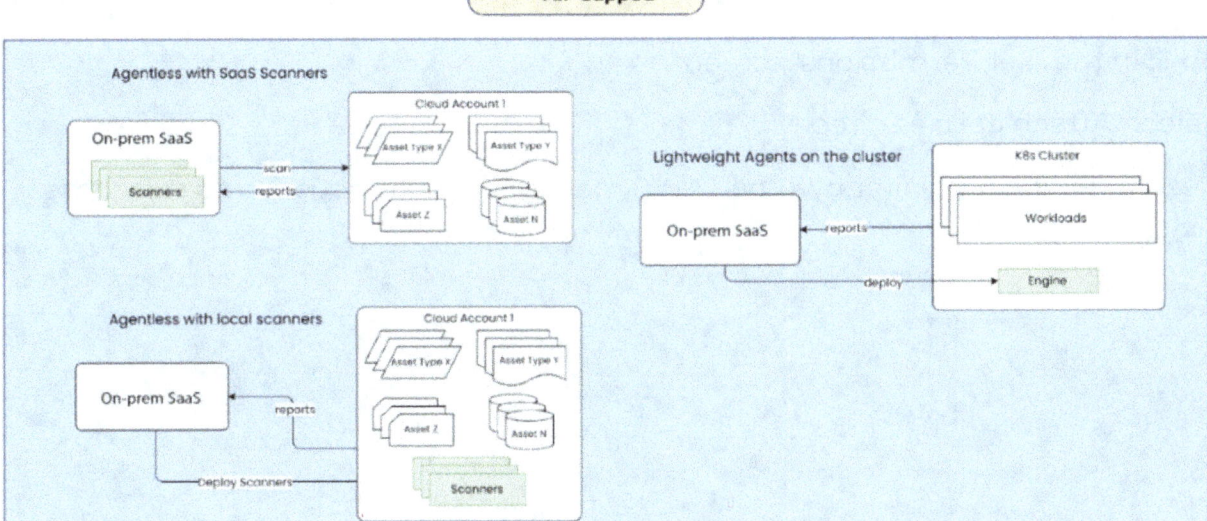

FIGURE 67. DEPLOYMENT METHODS SUPPORTED BY ACCUKNOX ENTERPRISE CNAPP

Section 9.1.   Deployment Models - Public Cloud

AWS

AWS onboarding requires creation of an IAM user. Please follow the following steps to provide a user with appropriate read access:

Step 1: Navigate to IAM → Users and click on Add Users

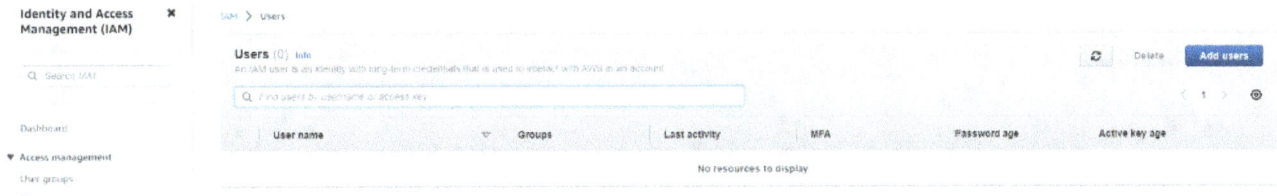

Step 2: Provide a username to identify the user

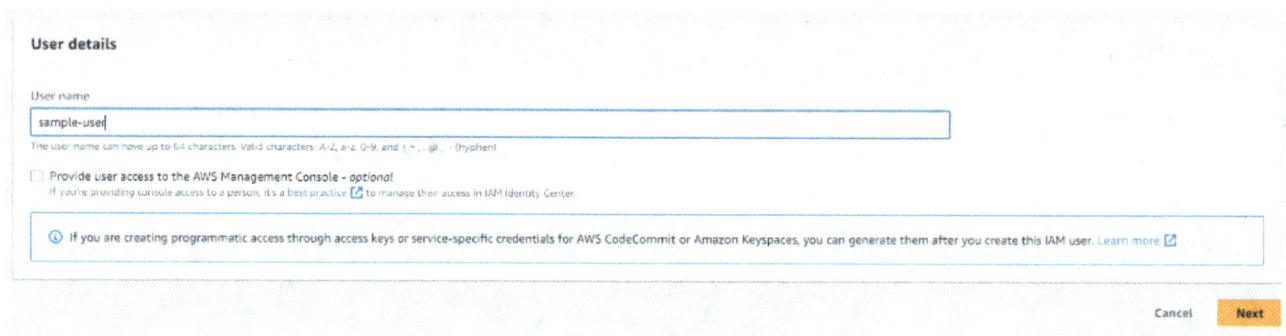

Step 3: In the "Set Permissions" screen:

a. Select "Attach policies directly"

b. Search "ReadOnly", Filter by Type: "AWS managed - job function" and select the policy

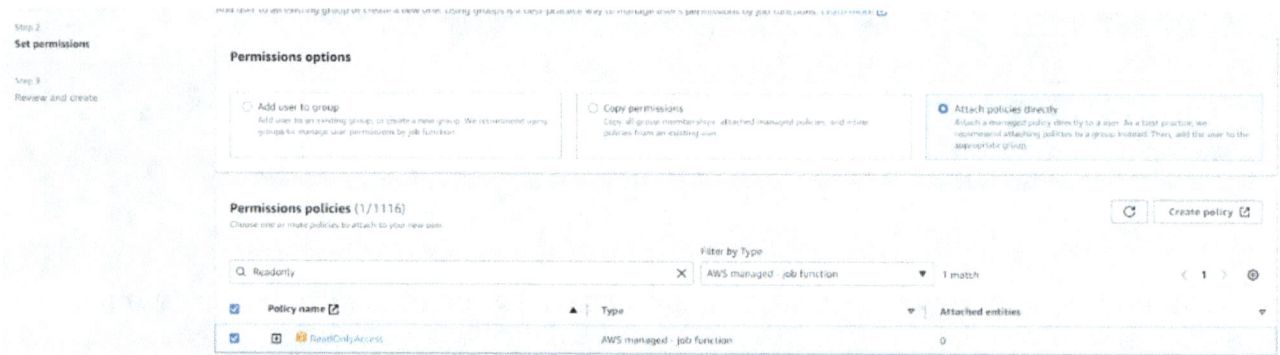

c. Search "SecurityAudit", Filter by Type: "AWS managed - job function" and select the policy

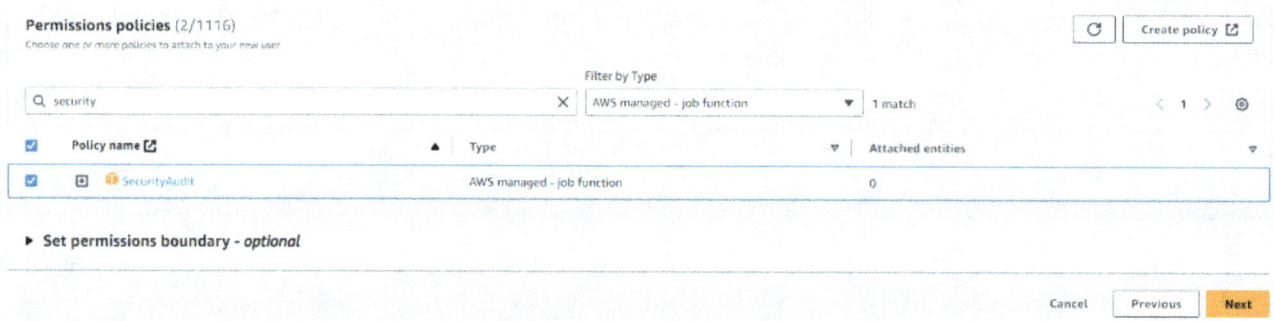

Step 4: Finish creating the user. Click on the newly created user and create the Access key and Secret Key from the Security Credentials tab to be used in the Accuknox panel

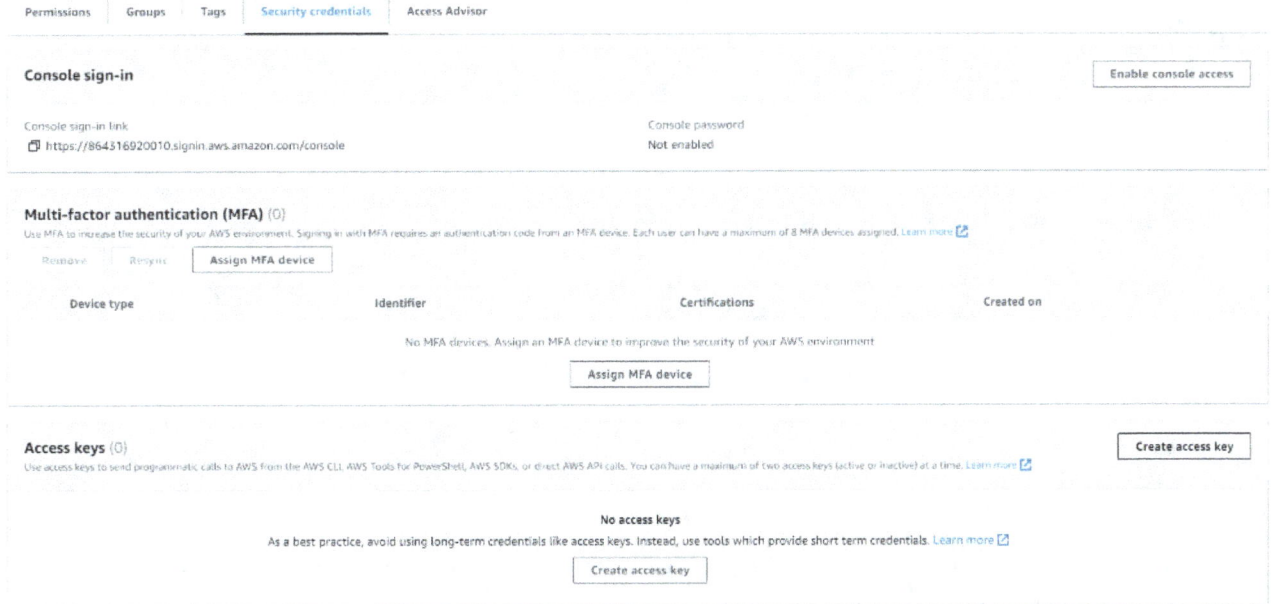

Azure

For Azure Onboarding it is required to register an App and give Security read access to that App from the Azure portal.

Step 1: Go to your Azure Portal search for App registrations and open it

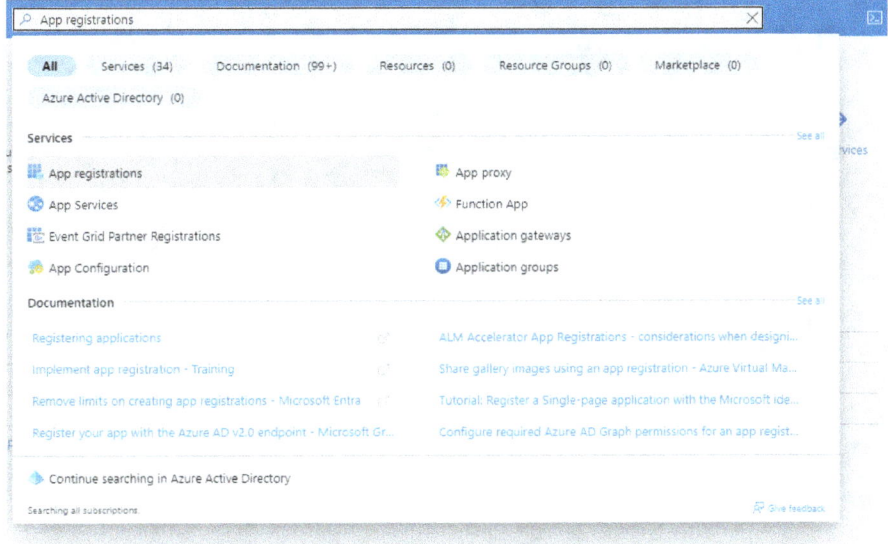

Step 2: Here click on New registration

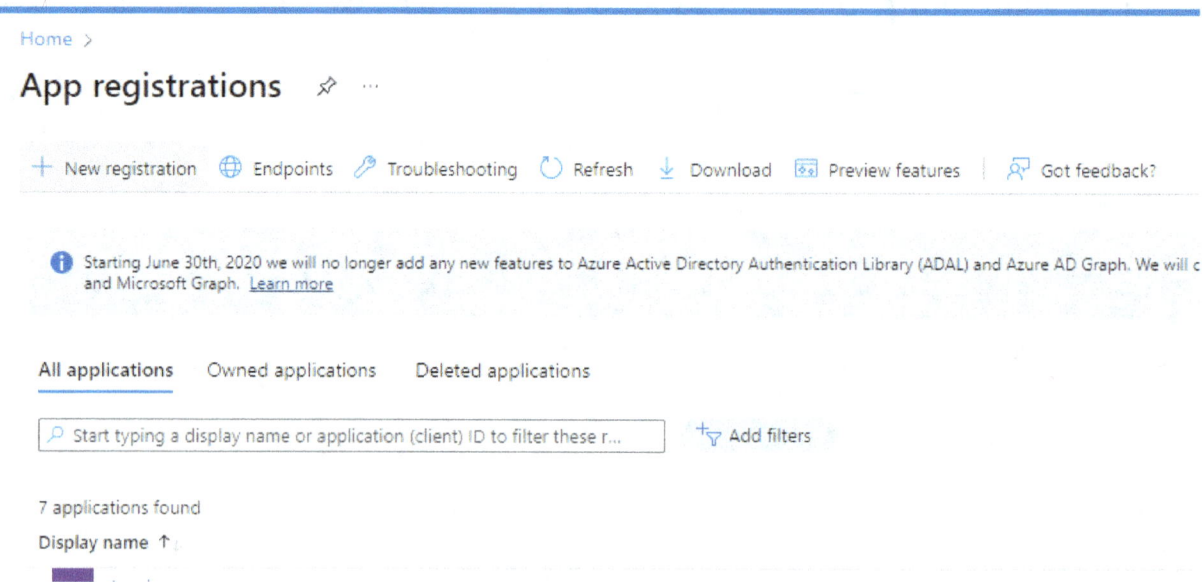

Step 3: Give your application a name, remember this name as it will be used again later, For the rest keep the default settings

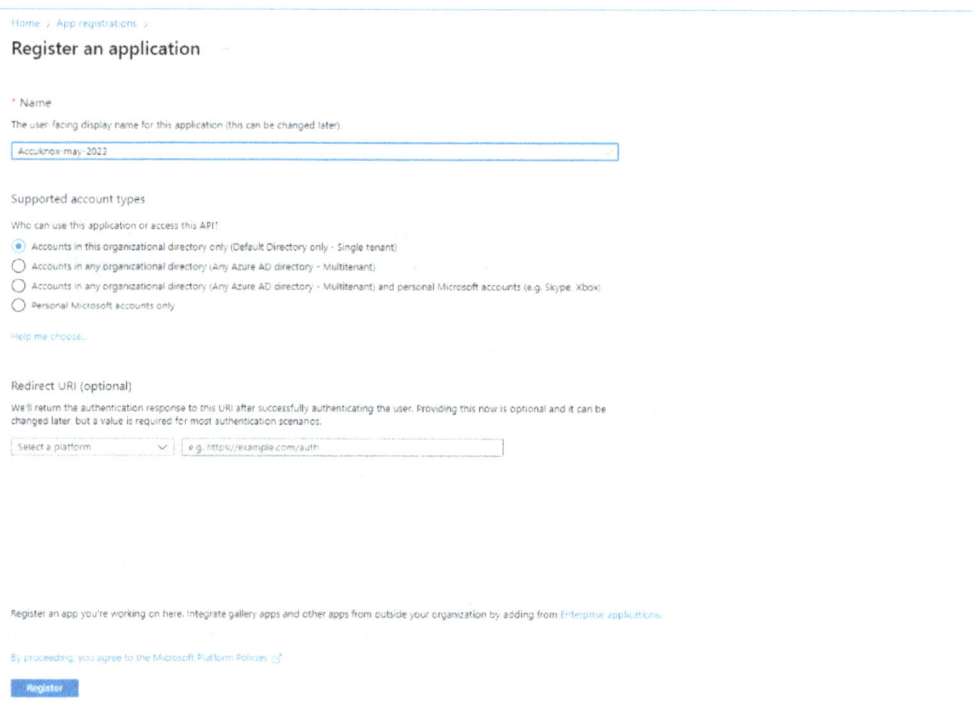

AccuKnox CNAPP Definitive Guide

Step 4: Now your application is created, save your *Application ID* and *Directory ID* as they will be needed for onboarding on Accuknox Saas and then click on 'Add a certificate or secret'

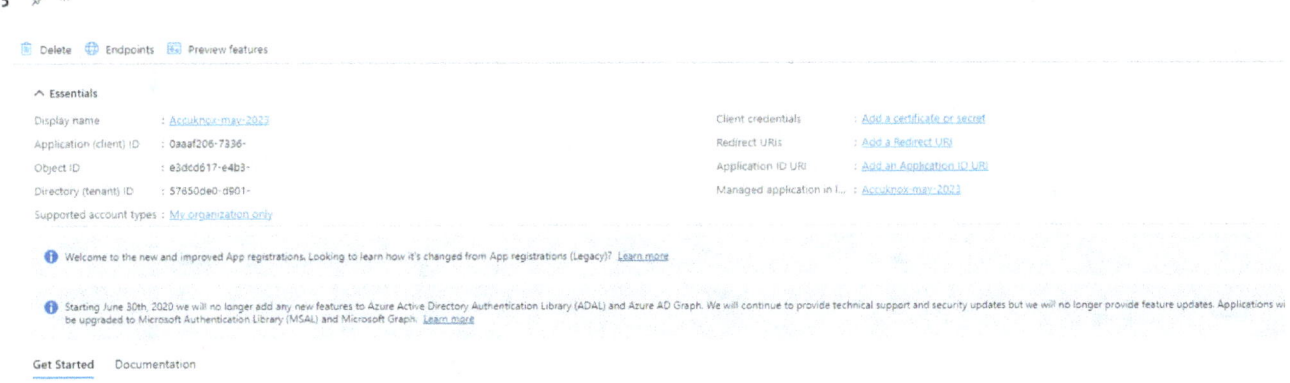

Step 5: Click on new client secret and enter the name and expiration date to get the *secret id* and *secret value*, save this secret value as this will also be needed for onboarding.

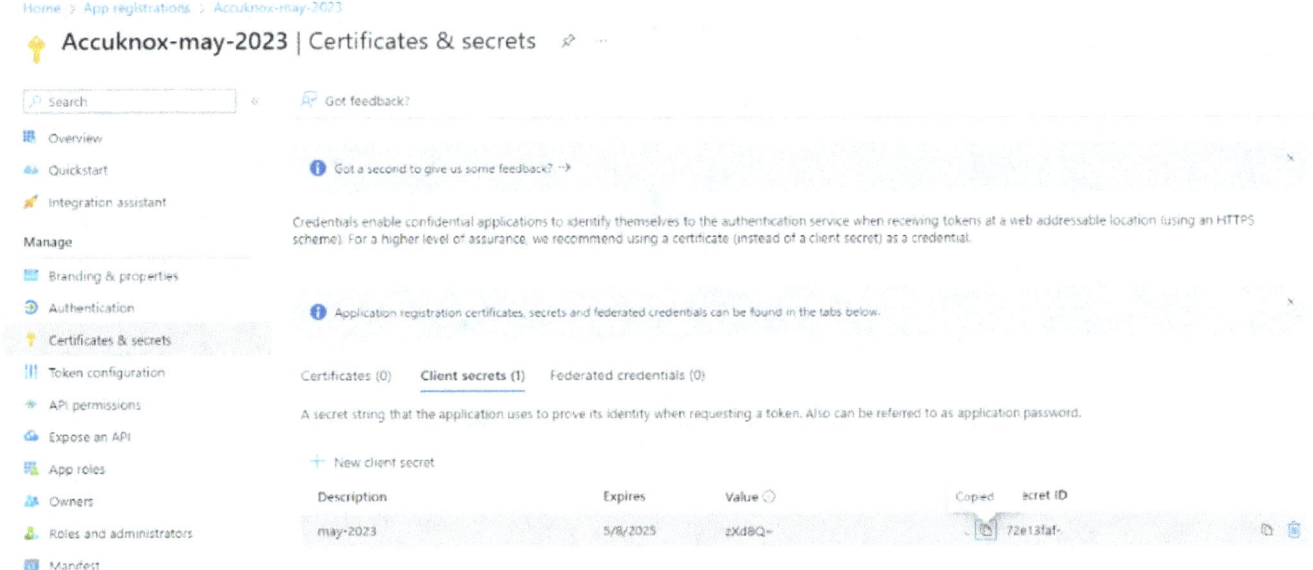

Step 6: Next, go to the *API permissions* tab and click on 'Add permission'

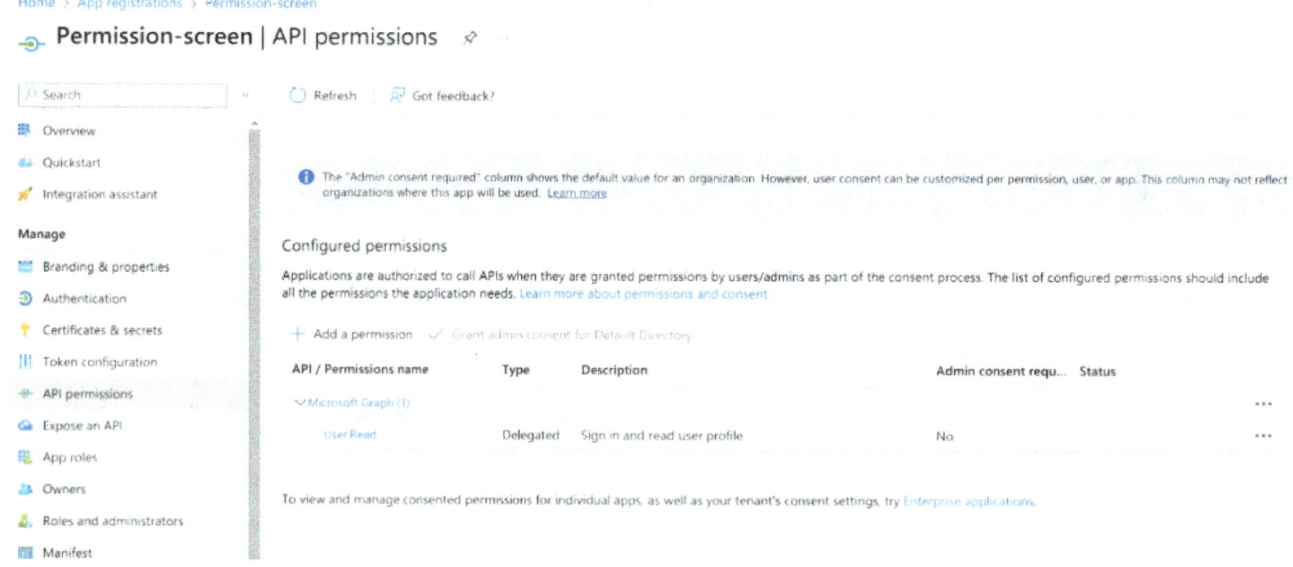

Step 7: On the screen that appears, click on 'Microsoft Graph'

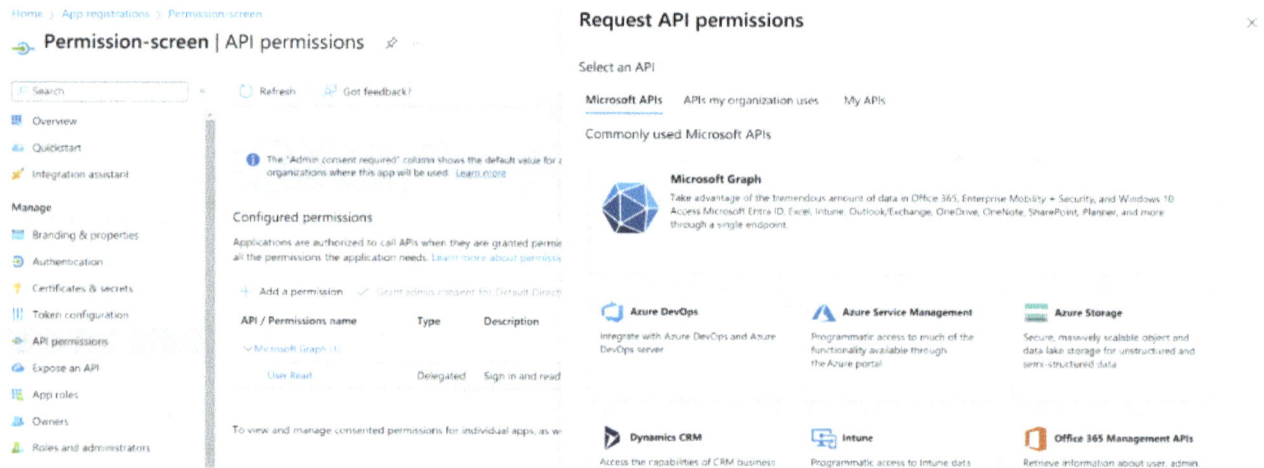

Step 8: Next, select Application Permissions and then search for Directory.Read.All and click on Add permissions

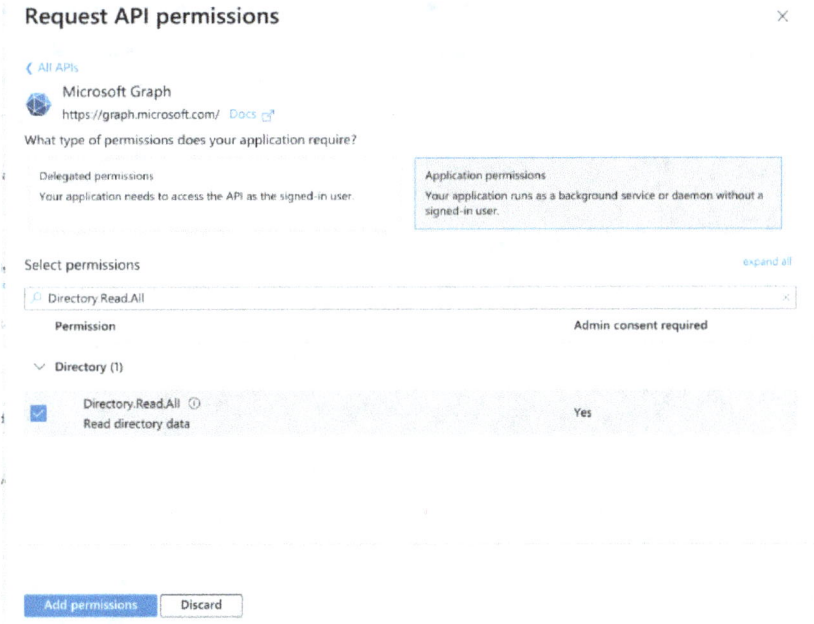

Step 9: Select 'Grant Admin Consent' for Default Directory and click on 'Yes'

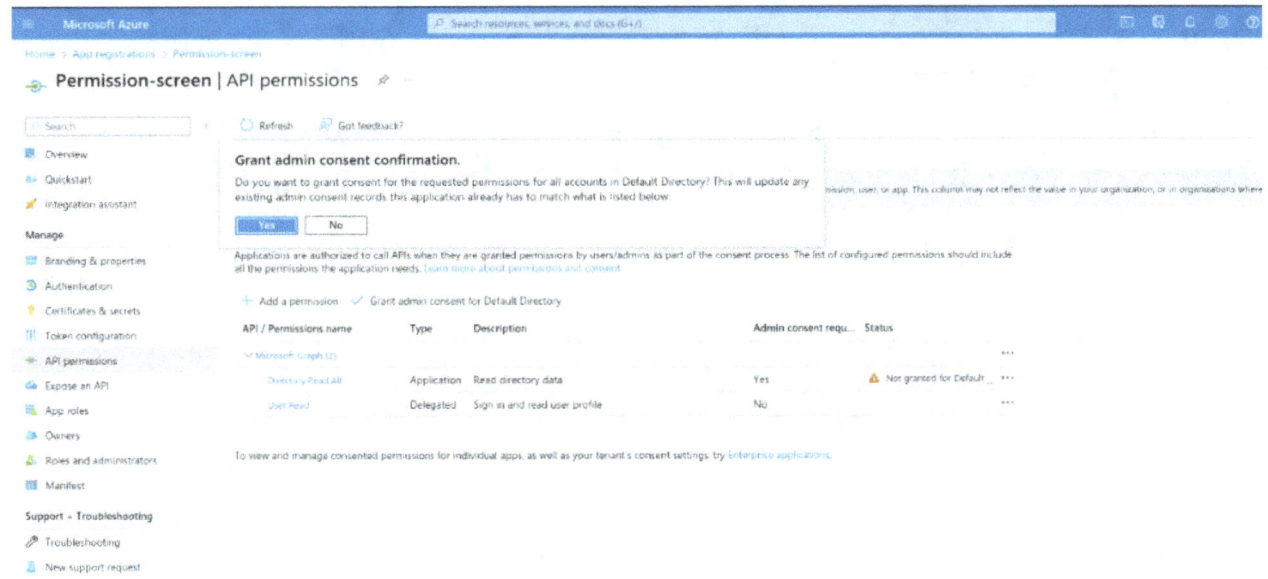

Step 10: Now we need to give Security read permissions to this registered Application, to do that go to subscriptions

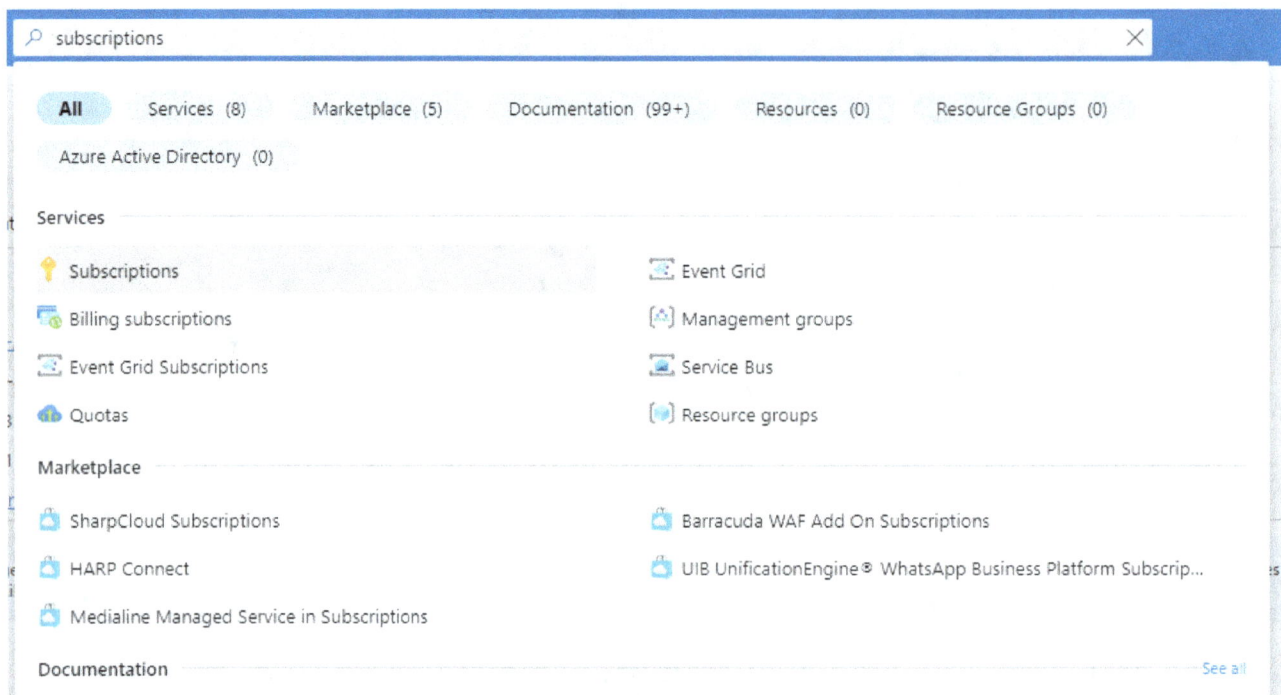

Step 11: First save the subscription ID and click on the subscription name, here it is "Microsoft Azure Sponsorship"

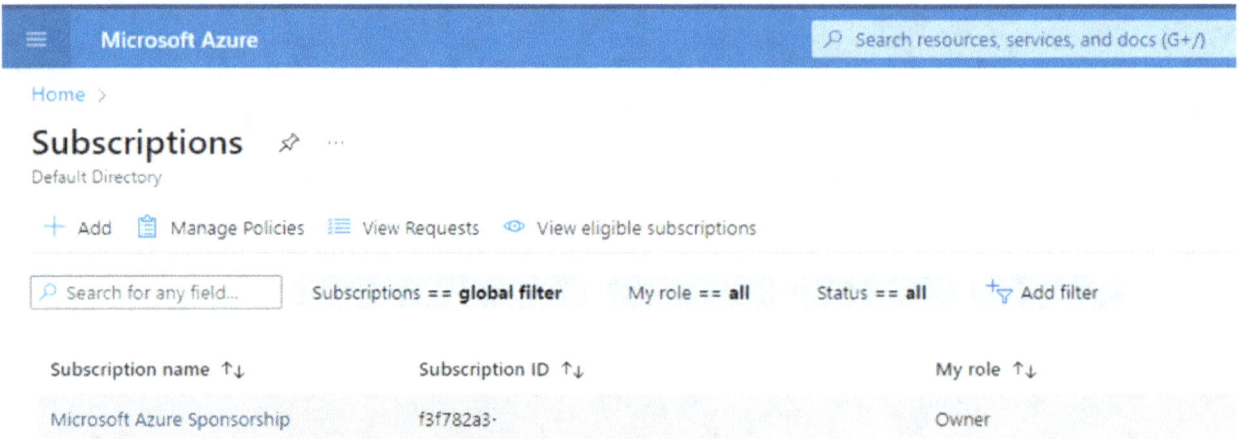

Step 12: Navigate to Access Control (IAM) and go to Roles, here select Add and Add role assignment

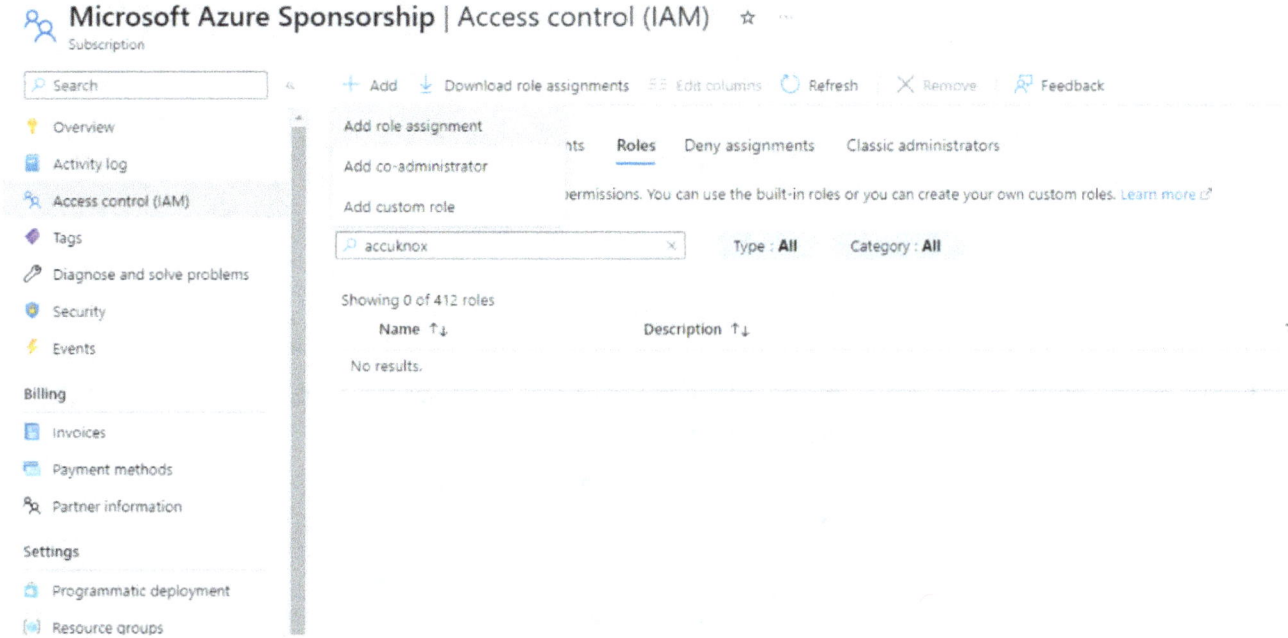

Step 13: Search for the "Security Reader" Job function Role, select it and press the *next*

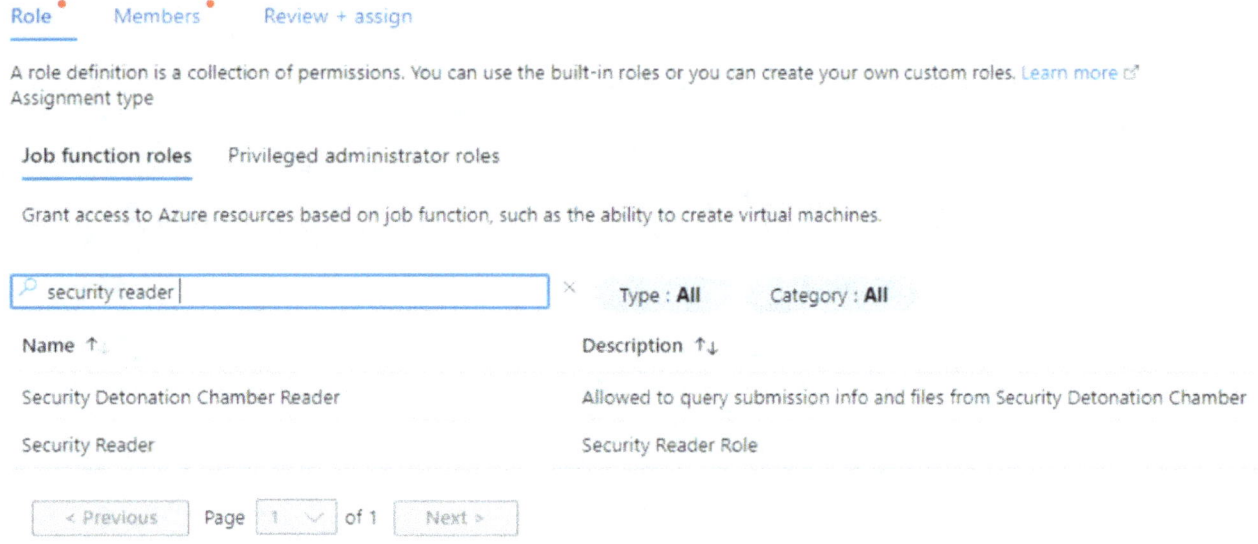

Step 14: In the member section click on Select *members* it will open a dropdown menu on the right-hand side

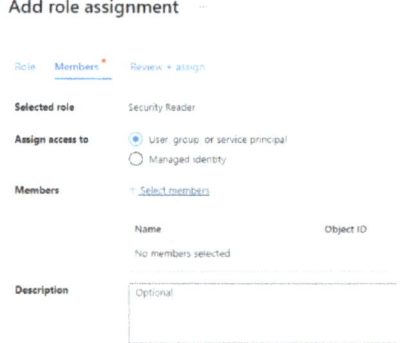

Step 15: Here search for the Application that you registered in the beginning, select the application and click on *review and assign*.

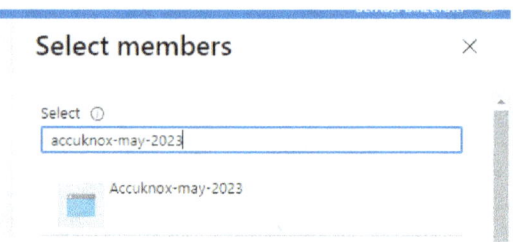

Step 16: Similarly, we must add another role. This time, search for *Log Analytics Reader*. Select it and click *next*

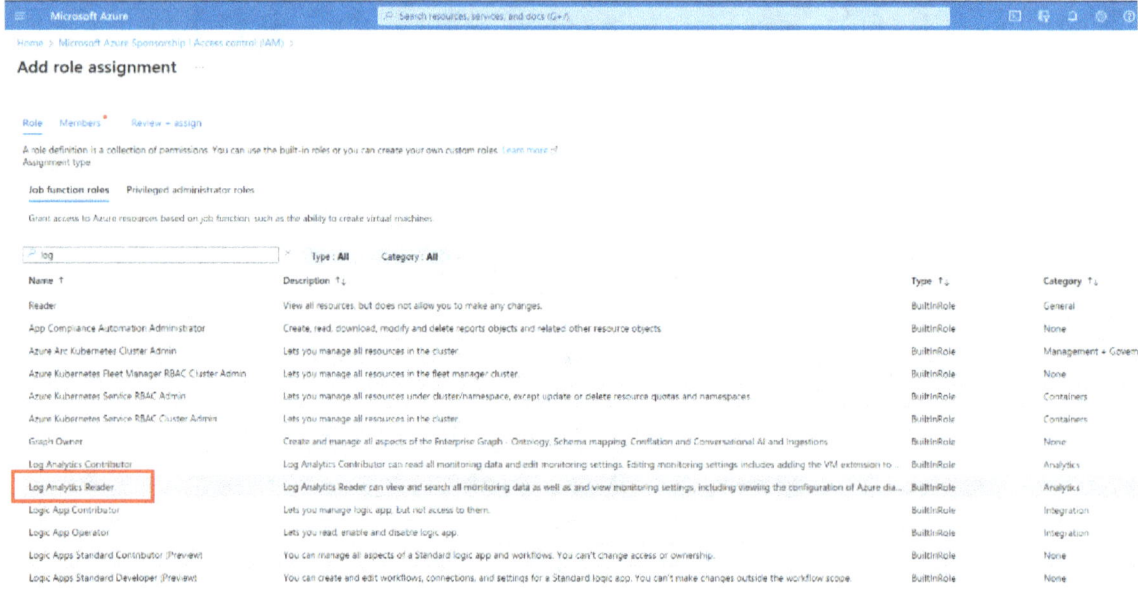

Step 17: Now, click on *Select members*, and select the application that was created similar to the previous role. Finally, click on *Review and Assign*.

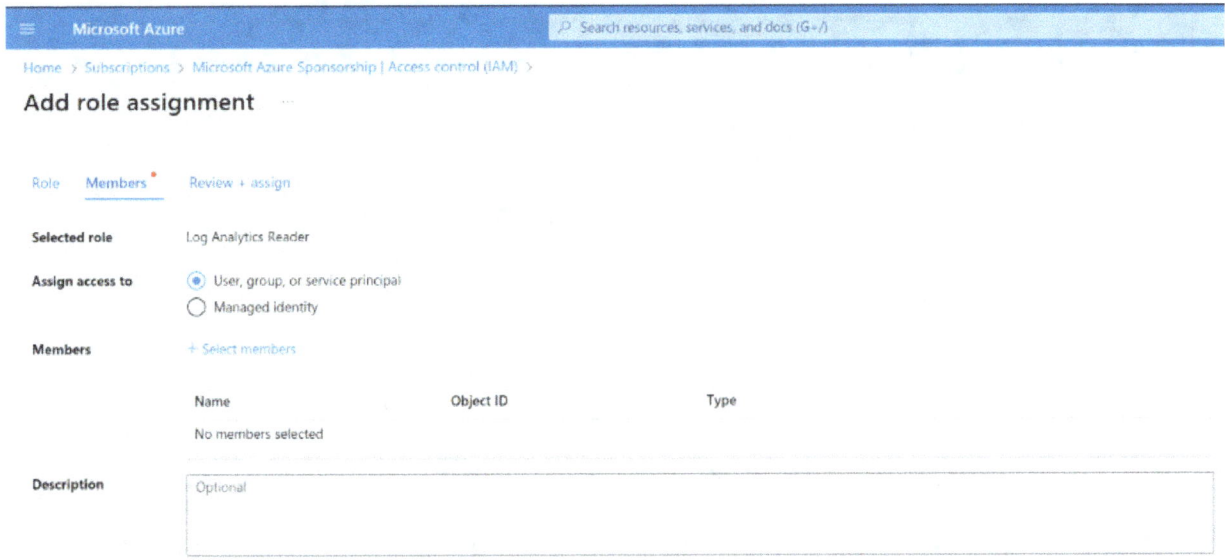

GCP

Make sure the Below API Library is enabled in your GCP Account for onboarding into Accuknox SaaS:

1. Compute Engine API
2. Identity and Access Management (IAM) API
3. Cloud Resource Manager API
4. Cloud Functions API
5. KMS API
6. Kubernetes API
7. Cloud SQL Admin API

For GCP there is a requirement for IAM Service Account Access.

Step 1: Log into your Google Cloud console and navigate to IAM & Admin choose "Roles", and Click "Create Role"

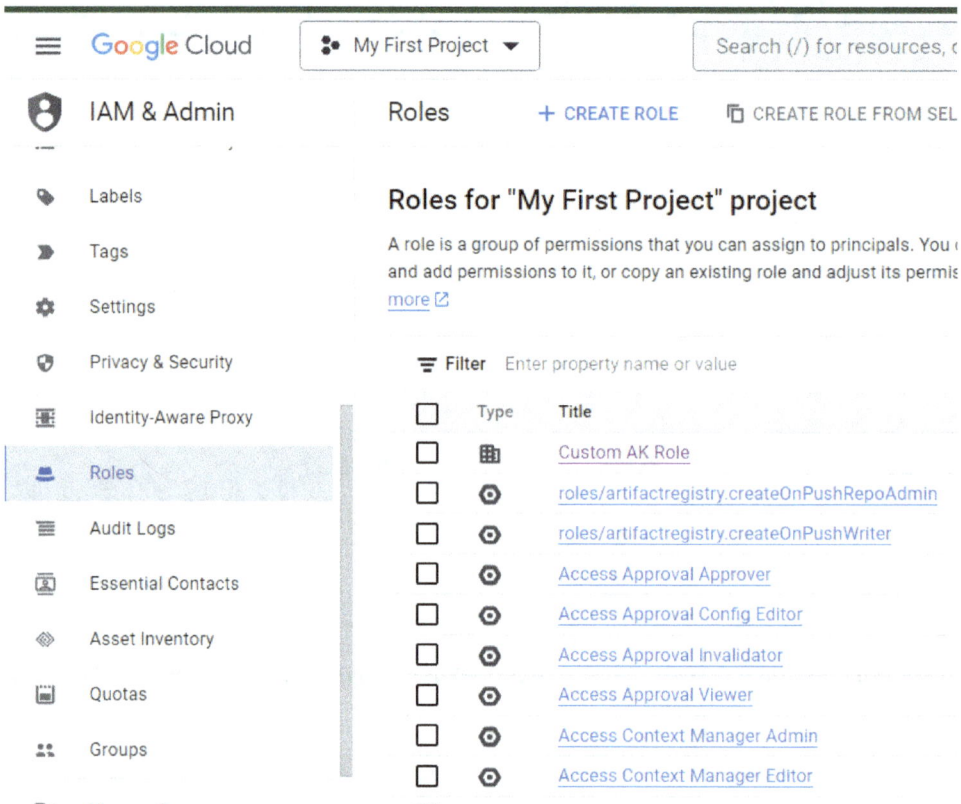

Step 2: Name the "Role" and Click "Add Permission"

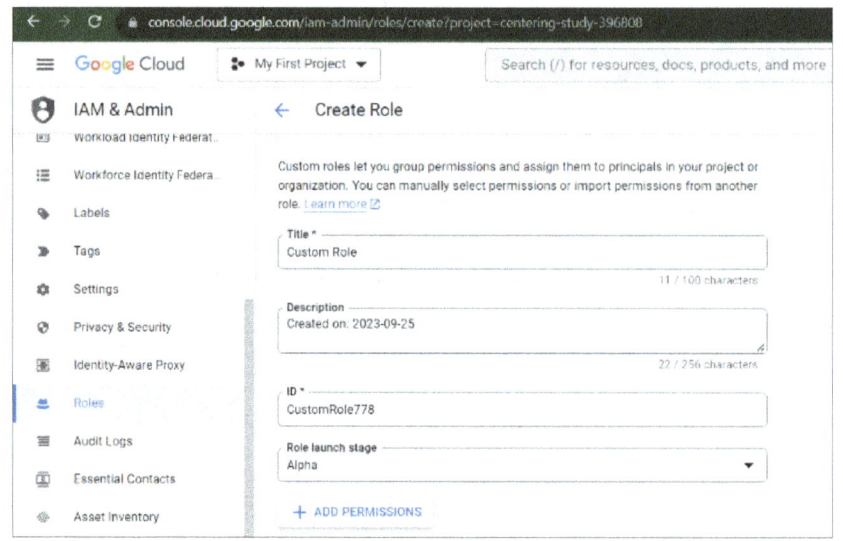

Step 3: Use the Service: storage filter then value as "storage.buckets.getIamPolicy"

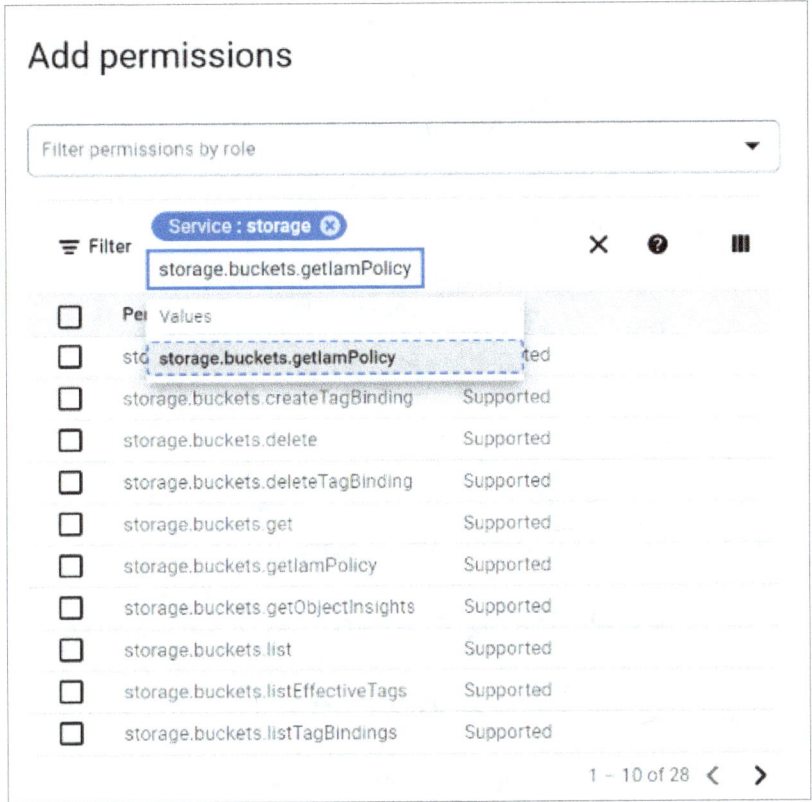

Step 4: Choose the permission and Click "Add" then Click Create in the same page.

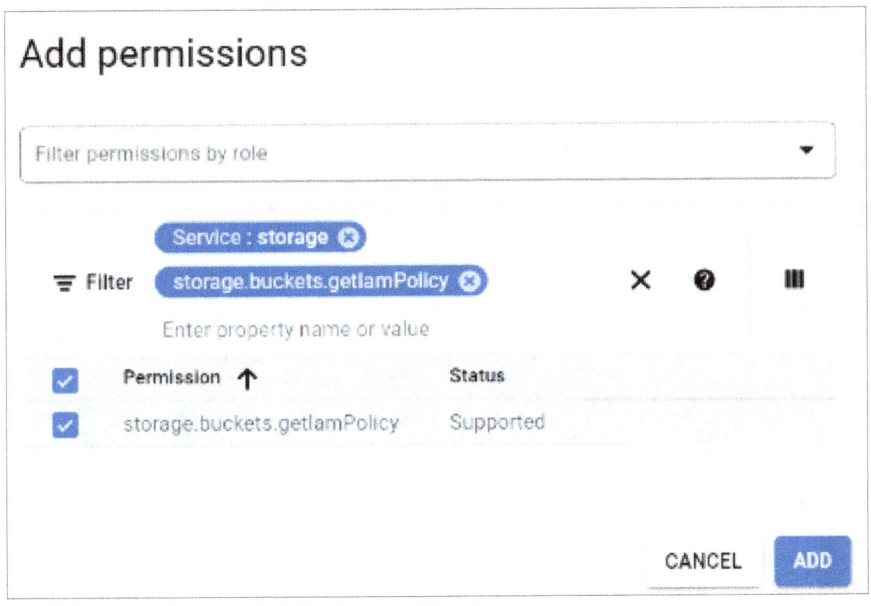

Step 5: In the Navigation Panel, navigate to IAM Admin > Service Accounts.

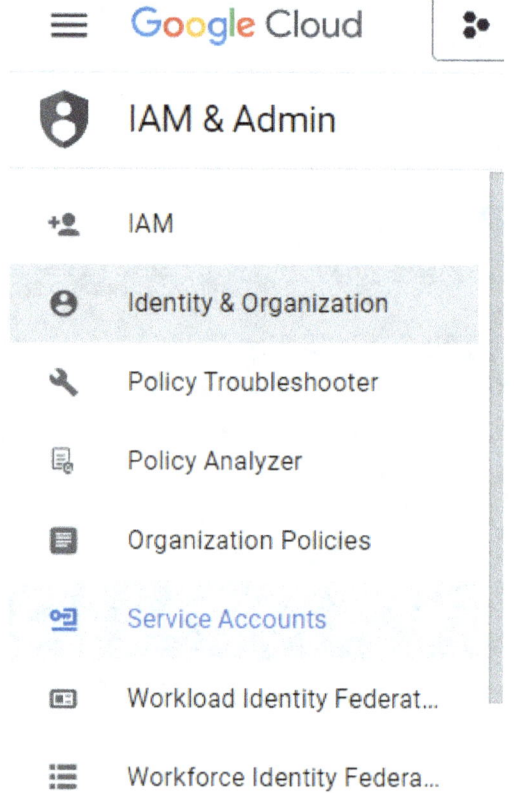

Step 6: Click on "Create Service Account"

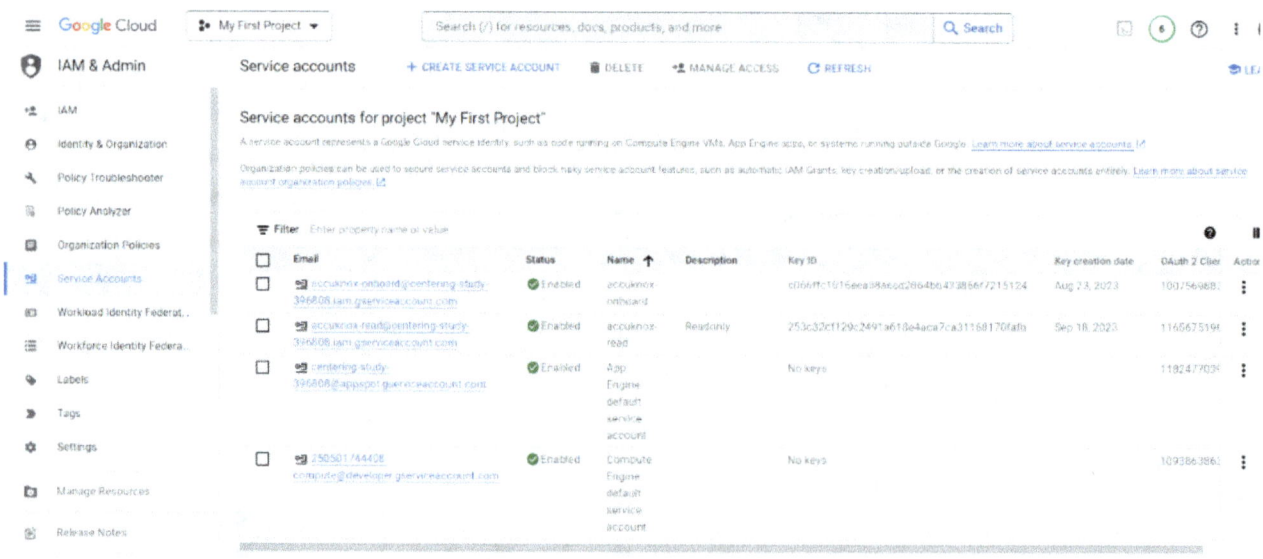

Step 7: Enter any name that you want on Service Account Name.

Step 8: Click on Continue.

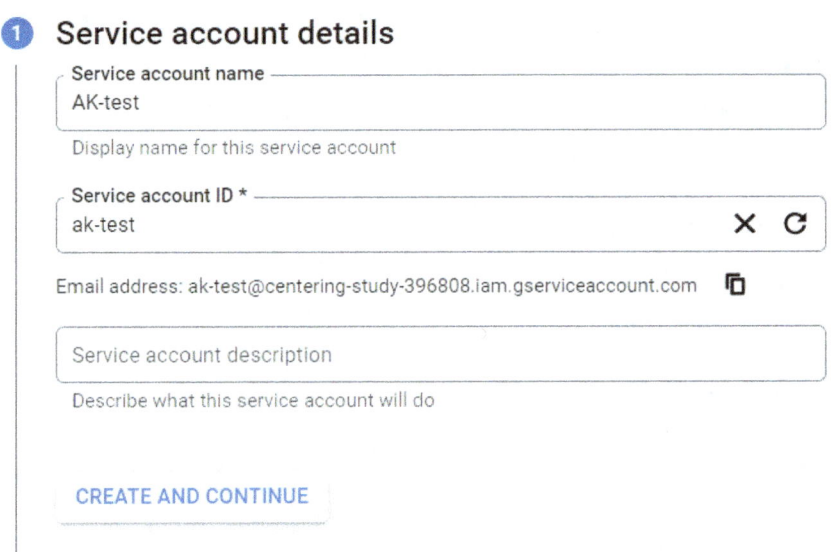

Step 9: Select the role: Project > Viewer and click Add another Role.

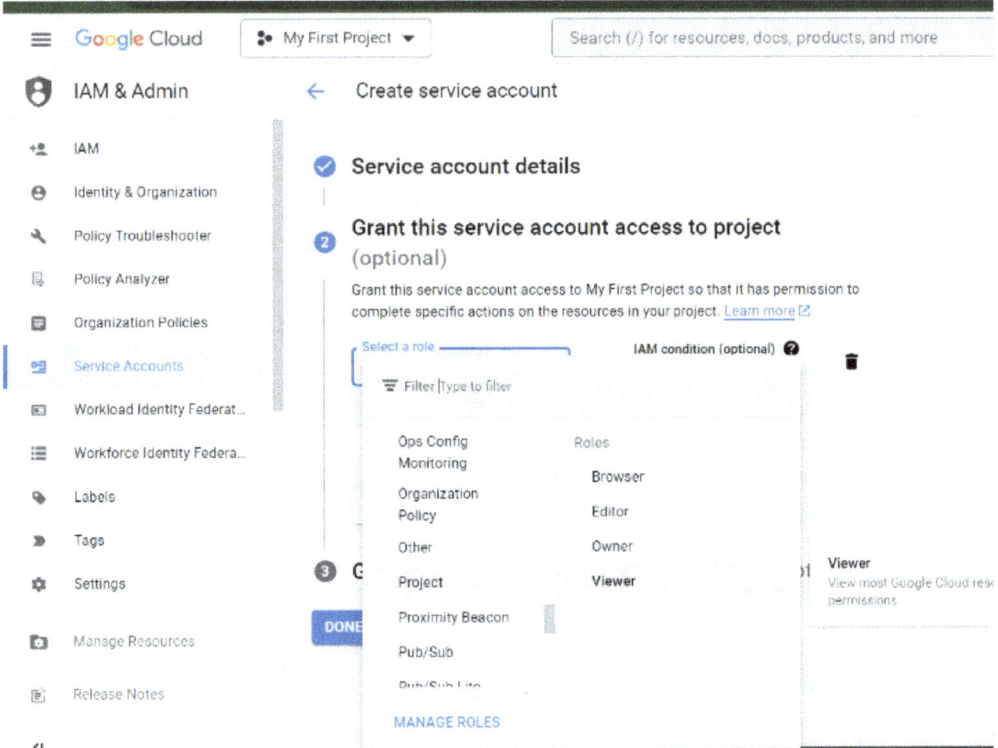

Step 10: Click "Add Another Role" Choose "Custom" Select the created Custom Role.

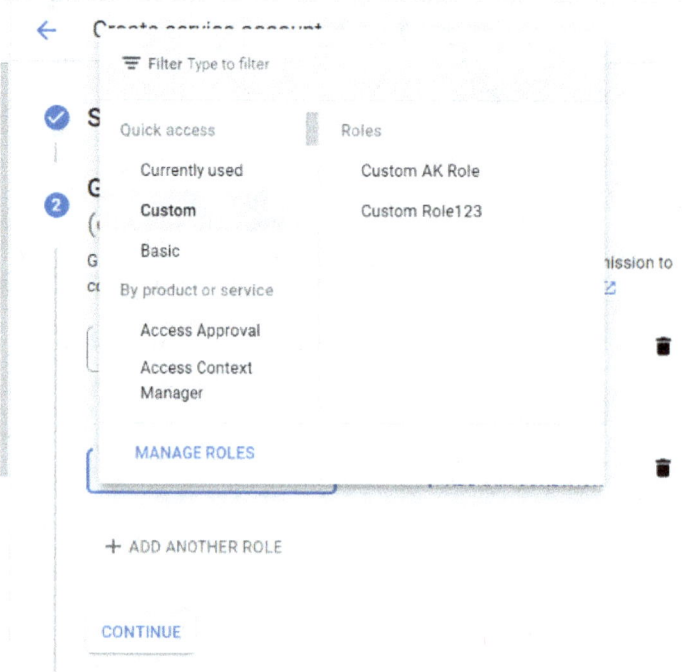

Step 11: Click on "Continue" and "Done"

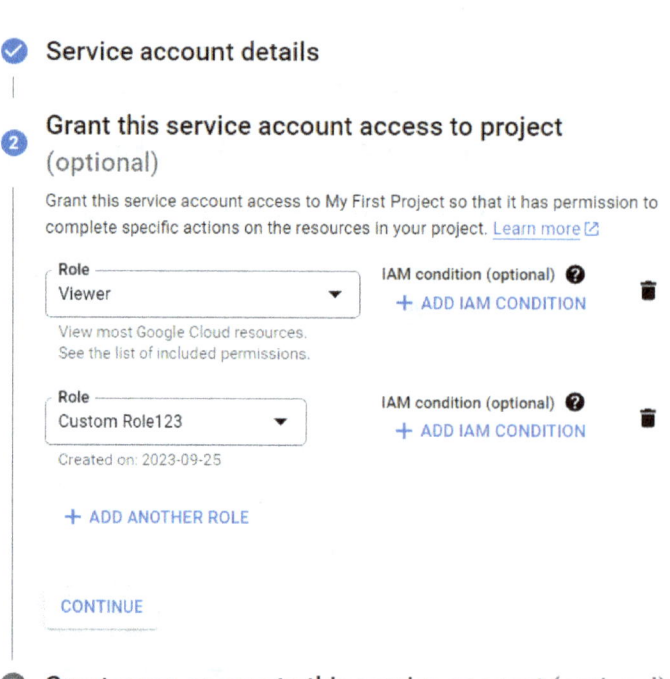

Step 12: Go to the created Service Account, click on that Service Account navigate to the "Keys" section.

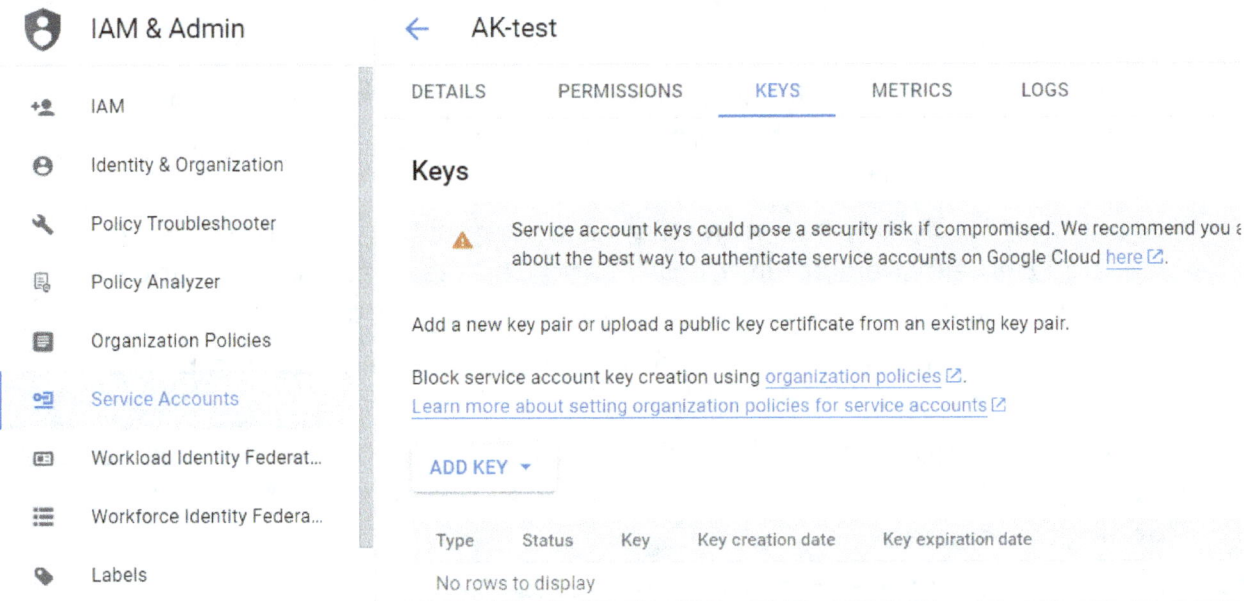

Step 13: Click the "Add key" button and "Create new key". Chosen Key type should be in JSON format.

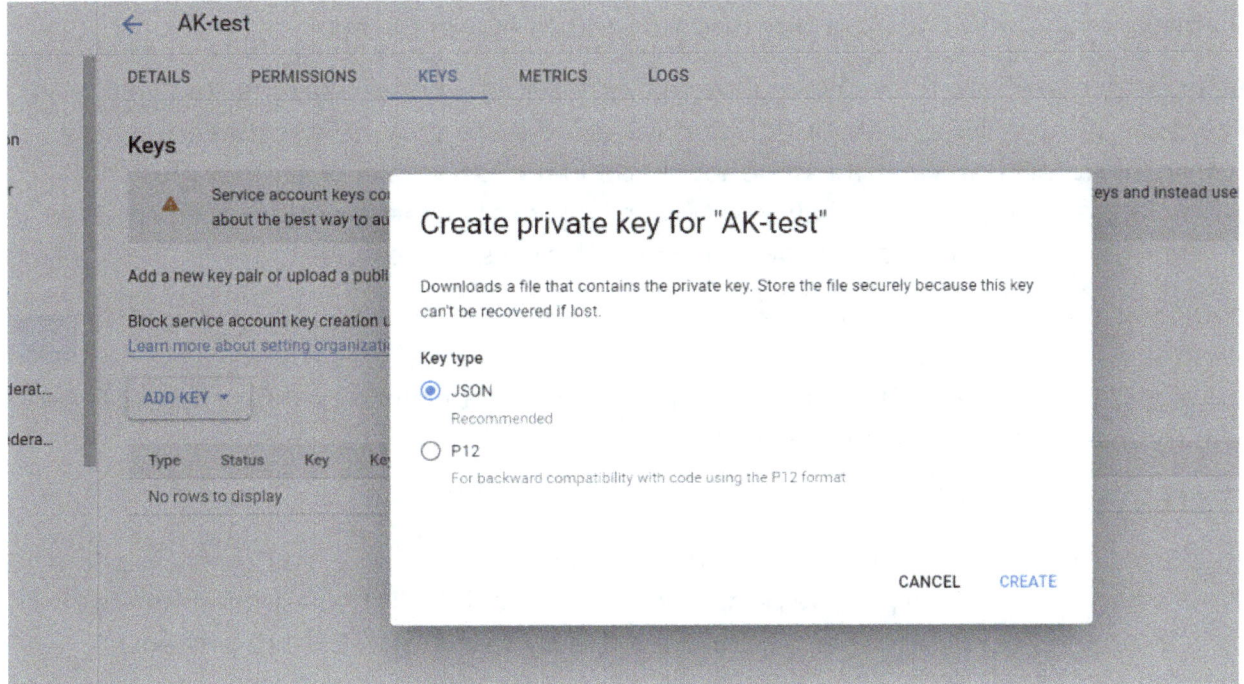

Step 14: Click the "Create" button it will automatically download the JSON key.

- Oracle Container Engine for Kubernetes (OKE) is a managed Kubernetes service that simplifies containerized application operations, offering scalability, reliability, and automation.
- Oracle Linux, the chosen distribution for OKE, is supported by the Unbreakable Enterprise Kernel (UEK) and provides a stable and secure environment for enterprise applications.
- AccuKnox, a CNCF sandbox project, is a runtime security engine that leverages extended Berkeley Packet Filter (eBPF) and Berkeley Packet Filter-Linux Security Module (BPF-LSM) to protect Kubernetes pods and containers.
- AccuKnox now supports OKE to secure pods and containers using BPF-LSM for inline attack mitigation and prevention.
- AccuKnox is a Kubernetes-native solution that uses Linux kernel primitives on the Unbreakable Enterprise Kernel (UEK) to harden the pods, further fortifying the Kubernetes engine.

What is Oracle Container Engine for Kubernetes (OKE)?

Oracle Container Engine for Kubernetes (OKE) is a managed Kubernetes service that simplifies containerized application operations, offering scalability, reliability, and automation. OKE enables you to deploy Kubernetes clusters instantly and ensure reliable operations with automatic updates, patching, and scaling.

The chosen distribution for OKE is Oracle Linux, which is based on the Red Hat Enterprise Linux (RHEL) distribution and is designed to provide a stable and secure environment for running enterprise-level applications. Oracle Linux includes the Unbreakable Enterprise Kernel (UEK), which delivers business-critical performance and security optimizations for cloud and on-premises deployment.

AccuKnox is a CNCF (Cloud Native Computing Foundation) sandbox project that provides enhanced security for Kubernetes environments. It leverages extended Berkeley Packet Filter (eBPF) and Berkeley Packet Filter-Linux Security Module (BPF-LSM) to protect Kubernetes pods and containers.

Why is this important?

While the Unbreakable Enterprise Kernel (UEK) in Oracle Linux is a heavily fortified kernel image, the security of the pods and containers is still the responsibility of the application developer. AccuKnox addresses this by using BPF-LSM to protect

Kubernetes pods hosted on OKE, limiting system behavior concerning processes, files, and the use of network primitives.

AccuKnox is a Kubernetes-native solution that uses Linux kernel primitives on the Unbreakable Enterprise Kernel (UEK) to harden the pods, further fortifying the Kubernetes engine. This helps to mitigate and prevent attacks at runtime, providing a robust security layer for containerized applications running on OKE.

How is this accomplished?

AccuKnox integrates with BPF-LSM, a new Linux Security Module introduced in kernel versions above 5.7. This allows AccuKnox to attach BPF bytecode to LSM hooks, enabling user-specified policy controls for pod and container-based enforcement.

Some key features of AccuKnox's integration with OKE:

1. **Sensitive Data Protection**: AccuKnox can restrict access to sensitive information, such as Kubernetes secrets and x509 certificates, within the containers. You can specify policy rules to prevent unauthorized modifications to critical certificates.

2. **Binary Execution Control**: AccuKnox can restrict the execution of certain binaries within the containers, providing real-time insights into system behavior, resource utilization, and application performance.

3. **Observability and Monitoring**: AccuKnox leverages eBPF for comprehensive observability, enabling real-time monitoring and analysis of system activities, including process runs, sensitive asset access, network interactions, and security-sensitive system call activities.

4. **Network Microsegmentation**: AccuKnox integrates with Kubernetes network policies, Cilium, Container Network Interface (CNI), and Project Calico to enhance security measures and provide comprehensive insights and control within your OKE Ampere A1-based deployments.

5. **Workload Hardening**: AccuKnox includes hardening strategies based on industry-leading compliance and attack frameworks, such as CIS, MITRE, NIST-800-53, and STIGs. These policies help secure workloads and reduce attack surfaces by implementing block-based policies.

6. **Zero-Trust Policies**: AccuKnox enforces a zero-trust approach, where every action is rigorously logged and inspected. It allows declaring which actions are allowed and which are denied or audited, ensuring a strong security posture.

AccuKnox CNAPP Definitive Guide

In this architecture, AccuKnox leverages the Unbreakable Enterprise Kernel (UEK) in Oracle Linux, BPF-LSM, and eBPF to provide enhanced security and observability for containerized workloads running on OKE Ampere A1 shapes.

OKE Ampere A1 AccuKnox Support

Feature	Description
Sensitive Data Protection	AccuKnox can restrict access to sensitive information, such as Kubernetes secrets and x509 certificates, within the containers.
Binary Execution Control	AccuKnox can restrict the execution of certain binaries within the containers.
Observability and Monitoring	AccuKnox leverages eBPF for comprehensive observability, providing real-time insights into system activities.
Network microsegmentation	AccuKnox integrates with Kubernetes network policies, Cilium, CNI, and Project Calico to enhance network security.
Workload Hardening	AccuKnox includes hardening strategies based on industry-leading compliance and attack frameworks.
Zero-Trust Policies	AccuKnox enforces a zero-trust approach, where every action is rigorously logged and inspected.

Key Differentiators

1. AccuKnox is a Kubernetes-native solution that leverages Linux kernel primitives to harden the pods, further fortifying the Kubernetes engine.
2. Integration with eBPF-LSM enables inline attack mitigation and prevention, safeguarding containerized workloads at runtime.
3. eBPF-based observability provides deep insights into system activities, enabling proactive threat detection and response.
4. Hardening strategies and zero-trust policies allow for granular control and enforcement of security measures.
5. Integration with Kubernetes network policies, Cilium, CNI, and Project Calico ensures a cohesive security solution for OKE Ampere A1-based deployments.

AccuKnox CNAPP Definitive Guide

Key Takeaways

- AccuKnox improves OKE's use of BPF-LSM for inline attack prevention and mitigation, securing pods and containers.
- AccuKnox uses Oracle Linux's Unbreakable Enterprise Kernel to strengthen the Kubernetes engine and harden individual pods.
- Get enhanced security features like workload hardening, zero-trust rules, network micro-segmentation, binary execution control, and data protection.
- AccuKnox's partnership with Oracle on Ampere A1 and KubeArmor in OKE offers a robust security solution for high-performance, affordable cloud infrastructure, demonstrating a proactive approach to cloud-native environment security.

Section 9.2.   Deployment Models - Private Cloud

In a SaaS model of deployment, the Accuknox CNAPP will be hosted in our cloud environment and the agents deployed on the workloads will connect with the SaaS.

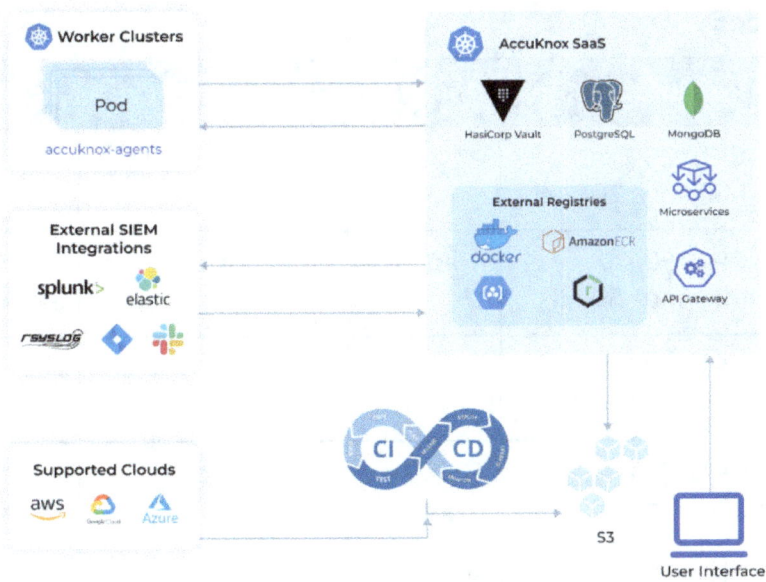

FIGURE 68. PRIVATE CLOUD DEPLOYMENT ARCHITECTURE

AccuKnox Agents

Deployments	Deployment Type
KubeArmor	DaemonSet

Deployments	Deployment Type
Shared Informer Agent	Deployment
Feeder Service	Deployment
Policy Enforcement	Deployment
Discovery Engine Agent	Deployment

It is assumed that the user has some basic familiarity with Kubernetes, kubectl and helm. It also assumes that you are familiar with the AccuKnox open-source tool workflow. If you're new to AccuKnox itself, refer first to the [opensource installation (https://help.accuknox.com/getting-started/open-source/)](https://help.accuknox.com/getting-started/open-source/)

It is recommended to have the following configured before onboarding:

- [Kubectl (https://kubernetes.io/docs/tasks/tools/)](https://kubernetes.io/docs/tasks/tools/)
- [Helm (https://helm.sh/docs/intro/install/)](https://helm.sh/docs/intro/install/)

Minimum Resources

Deployments	Resource Usage	Port	Connection Type	AccuKnox Endpoint
KubeArmor	CPU: 200 m, Memory: 200 Mi	-	-	-
Agents Operator	CPU: 50 m, Memory: 50 Mi	8081	Outbound	*.accuknox.com:8081 → SPIRE Access
Discovery Engine	CPU: 200 m, Memory: 200 Mi	-	-	-
Shared Informer Agent	CPU: 20 m, Memory: 50 Mi	3000	Outbound	*.accuknox.com:3000 → knox-gateway
Feeder Service	CPU: 50 m, Memory: 100 Mi	3000	Outbound	*.accuknox.com:3000 → knox-gateway
Policy Enforcement	CPU: 10 m, Memory: 20 Mi	443	Outbound	*.accuknox.com:443 → Policy Provider Service

These ports need to be allowed through a firewall.

AccuKnox CNAPP Definitive Guide

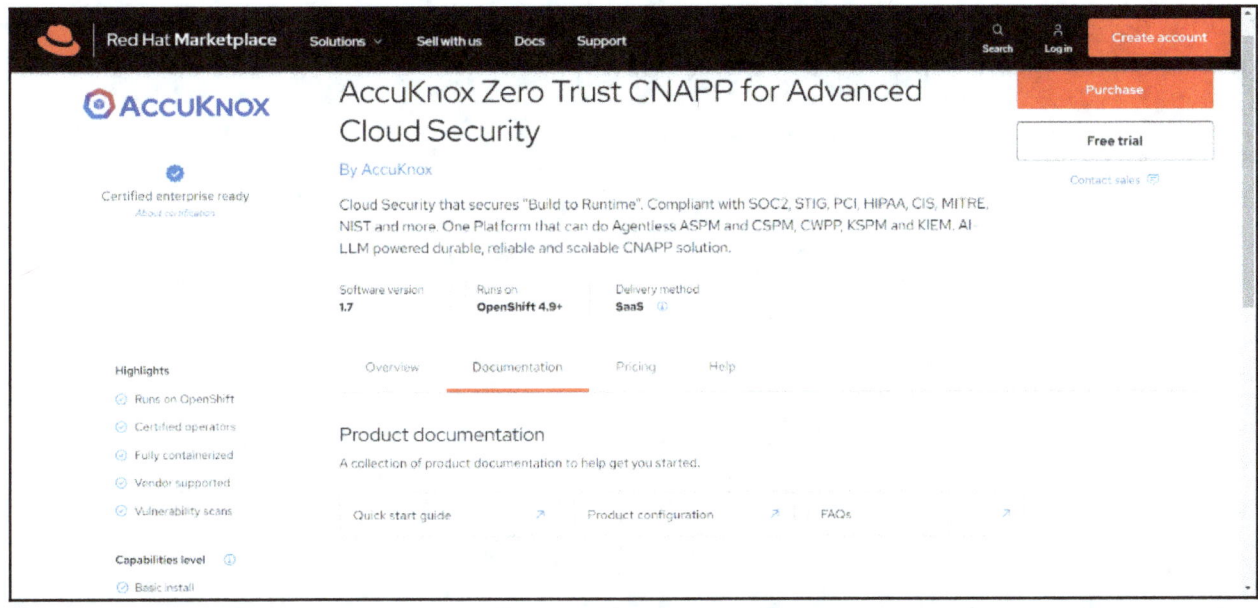

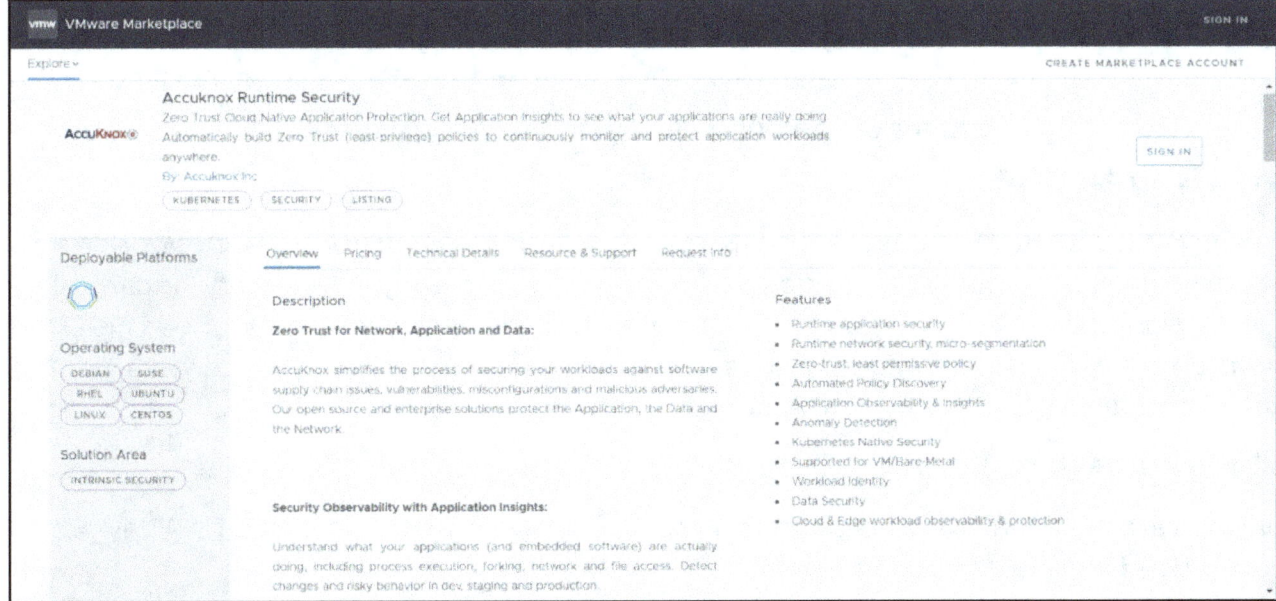

In addition to this AccuKnox also supports other private clouds like Nutanix, Mirantis, and Rafay.

Air Gapped

AccuKnox's air-gapped security via on-prem installation protects your critical systems from cyber threats. By physically isolating systems and data, air gaps prevent unauthorized access and eliminate the risk of network-based attacks. This approach defends sensitive information and mission-critical infrastructure in industries such as finance, military, government, and power utilities.

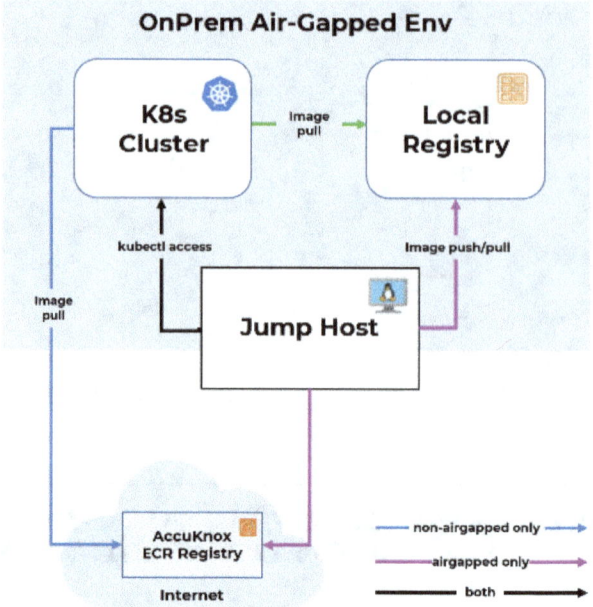

FIGURE 69. ON-PREM AIR GAPPED ENVIRONMENTS

What is an Air Gap?

An air gap is a security measure that physically separates a computer or network from any external connectivity. An air-gapped system is completely isolated and incapable of establishing wireless or wired connections with other devices or networks. This isolation prevents the spread of malware, ransomware, and other cyber threats, as there is no digital pathway for attackers to infiltrate the system.

Why is Air Gapping Important?

Air gaps are essential for protecting the most sensitive and critical systems. They are widely used in industries such as:

- **Stock markets**: To safeguard stock trading systems and financial data
- **Military and government agencies**: To secure classified information and mission-critical systems
- **Industrial control systems**: To shield industrial plants and power grids from cyber attacks

By completely isolating systems, air gaps eliminate the risk of remote access and network-based attacks. This is crucial for organizations that handle sensitive data or operate critical infrastructure where a breach could have severe consequences.

How is Air Gapping Accomplished?

Microservices

Microservices implement the API logic and provide the corresponding service endpoints. AccuKnox uses Golang-based microservices for handling any streaming data (such as alerts and telemetry) and Python-based microservices for any other control-plane services.

Databases

PostgreSQL is used as a relational database and MongoDB is used for storing JSON events such as alerts and telemetry. Ceph storage is used to keep periodic scanned reports and the Ceph storage is deployed and managed using the Rook storage operator.

Secrets Management

Within the on-prem setup, there are several cases where sensitive data and credentials have to be stored. Hashicorp's Vault is made use of to store internal (such as DB username/password) and user secrets (such as registry tokens). The authorization is managed purely using k8s native model of service accounts. Every microservice has its service account and uses its service account token automounted by k8s to authenticate and subsequently authorize access to the secrets.

Scaling

K8s native horizontal and vertical pod autoscaling is enabled for most microservices with upper limits for resource requirements.

AccuKnox-Agents

Agents need to be deployed in target k8s clusters and virtual machines that have to be secured at runtime and to get workload forensics. Agents use Linux native technologies such as eBPF for workload telemetry and LSMs (Linux Security Modules) for preventing attacks/unknown execution in the target workloads. The security policies are orchestrated from the AccuKnox on prem control plane. AccuKnox leverages SPIFFE/SPIRE for workload/node attestation and certificate provisioning. This ensures that the credentials are not hardcoded and automatically rotated. This also ensures that if the cluster/virtual machine has to be deboarded then the control lies with the AccuKnox control plane.

To install AccuKnox, you need to have the following tools installed on your machine: jq, unzip, yq, helm, kubectl, aws, and docker. The machine should have at least 80GB of storage. The installation package includes the On prem Deployment Installation

AccuKnox CNAPP Definitive Guide

Document and Helm Charts Archive. To use the private/local container registry, you need to install the accuknox-onmprem-mgr component first. The package also includes instructions on how to configure AWS cli with AccuKnox-provided secrets, connect to the Docker Accuknox Docker registry, upload images to the private registry, create a namespace, update override values, and configure SSL certificates. The package contains an override-values.yaml file with installation-specific options to be configured.

To install AccuKnox, you need to override your domain and set your SSL preferences in the override values. The installation package will contain an override-values.yaml file that contains installation-specific options to be configured. The user must also install the AccuKnox base dependencies and the AccuKnox microservices chart.

OpenCNAPP uses an air-gapped security strategy, real-time attack prevention, and a zero trust model—all required by CISA—to guarantee that federal government workloads remain secure.

Key Differentiators

1. **Comprehensive Isolation**: AccuKnox ensures complete physical and logical isolation of critical systems, leaving no digital attack surface exposed.
2. **Secure Data Transfer**: AccuKnox's manual, removable media-based data transfer process is highly secure and auditable, minimizing the risk of data breaches.
3. **Granular Access Control**: AccuKnox enforces strict access controls and the principle of least privilege, reducing the attack surface and the potential for unauthorized access.
4. **Continuous Monitoring**: AccuKnox's monitoring and management console provides real-time visibility and control over the air-gapped environment, enabling proactive threat detection and response.

Key Takeaways

- AccuKnox's air-gapped security features provide a robust solution to protect mission-critical systems and data from cyber threats.
- By physically isolating systems and data, air gaps eliminate the risk of network-based attacks, ensuring the highest levels of security.
- AccuKnox's air-gapped architecture, secure data transfer process, and granular access controls make it an ideal choice for organizations in industries with stringent security requirements.

AccuKnox CNAPP Definitive Guide

- AccuKnox's air-gapped security features are a crucial component of its comprehensive cybersecurity offering, enabling customers to maintain the integrity and availability of their most sensitive systems and data.

Chapter 10 ADVANCED CAPABILITIES

Leveraging AI/LLM to streamline Security Operations - AskADA

AccuKnox Ask Ada: Simplifying Cloud Security with Generative AI

AccuKnox Ask Ada is a groundbreaking cloud security assistant powered by generative AI. It enables users to ask questions in plain language and receive detailed recommendations to overcome cloud security challenges, automating the mundane and empowering diverse personas towards a stronger security posture.

What is it?

Ask Ada is one of the first Gen-AI LLM-based cloud security assistants, designed to simplify cloud security and enable innovation without sacrificing resilience or compliance. It allows users to interact conversationally with the AccuKnox platform, obtaining just-in-time insights, prioritized recommendations, and automated security actions.

The tool is built on top of the AccuKnox CNAPP (Cloud-Native Application Protection Platform), leveraging its comprehensive visibility, security controls, and remediation capabilities. By integrating with the CNAPP, Ask Ada can access detailed information about the user's cloud environment, including workloads, configurations, and security events.

Ask Ada's core functionality revolves around four key areas:

- **Discovering Misconfigurations**: Users can ask questions about their cloud infrastructure and receive insights on security misconfigurations, vulnerabilities, and policy violations.
  Example: "What are the top 5 most critical misconfigurations in my Kubernetes clusters?"

- **Fetching Actionable Insights from Logs and Alerts**: Ask Ada can analyze logs and security events, providing prioritized recommendations to address security issues and comply with industry standards.
  Example: "Show me the top 10 security alerts from the past week and how to resolve them."

- **Obtaining Assistive Remediation Guidance**: The tool offers step-by-step guidance to help users resolve security gaps, tailored to their specific environment and persona.
  Example: "How do I harden the security of my AWS Lambda functions?"

- **Auto-Generating Customized Security Actions**: Users can generate policies, notifications, scans, and other security controls directly from natural language requests.
  Example: "Create a new policy to enforce multi-factor authentication for all admin users."

By covering these key areas, Ask Ada aims to simplify cloud security tasks, empower diverse personas, and enable organizations to focus on strategic initiatives rather than mundane security operations.

Why is this important?

Traditional cloud security approaches can be complex, time-consuming, and require deep technical expertise. Ask Ada aims to democratize cloud security by making it accessible to a wider range of users, from security analysts to DevOps teams. By automating routine tasks and providing tailored guidance, Ask Ada helps organizations strengthen their security posture, ensure compliance, and focus on strategic initiatives.

One of the primary challenges in cloud security is the sheer volume of data and the need to constantly monitor and respond to security events. Security teams often struggle to keep up with the pace of cloud-native infrastructure changes, leading to misconfigurations, vulnerabilities, and compliance gaps. Ask Ada addresses this challenge by providing a conversational interface that can rapidly analyze the user's environment, identify security issues, and recommend appropriate actions.

Moreover, cloud security often requires coordination across multiple teams, including security, DevOps, and application development. Ask Ada's persona-driven approach ensures that users from different backgrounds can leverage the tool to address their specific needs, ultimately improving cross-functional collaboration and driving a stronger security culture.

How is this accomplished?

Ask Ada leverages the power of generative AI to understand natural language queries and provide relevant, actionable responses. The tool is integrated with the AccuKnox CNAPP, allowing it to access a comprehensive view of the user's cloud environment, including workloads, configurations, and security events.

The Ask Ada architecture consists of the following key components:

1. **Natural Language Processing (NLP) Engine**: This component is responsible for understanding user queries and translating them into actionable requests. The

NLP engine uses advanced language models and techniques, such as intent recognition, entity extraction, and contextual understanding, to interpret the user's intent and gather the necessary information to formulate a response.

2. **Knowledge Base**: Ask Ada's knowledge base is a curated database of cloud security best practices, threat intelligence, and remediation steps. This knowledge base is powered by the extensive data and insights gathered by the AccuKnox CNAPP, ensuring that the recommendations and guidance provided by Ask Ada are up-to-date and tailored to the user's specific cloud environment.

3. **Response Generation**: The response generation component leverages the knowledge base and the user's context to generate tailored recommendations and instructions. This includes prioritizing security issues based on risk, compliance requirements, and potential impact, as well as providing step-by-step remediation guidance that is customized to the user's environment and persona.

4. **Integration with AccuKnox CNAPP**: The seamless integration between Ask Ada and the AccuKnox CNAPP is a key aspect of the tool's architecture. This integration allows Ask Ada to retrieve relevant data, execute security actions, and provide users with a comprehensive view of their cloud security posture.

To ensure the reliability and security of the Ask Ada system, the architecture also includes robust anti-hallucination safeguards. These measures protect against potential misuse or malicious attacks on the generative AI system, ensuring that the recommendations and actions provided by Ask Ada are trustworthy and reliable.

Architecture

The Ask Ada architecture consists of the following key components:

1. **Natural Language Processing (NLP) Engine:**
   - Responsible for understanding user queries and translating them into actionable requests
   - Uses advanced language models and techniques, such as intent recognition, entity extraction, and contextual understanding
   - Interprets the user's intent and gathers the necessary information to formulate a response

2. **Knowledge Base:**
   - Curated database of cloud security best practices, threat intelligence, and remediation steps

- Powered by the extensive data and insights gathered by the AccuKnox CNAPP
- Ensures that the recommendations and guidance provided by Ask Ada are up-to-date and tailored to the user's specific cloud environment

3. **Response Generation:**
    - Leverages the knowledge base and the user's context to generate tailored recommendations and instructions
    - Prioritizes security issues based on risk, compliance requirements, and potential impact
    - Provides step-by-step remediation guidance that is customized to the user's environment and persona

4. **Integration with AccuKnox CNAPP:**
    - Seamless integration between Ask Ada and the AccuKnox CNAPP
    - Allows Ask Ada to retrieve relevant data, execute security actions, and provide users with a comprehensive view of their cloud security posture

5. **Anti-Hallucination Safeguards:**
    - Robust security measures to protect against potential misuse or malicious attacks on the generative AI system
    - Ensures that the recommendations and actions provided by Ask Ada are trustworthy and reliable

Table: Key Features and Benefits of Ask Ada

Feature	Benefit
Natural Language Queries	Users can ask questions in plain language, without the need for complex syntax or technical expertise. This lowers the barrier to entry and makes cloud security more accessible.
Prioritized Recommendations	Ask Ada to analyse the user's environment and provide prioritized recommendations based on risk, compliance, and potential impact. This helps users focus on the most critical security issues.
Guided Remediation	Ask Ada provides detailed, step-by-step guidance to help users resolve security issues and maintain a strong security posture. This includes recommended

Feature	Benefit
	actions, configuration changes, and policy updates.
Automated Security Actions	Users can generate policies, notifications, scans, and other security controls with simple text-based requests. This streamlines security operations and reduces the risk of manual errors.
Multi-Persona Support	Ask Ada is designed to cater to the needs of different roles, from security analysts to DevOps teams. Each user can leverage the tool to address their specific cloud security challenges.
Anti-Hallucination Safeguards	Robust security measures protect against potential misuse or malicious attacks on the generative AI system, ensuring the reliability and trustworthiness of the recommendations and actions provided by Ask Ada.

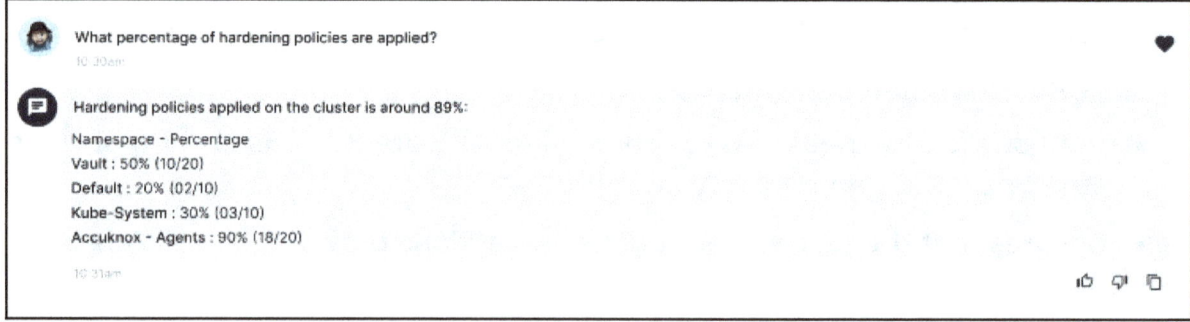

FIGURE 70. GEN-AI BASED LLM CHAT INTERFACE (ASK ADA)

Ask Ada to provide a detailed response, highlighting the specific issues and recommending steps to resolve them.

Key Differentiators

- **Gen-AI Powered**: Ask Ada leverages the latest advancements in generative AI to provide a conversational, user-friendly experience. This sets it apart from traditional, rule-based cloud security tools.
- **Integrated with AccuKnox CNAPP**: Tight integration with the AccuKnox platform allows Ask Ada to access comprehensive cloud security data and execute actions directly. This provides users with a seamless, end-to-end cloud security experience.

- **Anti-Hallucination Safeguards**: Robust security measures protect against potential misuse or malicious attacks on the generative AI system. This ensures the reliability and trustworthiness of the recommendations and actions provided by Ask Ada.
- **Persona-Driven Approach**: Ask Ada is designed to cater to the needs of diverse personas, from security analysts to DevOps teams. This allows organizations to democratize cloud security and empower different stakeholders.

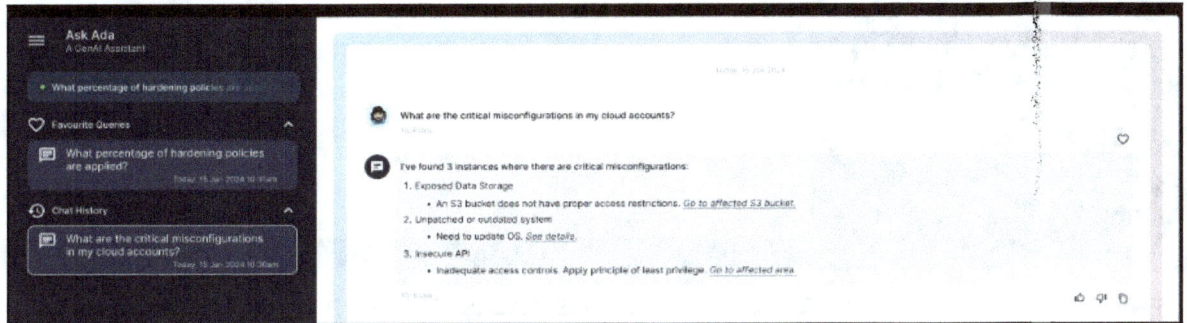

FIGURE 71. GET SIMPLIFIED ANSWERS ABOUT MISCONFIGURATIONS, ASSETS, POLICIES, ETC.

Example Use Cases

1. **Discovering Misconfigurations**: A security analyst can ask Ask Ada, "What are the top 5 most critical misconfigurations in my Kubernetes clusters?" The tool will analyze the user's cloud environment, identify the most severe configuration issues, and provide detailed recommendations on how to resolve them.
2. **Fetching Actionable Insights from Logs and Alerts**: A DevOps engineer can inquire, "Show me the top 10 security alerts from the past week and how to resolve them." Ask Ada will review the relevant logs and alerts, prioritize the security issues based on risk, and offer step-by-step guidance to address them.
3. **Obtaining Assistive Remediation Guidance**: A cloud architect can ask, "How do I harden the security of my AWS Lambda functions?" Ask Ada will provide detailed instructions on implementing security best practices, such as enabling encryption, configuring least-privilege access, and setting up logging and monitoring.
4. **Auto-Generating Customized Security Actions**: A compliance manager can request, "Create a new policy to enforce multi-factor authentication for all admin users." Ask Ada will automatically generate the necessary policy, configuration changes, and notifications to implement this security control across the organization.

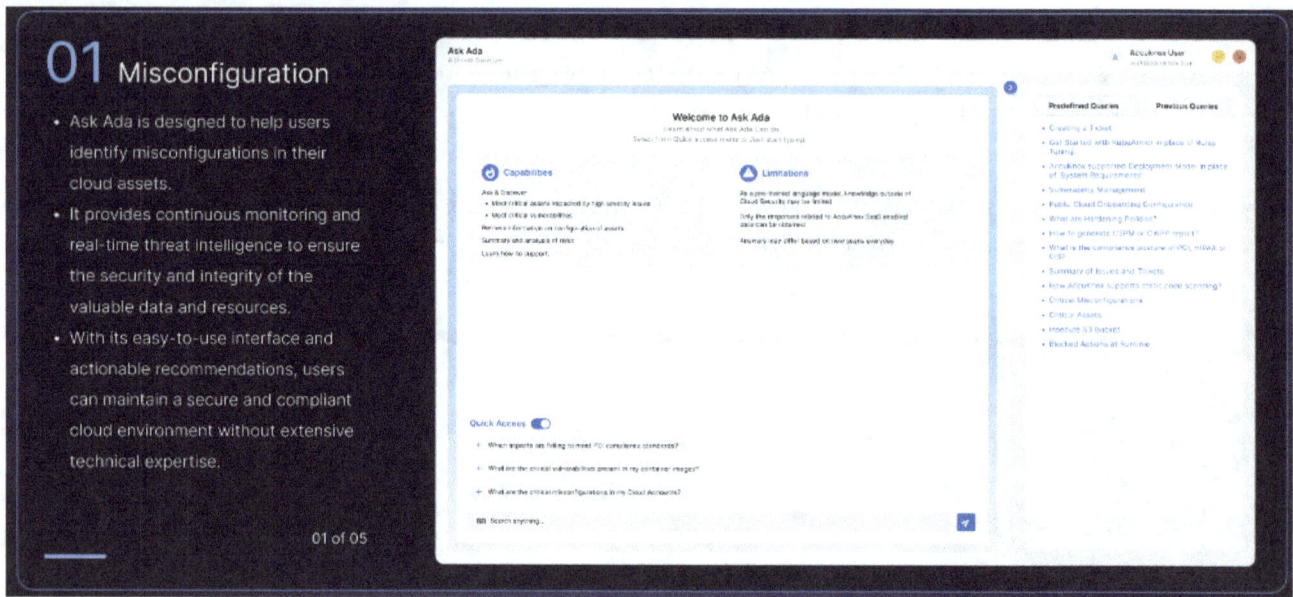

FIGURE 72. ASK ADA CAN SERVE MULTIPLE USER PERSONAS FOR DIFFERENT LEVELS OF GRANULAITY

Key Takeaways

- Ask Ada democratizes cloud security by making it accessible to a wider range of users, from security analysts to DevOps teams.
- The tool leverages generative AI to understand natural language queries and provide tailored recommendations, prioritized based on risk, compliance, and potential impact.
- Tight integration with the AccuKnox CNAPP platform allows Ask Ada to access comprehensive cloud security data and execute actions directly, offering a seamless, end-to-end cloud security experience.
- Robust anti-hallucination safeguards protect against potential misuse or malicious attacks on the generative AI system, ensuring the reliability and trustworthiness of the recommendations and actions provided by Ask Ada.
- Ask Ada's persona-driven approach ensures that users from different backgrounds can leverage the tool to address their specific cloud security challenges, improving cross-functional collaboration and driving a stronger security culture.

Section 10.1. Securing Edge/IoT Assets

The rise of edge computing and the increase in IoT devices has led to more data being created from more locations than ever before. This creates a need for securing these edge workloads, as data at the edge can be difficult to handle when it's being collected from multiple sources that might not be as secure as a centralized system. AccuKnox provides deep observability and granular policy enforcement to protect these edge workloads.

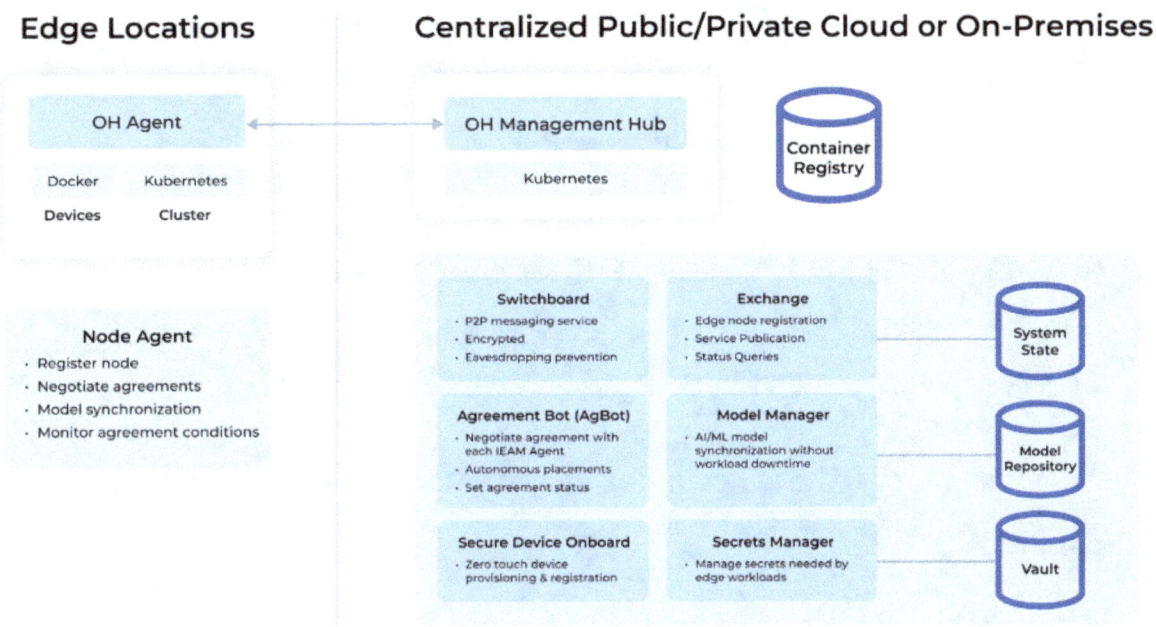

FIGURE 73. MAIN OPEN HORIZON COMPONENTS

How is this accomplished?

AccuKnox leverages Linux Security Modules (LSMs) like AppArmor, BPF-LSM and SELinux to provide kernel-level security enforcement. It uses eBPF-based system monitoring to provide container-aware logs for policy violations. The AccuKnox Discovery Engine can automatically generate the least permissive security policies based on observed behavior.

Architecture

AccuKnox can be deployed on the Open Horizon management hub and agents as a system service or in container mode. It provides enforcement capabilities to restrict the behavior of containers and nodes, as well as rich observability into the operations happening within the workloads, between containers and the agent edge node, and from the agent node to the management hub. The AccuKnox Discovery Engine leverages the visibility provided by AccuKnox and Cilium to automatically discover the network and system security posture, and generate the least-permissive allowed policies.

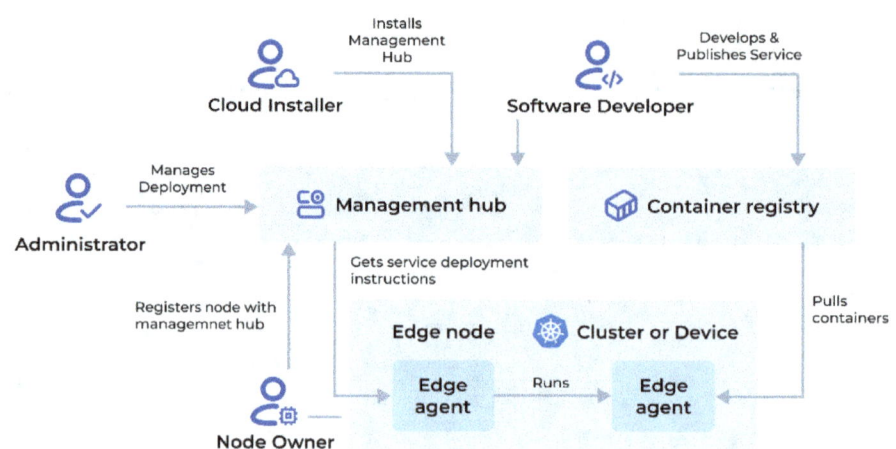

FIGURE 74. DEPLOYING ACCUKNOX ON OPEN HORIZON MANAGEMENT HUB

Key Capabilities

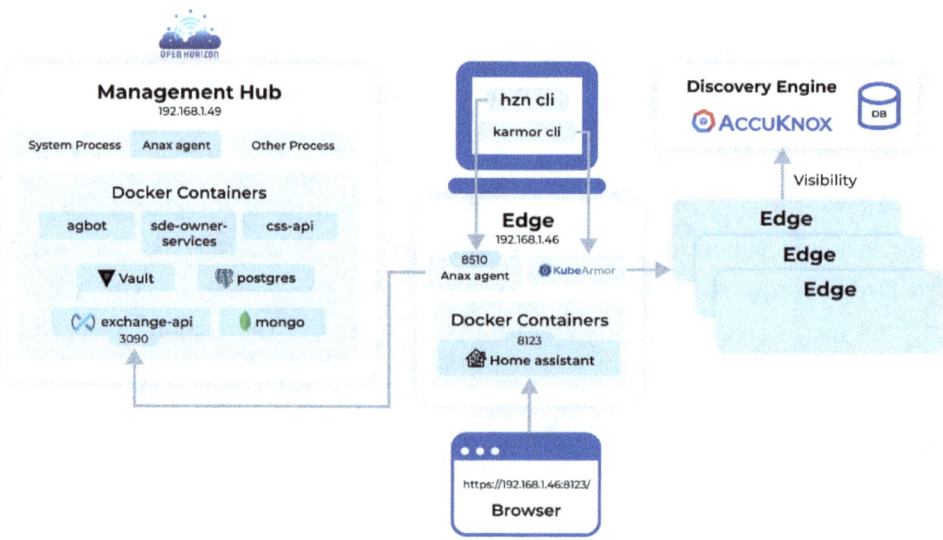

FIGURE 75. ACCUKNOX PROVIDES VISIBILITY INTO EDGE/IOT DEVICES VIA DISCOVERY ENGINE

- Kernel-level security enforcement using Linux Security Modules
- Container-aware observability using eBPF-based system monitoring

- Automatic generation of least-permissive security policies using Discovery Engine
- Support for un-orchestrated containers, Kubernetes workloads, and bare metal VMs

Let's apply a sample policy to prevent unauthorized updates to root certificates and restrict access to certificate folders:

```yaml
apiVersion: security.kubearmor.com/v1
kind: KubeArmorPolicy
metadata:
  name: block-certificates-access
spec:
  severity: 10
  message: "a critical file was accessed"
  tags:
  - WARNING
  selector:
    matchLabels:
      kubearmor.io/container.name: homeassistant
  process:
    matchPaths:
      - path: /usr/sbin/update-ca-certificates
  file:
    matchDirectories:
    - dir: /usr/share/ca-certificates/
      recursive: true
    - dir: /etc/ssl/
      recursive: true
  action:
    Block
```

This policy will:

1. Block the /bin/bash process from executing the /usr/sbin/update-ca-certificates command, to prevent unauthorized updates to root certificates.

2. Restrict access to the /etc/ssl/certs/ folder, to prevent unauthorized access to certificate files.

The subsequent alert generated on violation of the above policy would look like this:

```
HostName: knownymousagent-VirtualBox
NamespaceName: container_namespace
PodName: homeassistant
ContainerName: homeassistant
ContainerID: 77c3916a24f74915cd7d2eb51ff6a2425c3b4d6e72b805f735800d023d355338
Type: MatchedPolicy
PolicyName: block-certificates-access
Severity: 10
Message: a critical file was accessed
Source: /bin/bash
Resource: /usr/sbin/update-ca-certificates
Operation: Process
Action: Block
Data: syscall=SYS_EXECVE
Enforcer: AppArmor
Result: Permission denied
HostPID: 4922
HostPPID: 4912
PID: 116
PPID: 110
ParentProcessName: /bin/bash
ProcessName: /usr/sbin/update-ca-certificates
Tags: WARNING
```

Key Differentiators

- Kernel-level security enforcement using LSMs for both host and workloads
- Container-aware observability using eBPF-based system monitoring
- Automatic generation of least-permissive security policies using Discovery Engine
- Support for un-orchestrated containers, Kubernetes workloads, and bare metal VMs

Key Takeaways

- AccuKnox provides deep observability and granular policy enforcement to secure edge and IoT workloads
- It leverages kernel-level security mechanisms and eBPF-based monitoring to deliver comprehensive protection
- The Discovery Engine can automatically generate least-permissive security policies based on observed behavior
- AccuKnox is a universal security engine that can protect containers, Kubernetes workloads, and bare metal VMs

By integrating AccuKnox with Open Horizon, you can ensure the security and integrity of your edge computing infrastructure, even in disconnected or intermittently connected environments.

Section 10.2. Securing 5G Assets

AccuKnox is a cloud-native security platform that offers a holistic solution for securing 5G workloads and assets. It leverages a zero-trust security model, automating the deployment of security policies and controls across the entire application lifecycle, from code to runtime. By integrating with various 5G components, AccuKnox provides a unified and streamlined approach to securing the diverse elements of the 5G network.

Why is this important?

The 5G ecosystem is rapidly expanding, with the number of 5G connections expected to reach 3.2 billion by 2026. As 5G technologies become more widely adopted, the need to secure the cloud, edge/IoT, and core infrastructure of the 5G network becomes increasingly critical. Traditional security approaches often struggle to keep up with the dynamic nature and distributed architecture of 5G networks, making automated and intelligent security solutions like AccuKnox essential.

How is this accomplished?

AccuKnox's intent-driven security automation framework translates high-level security goals and intents into actionable policies and controls. It generates security policies for the network, transport, pre-container instantiation, and application layers, providing a multi-layered defense against a wide range of threats.

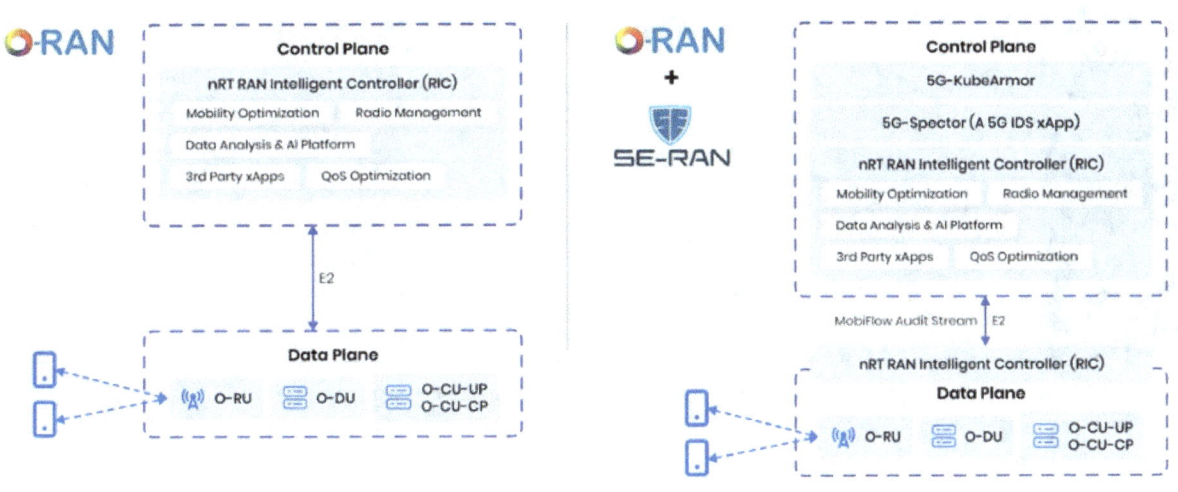

FIGURE 76. O-RAN ARCHITECTURE

AccuKnox CNAPP Definitive Guide

Key 5G Security Challenges

1. **O-RAN Threats**: The open and modular nature of O-RAN introduces new attack vectors, such as exploiting insecure designs (T-O-RAN-01) and targeting misconfigurations (T-O-RAN-02).
2. **RIC Threats**: The Near-RT RIC (T-NEAR-RT-01) is susceptible to malicious xApps that can compromise the network and user privacy.
3. **Distributed Architecture**: The distributed nature of 5G networks, with edge computing and IoT devices, increases the attack surface and complexity of securing the entire ecosystem.

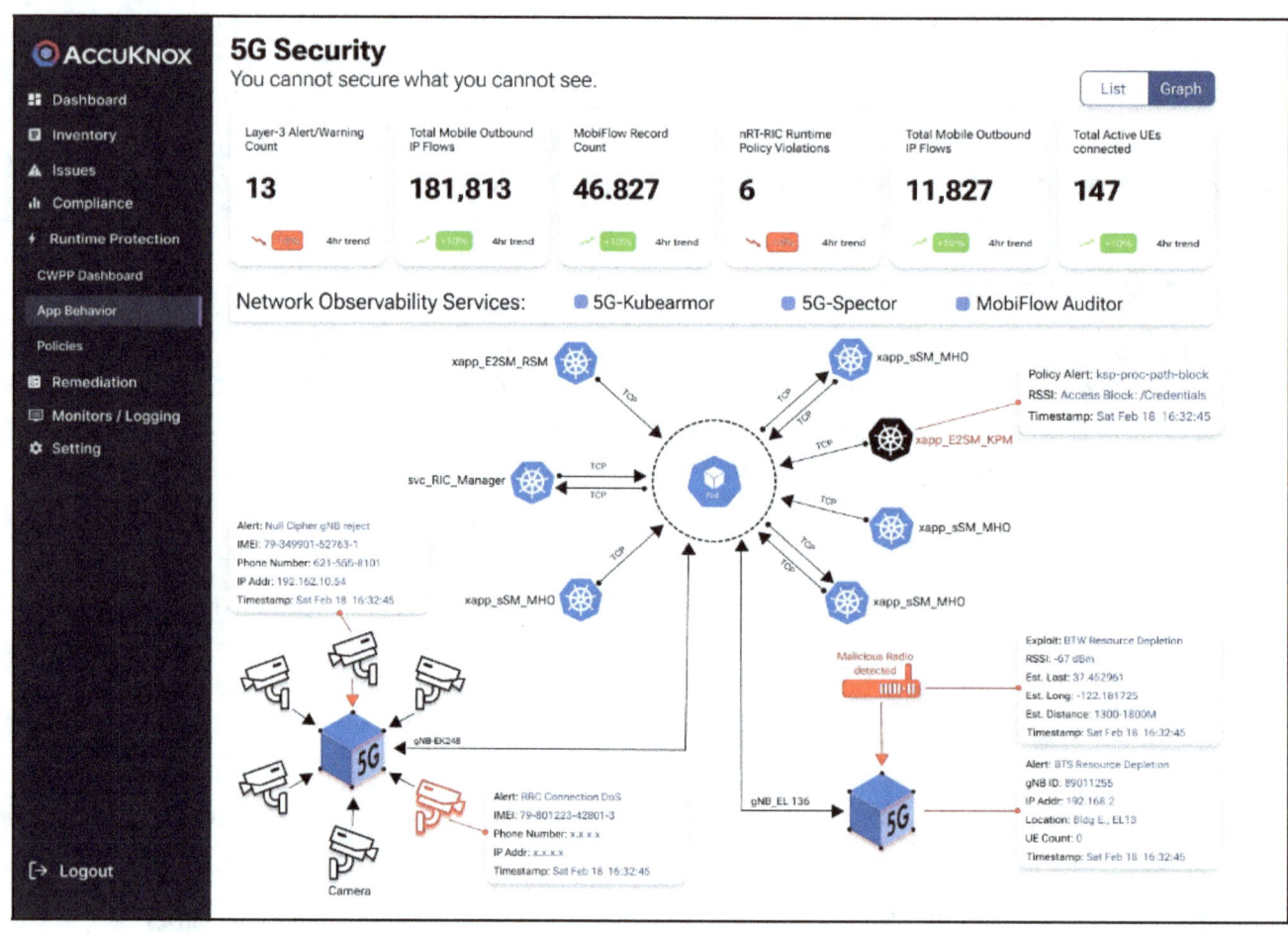

FIGURE 77. ACCUKNOX 5GNAPP FOR 5G SECURITY

AccuKnox's Approach to 5G Security

1. **Validation of Configurations**: AccuKnox rigorously validates the Kubernetes configurations of the SD-RAN to ensure adherence to best practices and security standards.
2. **xApp and RIC Security Compliance**: AccuKnox autonomously generates YAML policies for xApps and the Near-RT RIC, simplifying compliance with security policies.
3. **Control Plane Compliance Enforcement**: Leveraging 5G-KubeArmor, AccuKnox aids in the continuous monitoring and enforcement of control plane policies, preventing security breaches in real-time.
4. **Live RF-Threat Monitoring**: By integrating 5G-Spector, AccuKnox offers real-time 5G Intrusion Detection System (IDS) analysis, promptly detecting RF-based attacks and anomalies in RAN operations.
5. **Governance of Audits**: AccuKnox consolidates security-relevant statistics at the base station layer, including policy violations, warning alerts, RF-attack detection, and SD-RAN configuration validations.

Architecture

1. **Security Intents**: High-level security goals and requirements that serve as inputs to the platform.
2. **Policy Engines**: Responsible for generating and enforcing security policies based on the defined intents.
3. **Deployment Abstraction**: Translates the security policies into environment-specific configurations, enabling seamless deployment across various platforms.
4. **Monitoring and Threat Detection**: Continuously monitors the environment and detects anomalies or threats, triggering appropriate security responses.

Mapping 5G Attack Vectors and AccuKnox Protection

Attack Vector	AccuKnox Protection
T-O-RAN-01: Exploits insecure designs	Advanced threat detection and containment measures, safeguarding against malware and unauthorized access
T-O-RAN-02: Targets misconfigurations	Enforces stringent configuration policies, minimizing the risk of misconfigurations and enhancing overall system resilience

Attack Vector	AccuKnox Protection
T-NEAR-RT-01: Explores malicious xApps	Behavioral analysis to detect and prevent unauthorized activities, secure against malicious xApps and ensure UE privacy

Key Differentiators

1. **Intent-driven security automation**: AccuKnox's unique approach translates high-level security goals and intents into actionable policies, simplifying the deployment and management of security controls across complex 5G environments.

2. **Multi-layered zero-trust approach**: AccuKnox provides security at the network, transport, pre-container, and application layers, ensuring a comprehensive defence-in-depth strategy to address the diverse attack vectors in 5G networks.

3. **Seamless integration**: AccuKnox seamlessly integrates with various 5G components, including the O-RAN and RIC, to provide a unified security solution that enhances visibility and control across the entire 5G infrastructure.

4. **Threat detection and response**: AccuKnox's continuous monitoring and threat detection capabilities enable proactive security measures, helping organizations stay ahead of emerging threats and ensuring the ongoing protection of their 5G assets.

Key Takeaways

1. The rapid growth of the 5G ecosystem has introduced new security challenges, with the distributed architecture and open standards of 5G networks creating a complex attack surface that requires a comprehensive security solution.

2. AccuKnox addresses these challenges by providing a zero-trust, cloud-native security platform that automates the deployment of security policies and controls across the entire 5G infrastructure, from the cloud and edge/IoT to the core network.

3. AccuKnox's unique security capabilities, such as configuration validation, xApp and RIC security compliance, control plane monitoring, and RF-threat detection, enable organizations to secure their 5G assets effectively and efficiently.

4. By integrating with various 5G components and providing a unified security solution, AccuKnox simplifies the management and governance of 5G security,

empowering organizations to stay ahead of emerging threats and ensure the ongoing protection of their 5G investments.

Section 10.3. Securing LLMs (Large Language Models)

LLM security refers to the set of practices and technologies employed to protect large language models from various security threats, including prompt injection, insecure output handling, training data poisoning, model denial of service, and more. Ensuring the security of LLMs is crucial as they become increasingly prevalent in a wide range of applications.

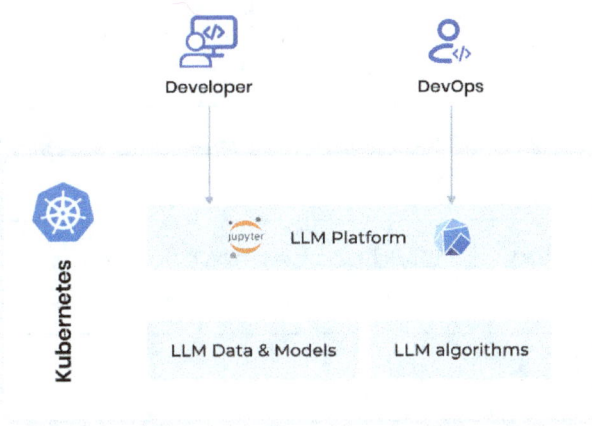

FIGURE 78. LLM PLATFORMS BASED ON USER PERSONA

Why is this important?

LLMs are powerful tools that can generate highly convincing and influential text, but they can also be vulnerable to various security threats. Securing LLMs is essential to prevent malicious actors from exploiting these vulnerabilities and causing harm, such as generating misinformation, leaking sensitive information, or disrupting critical systems.

How is this accomplished via AccuKnox?

AccuKnox is a security platform that provides a comprehensive solution for securing LLMs. It employs a range of techniques, including input validation, output filtering, data quality checks, rate limiting, and runtime processing monitoring, to mitigate the various security risks associated with LLMs.

Feature	Description
Sandboxing with Pre-emptive Mitigation	Isolating and proactively addressing potential vulnerabilities.
SBOM Verification	Ensuring the integrity and security of system components.
Container Scanning	Detecting and mitigating vulnerabilities, malware, and other issues in containers.
Malware Protection	Detecting and blocking malicious code or activity.
Workload Hardening	Strengthening the security posture of individual workloads.
Fencing Data Assets in Workloads	Isolating and protecting sensitive data within workloads.
Network Microsegmentation	Dividing the network into isolated segments to limit threat movement.

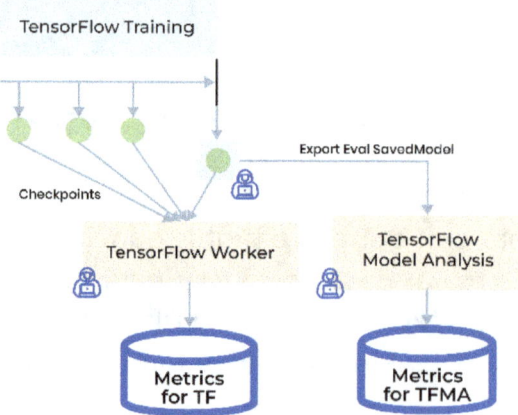

FIGURE 79. TENSORFLOW TRAINING FOR LLMS AND POSSIBLE INJECTION/TAKEOVER FROM ATTACKERS

1. **Input Validation**: Advanced techniques to validate user prompts, filtering out potential malicious inputs and preventing prompt injection attacks.
2. **Output Filtering**: The platform applies post-processing filters to the generated outputs, ensuring that they do not contain inappropriate or biased content.

3. **Data Quality Checks**: Rigorous data quality checks to identify and remove malicious or biased samples from the training data, preventing training data poisoning attacks.
4. **Rate Limiting**: The platform employs rate limiting mechanisms to restrict the number of model queries from a single source, mitigating denial of service attacks.
5. **Secure Data Storage**: AccuKnox ensures that the data used for training and inference is stored securely, preventing unauthorized access and sensitive information disclosure.
6. **Plugin Isolation**: The platform conducts security audits and isolates plugins or additional components to address insecure plugin design vulnerabilities.
7. **Overreliance Mitigation**: Helps reduce overreliance on LLM outputs by integrating multiple models or ensembles and promoting the use of diverse training data and model architectures.

How AccuKnox Mitigates LLM Security Risks

Security Risk	AccuKnox Mitigation Technique
Prompt Injection	Input Validation
Insecure Output Handling	Output Filtering
Training Data Poisoning	Data Quality Checks
Model Denial of Service	Rate Limiting
Supply Chain Vulnerabilities	Secure Data Storage
Sensitive Information Disclosure	Redaction and Privacy-Preserving Techniques
Insecure Plugin Design	Plugin Isolation and Security Audits
Excessive Agency	Output Filtering and Overreliance Mitigation
Overreliance	Ensemble Models and Diverse Training Data

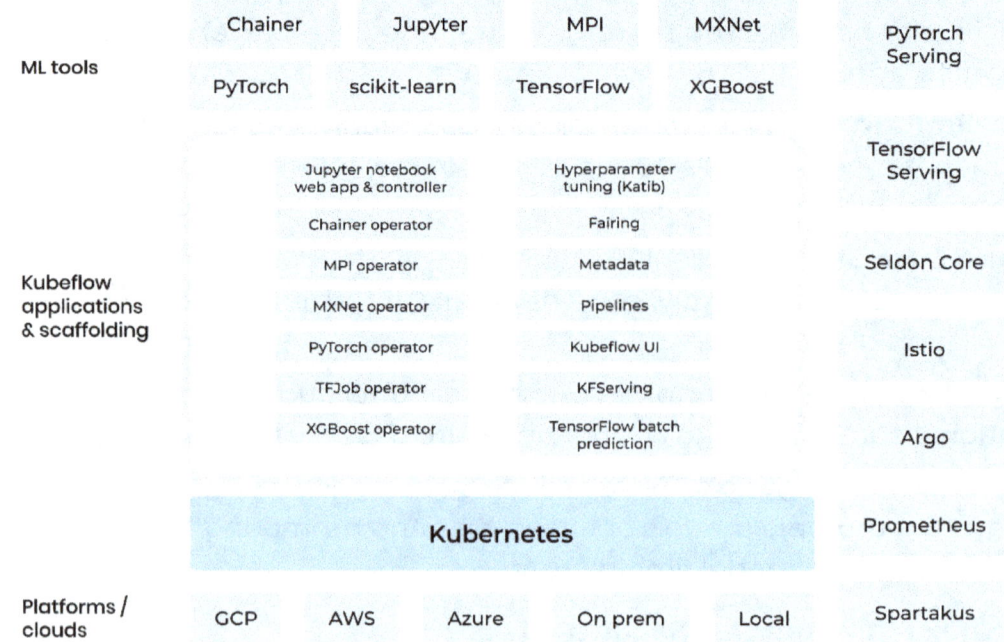

FIGURE 80. TOOLS, PLATFORMS AND APPS FOR LLM DEPLOYMENTS

Key Differentiators

The key differentiators of AccuKnox in securing LLMs include:

- Pre-emptive mitigation, No detect and respond
- Lower Deployment Cycles
- No custom AMIs needed
- No changes required at the host
- Works equally well with hardened distributions (Bottlerocket, COS)
- Minimal Performance Penalty
- <3% performance hit in control flows
- No impact on data flows

Key Benefits

1. **Full Security Coverage**: AccuKnox addresses a wide range of security risks associated with LLMs, providing a holistic security solution.

2. **Deployment Simplicity**: The platform's seamless integration and easy-to-use interface make it simple to implement and manage, even for organizations with limited security expertise.

3. **Adaptability**: AccuKnox is designed to be agile and adaptable, allowing it to keep up with the evolving security landscape and address new threats as they emerge.

4. **Scalability**: The platform can accommodate the growing demands of large-scale LLM deployments, ensuring robust security at scale.

Key Takeaways

1. LLM security is crucial to prevent malicious exploitation of vulnerabilities in large language models.

2. AccuKnox provides a comprehensive solution for securing LLMs, addressing a wide range of security risks through advanced techniques like input validation, output filtering, and data quality checks.

3. The platform's key differentiators, including its comprehensive security coverage, deployment simplicity, adaptability, and scalability, make it a valuable tool for organizations looking to secure their LLM deployments.

4. By implementing the security measures provided by AccuKnox, organizations can enhance the overall security and trustworthiness of their LLM-powered applications and services.

Chapter 11 CUSTOMER CASE STUDIES

 Large US Government Contractor — "We performed an extensive analysis of comparable industry offerings and selected AccuKnox due to its support for public and private cloud and highly differentiated capabilities in the areas of Risk Prioritization, Drift Detection, and Advanced Compliance. Furthermore, we were very impressed with AccuKnox's integration with leading Vulnerability Management platforms like Nessus."

 Large Cyber Insurance Provider — "Their comprehensive and integrated offering; flexible deployment options; ongoing R&D commitment; Open Source foundations; and their track record of successful partnerships made them a clear winner."

 Large Digital Health Provider — "Zero Trust security is a Clint Health imperative and commitment we have to our customers. AccuKnox's leading product combined with their successful track record of partnering with their customers forms the foundation for this objective."

 European Cyber Service Provider — "AccuKnox's powerful combination of CSPM and CWPP; OpenSource foundations; In-line Zero Trust Security; Support for Public and Private Clouds; made them the ideal partner for us. Our client, a Large European CyberSecurity agency, was looking for a Zero Trust Security Solution that supports Private Cloud platforms. Our win is a clear testament to the value our clients see in this partnership. We look forward to many more successes ahead."

Client	Cloud	Environment	AccuKnox Solution, Use Cases
US Data Analytics Provider	AWS	• Kubernetes, Virtual Machine	• Zero Trust Policy • Drift Detection • SOC2, HIPAA compliance
European Cyber Security Agency	Private Cloud	• Target Cluster & Management Plane - Air Gapped • Kubernetes - Pure K8s Platform • Virtual Machine - Oracle Linux and Debian, virtualization on ovirt	• Deploy complete CNAPP On-Prem (Air-Gapped) • Detect Application Behavior Dynamically and Govern via Fine-grained Policies • Ensure protection and mitigation from Zero Day attacks without affecting application behavior
US Medicare Medicaid Services Provider	Hybrid Cloud	• Public Cloud – AWS • On-Prem Deployment	• Comprehensive Security of Public Cloud • Drift Detection & Continuous Compliance • Compliance Posture & Reporting • Detect Misconfigurations & Vulnerabilities in the Cloud • Detect Drift in Configuration and Alert based on criticality • Generate Report on Compliance posture • Multi-Cloud Security & Vulnerability Management
Top 3 US Defense Systems Integrator	Hybrid Cloud	• Hybrid Cloud - AWS, On-Prem • Kubernetes - AKS, ACR • SIEM - Splunk, Elastic	• Zero Trust Security for Hybrid Cloud • Integrated ASPM, CSPM, CWPP • Continuous Diagnostic & Mitigation for MITRE, STIG compliance • On-Prem Air Gapped Deployment • SAST, SCA & Registry Scan for Vulnerabilities • Automated Zero Trust Posture for Application • Continuous Diagnostic & Mitigation against STIG, MITRE • On-Prem (Air-Gapped) Deployment
Top 5 Financial Services Leader	Hybrid Cloud	• Hybrid Cloud - AWS, On-Prem • VM - Ubuntu 22.04, RHEL {On-Prem} • Jupyter Notebook	• Zero Trust Security for "air gapped" Kubernetes Private Cloud • Proactive Mitigation for Control Plane Violations • Workload Hardening for KAAS (Kubernetes As A Service) • Data Access Security for AI/ML Jupyter Notebook users against RCEs, Privilege Escalations & Lateral Movement.

Case Study - AccuKnox's Inline Mitigation

Understanding the Difference: Inline vs. Post-Attack Mitigation The key difference between AccuKnox's inline mitigation and conventional post-attack mitigation lies in the context of enforcement and observability.

In the AccuKnox system, which is implemented within the open-source KubeArmor environment, an attacker process is thwarted at the operating system level using Linux Security Modules (LSMs). These LSMs deny the fork or execution of any unknown process, effectively stopping the attack before it can cause harm.

The corresponding observability of the process is provided by the eBPF functionality. eBPF enables probes into the underlying system behavior, offering visibility into the process. The resulting telemetry is then fed back into the KubeArmor environment, supporting security policy updates and host policies. The result is an inline security system that allows or denies processes, accesses, and other behaviors based on the defined security policies. In contrast, post-attack mitigation allows the unwanted behavior to occur, presumably some malicious intended execution. While eBPF can still provide visibility into the ongoing attack, the telemetry would only illustrate the attack, which could then be handled by event handlers (e.g., deleting or killing the process).

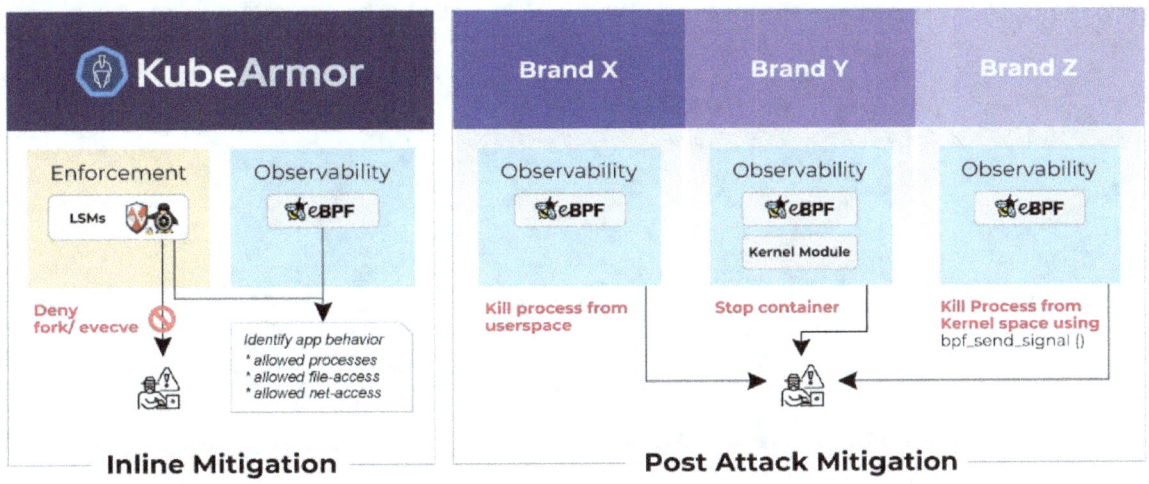

FIGURE 81. INLINE MITIGATION COVERS UP POST-ATTACK MITIGATION FLAWS

The Benefits of Inline Mitigation

The key advantage of AccuKnox's inline mitigation approach is that it stops the attack before it can cause any damage. By denying the fork or execution of unknown processes at the operating system level, AccuKnox effectively prevents malicious behavior from ever occurring. This contrasts with post-attack mitigation, which, while still useful, is inherently less desirable as it allows the unwanted behavior to take place before any remediation can be applied. AccuKnox's inline mitigation solution, integrated with the power of eBPF and the KubeArmor environment, represents a robust and innovative approach to runtime security. By stopping attacks at the source, AccuKnox empowers organizations to enhance their overall security posture and better protect their critical systems and assets.

Chapter 12 Analyst Accolades

"Zero Trust run-time Cloud Security has become an organizational imperative for Companies and Governments. Accuknox' highly differentiated approach, their eBPF foundations and their seminal innovations developed in partnership with Stanford Research Institute (SRI) positions them very well to deliver a highly efficient Zero Trust Cloud Security platform."

FRANK DICKSON
VICE PRESIDENT
SECURITY AND TRUST, IDC

"Run-time Cloud Security is extremely important to detect Zero Day attacks, Bitcoin Miners, DDOS attacks, etc. Accuknox delivers a critical component of the CWPP (Cloud Workload Protection Platform). Their ability to deliver Network, Application and Data Security makes Accuknox a unique and differentiated offering."

CHRIS DEPUY
TECHNOLOGY ANALYST
650 GROUP ANALYST

"Accuknox' foundational capabilities are innovative in the areas specific to Kubernetes security. By combining technologies like un-supervised Machine Learning and Data Provenance, Accuknox is positioned to deliver a comprehensive and robust cloud native Zero-Trust security platform to their customers."

CHASE CUNNINGHAM
RENOWNED CYBER SECURITY ANALYST AND ZERO-TRUST EXPERT

Chapter 13 PARTNERS

We are ardent believers in ensuring "best in class" partnerships to deliver the most comprehensive, efficient, and cost-effective solutions for our clients. To this goal, we align with key enabling partners in the industry. Our partnerships are based on technical, strategic, go-to-market leverage. The following outlines some of our key partnerships:

This is an evolving list and we seek to expand our partnerships to ensure the best value for our clients. These partnerships translate into immense benefits to customers:

- More complete and comprehensive solution
- Lower operating costs
- Lower cost of ownership

Chapter 14 DIFFERENTIATORS

6 Reasons to Choose AccuKnox for Your Zero-Trust Cloud Security

[1] Effortless	AccuKnox delivers layered security. AccuKnox offers agentless security to address most aspects of Cloud Security and leverages the industry's most open, high-performance engine, eBPF (Extended Berkeley Packet Filter) for advanced inline security. We deliver it in a DevSecOps model so organizations can integrate it into their development, and deployment workflow.
[2] Extensive	Accuknox secures modern assets (Kubernetes, IaC - Infrastructure as Code) and traditional (Virtual Machine) assets. AccuKnox CNAPP is a comprehensive platform that combines: CSPM/KSPM (Cloud/Kubernetes Security Posture Management) CWPP (Cloud Workload Protection Platform) KIEM (Kubernetes Identity and Entitlement Management) GRC (Governance Risk and Compliance) CDR (Cloud Detect and Response) and CloudDLP (Data Leak Prevention) Furthermore, we offer the most flexible deployment options. We support All Public Clouds (AWS, Azure, GCP, Oracle, AliCloud) All Private Clouds (RedHat OpenShift, VMWare Tanzu, Nutanix, OpenStack, etc.) and fully Air-gapped Clouds
[3] Effective	AccuKnox delivers security against advanced Zero Day attacks through inline security (as contrasted by post-attack mitigation offered by competing vendors)
[4] Open Source	AccuKnox is powered by KubeArmor, a CNCF (Linux Foundation) project developed by us. KubeArmor has achieved 750,000+ downloads and 1,000+ GitHub stars. AccuKnox is also a core contributor to leading OpenSource projects like eBPF, and Nephio. Consequently, we have the benefit of leveraging some of the best minds in the industry, globally
[5] Innovative	AccuKnox was developed in partnership with SRI International (Stanford Research Institute) and we have 10+ patents on different aspects of Zero Trust Cloud Security. Furthermore, the "Future Proof" Zero Trust security we deliver extends beyond the Cloud (Public and Private Cloud) and covers Edge/IoT, 5G and LLM
[6] AI-Powered	AccuKnox leverages AI/LLM techniques to streamline and simplify CloudSecOps. This is delivered via AskAda, which aims to automate the mundane and empower the expert

AccuKnox CNAPP Definitive Guide

FIGURE 82. A COMPLETE, UNIFIED, SOLUTION WITH DIVERSIFIED USE CASES

Chapter 15 APPENDIX

KubeArmor

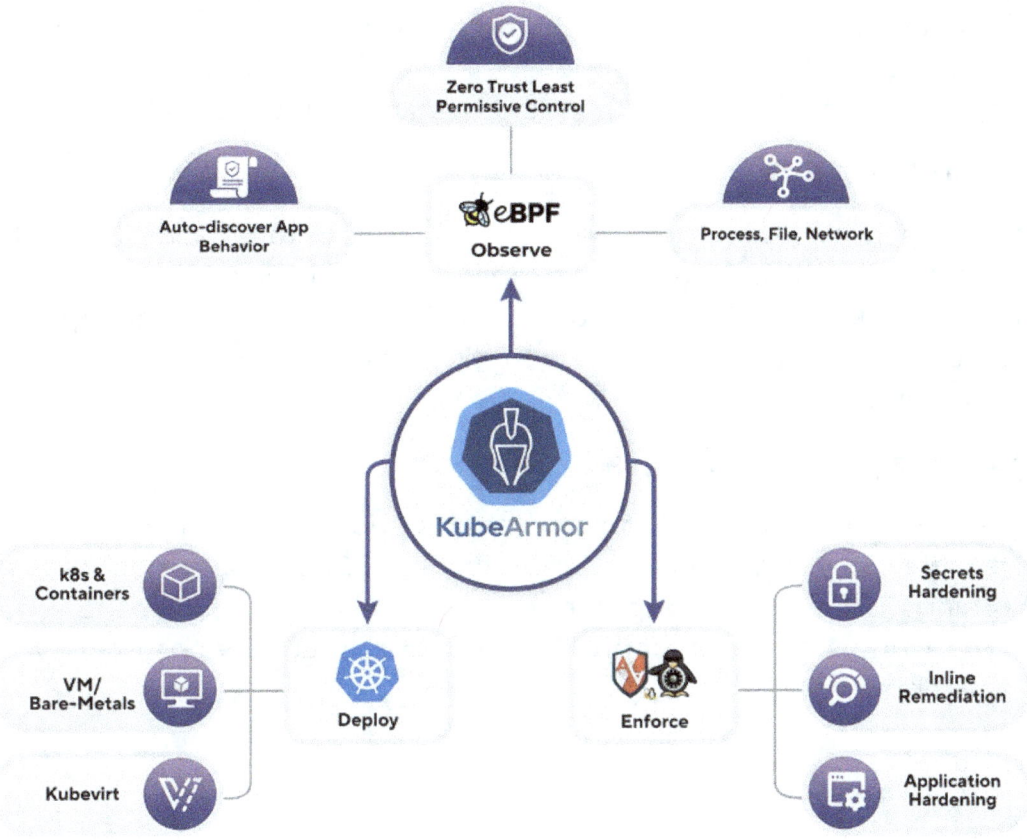

AccuKnox's KubeArmor: Powering Runtime Security Enforcement

As a core contributor to the KubeArmor project, AccuKnox has helped propel this open-source runtime Kubernetes security engine to over 750,000 downloads and 1,200 GitHub stars. KubeArmor leverages the power of eBPF (extended Berkeley Packet Filter) and Linux Security Modules (LSMs) to fortify workloads in cloud containers, IoT/Edge, and 5G networks, enforcing policy-based controls.

The First K8s Security Engine to Leverage BPF-LSM

KubeArmor is the first Kubernetes security engine to harness the combined capabilities of eBPF and LSMs, such as AppArmor, BPF-LSM, and SELinux, to provide robust security without modifying pods, containers, or the host environment.

Inline Mitigation: Proactive Security

KubeArmor's inline mitigation approach, powered by LSMs, helps to lessen the attack surface on pods, containers, and virtual machines. This proactive strategy stands in contrast to traditional post-attack mitigation, which reacts to observed malicious intent, allowing attackers to potentially evade detection and run malicious code.

Addressing Multi-Cloud Challenges

Dealing with pod security contexts can be challenging, as different cloud providers may use various default LSMs. KubeArmor simplifies these intricacies, making it easy to enforce security policies across your multi-cloud infrastructure. The platform functions as a non-privileged DaemonSet, providing host, pod, and container monitoring capabilities.

Enhancing Kubernetes Native Security

The Kubernetes native Pod Security Context has limitations, including difficulties in predicting available LSMs and a lack of support for BPF-LSM. KubeArmor addresses these shortcomings, providing a comprehensive solution that simplifies the enforcement of security policies and enhances the overall security posture of your Kubernetes environment.

AccuKnox CNAPP Definitive Guide

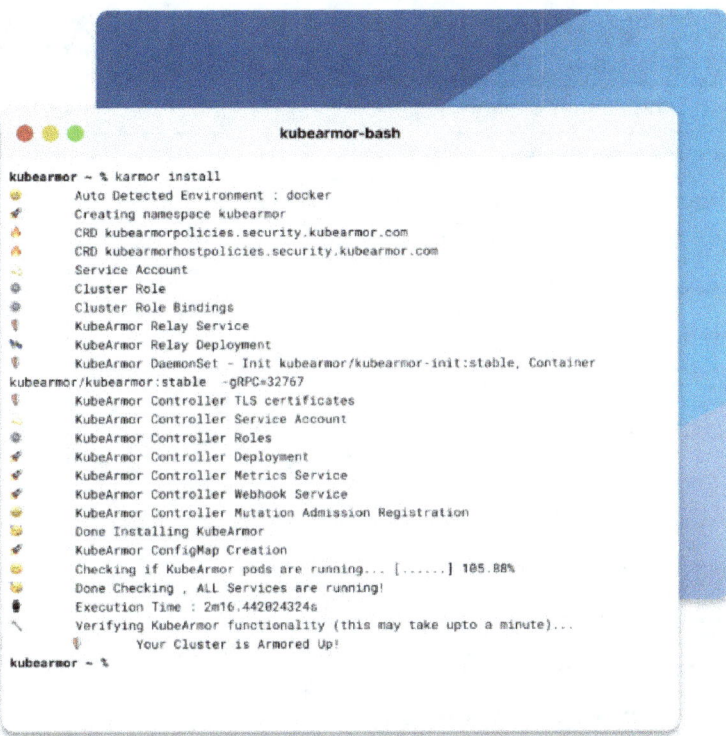

AccuKnox Enterprise vs. KubeArmor OpenSource

KubeArmor (Opensource)

KubeArmor is a cloud-native runtime security enforcement system that restricts the behavior (such as process execution, file access, and networking operations) of pods, containers, and nodes (VMs) at the system level.

Accuknox (Enterprise)

AccuKnox is one of the industry's most comprehensive and integrated CNAPP solutions which brings together multiple disparate security modules to deliver comprehensive Zero Trust security for Networks, Applications (K8s, VM), and Data across the Cloud.

AccuKnox CNAPP Definitive Guide

AccuKnox Runtime Security Features	KubeArmor Open Source	AccuKnox Enterprise
Observability into the workload at granular level	✓	✓
In-line remediation for Zero Day Attacks	✓	✓
Manual apply of Security Policies using CLI	✓	✓
Integration to SIEM for security events and Notification tool	✓	✓
Network security using CNI	✗	✓
Auto-Discovered Behavioural Policies	✗	✓
Recommendation of Hardening Policies based on standard compliance framework – MITRE, NIST, PCI-DSS, CIS	✗	✓
Inventory View of Application	✗	✓
Network Graph View of the Application	✗	✓
Network Microsegmentation in the application	✗	✓
Hardening of the Secrets Managers like HashiCorp Vault, CyberArk Conjur	✗	✓
GitOps based Version Control for Policy Lifecycle Management	✗	✓
Rollback of recently changed Policy governing App Behavior	✗	✓
On-the-fly detection of change in App Behavior through Policies	✗	✓
Multi-Tenant, Multi-Cluster, RBAC for user-management	✗	✓
Comprehensive Dashboard across workloads running in	✗	✓
Managed/Unmanaged Cluster, Containerized environment, VM or Bare Metal	✗	✓
Integration with Registries for Container Image Vuln Scan	✗	✓
Telemetry aggregation (Process executed, File accessed, Network connections made) and Alerts events (Audit, Block)	✗	✓

FIGURE 83. ACCUKNOX OPEN-SOURCE (KUBEARMOR) VS. ACCUKNOX ENTERPRISE COMPARISON TABLE

AccuKnox CNAPP Definitive Guide

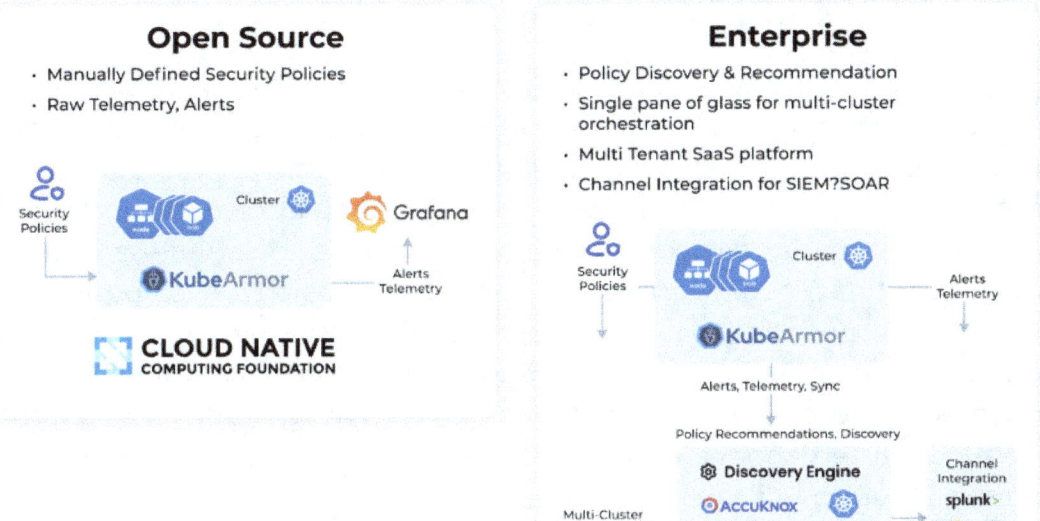

FIGURE 84. ACCUKNOX ENTERPRISE PACKAGE OUTWEIGHS THE OPEN SOURCE WITH "MUST-HAVE" FEATURES FOR PROFESSIONAL GRADE SECURITY

Chapter 16 ABOUT ACCUKNOX

Introducing One of the Most Comprehensive Zero Trust CNAPP Platforms in the Industry. Look no further for the ultimate solution – our platform provides unparalleled coverage. With support for public clouds like AWS, GCP, and Azure, as well as private clouds such as OpenStack and Tanzu, you can trust our platform to handle all your workload needs. We cater to modern workloads, like K8 and Serverless, and traditional workloads, like Virtual Machine and Bare Metal. Our platform is even equipped to handle futuristic workloads like IoT/Edge and 5G. We also deliver both Static and Runtime Security, anchored on innovations in Cloud Security and AI/ML-based Anomaly Detection. With over 15 patents, we're proud to offer an OpenSource, DevSecOps-led delivery model. To top it off, we have an ongoing R&D partnership with the esteemed Stanford Research Institute.

1. "AccuKnox has one of the most comprehensive, modern, Cloud Native CNAPP offerings" - Top 25 SAAS Software Company

2. *"AccuKnox and its capabilities in the areas of run-time security enforcement are unique. We like the fact that it is a CNCF-supported project. It has the support of the global community."* - Top 10 Telco

3. *"While researching solutions to the increasing and advanced attacks in the Cloud, we were impressed with AccuKnox's approach to Zero Trust and NSA/CISA hardening guidelines. With their contributions to OpenSource, AccuKnox is a clear winner."* - Top 50 Cloud Native Unicorn

www.ingramcontent.com/pod-product-compliance
Lightning Source LLC
Chambersburg PA
CBHW062104220526
45471CB00010B/3595